Also by E. Reid Gilbert

Trickster Jack

Shall We Gather at the River

What Matters

Valley Studio: More than a Place

The Twelve Houses of My Childhood

A Hundred Limericks for a Hundred Days of Trump

Stories Tell What Can't be Told: My Story

E. REID GILBERT
A Memoir

A3D IMPRESSIONS
TUCSON • MINNEAPOLIS

A3D Impressions™

A Division of Awareness3D, LLC
PO Box 57415, Tucson, AZ 85732

This is a work of creative nonfiction—a memoir.
The events are portrayed to the best of E. Reid Gilbert's memory. While all the stories in this book are true, some names and identifying details have been changed to protect the privacy of the people involved.
To this effect, the story, experiences and words are solely the author's.

Copyright © 2018 E. Reid Gilbert

All rights reserved, including the right to reproduce this book or portions thereof in any form whatsoever. Contact A3D Impressions Rights & Permission,
PO Box 57415, Tucson, AZ 85732.
awareness3d.com

First A3D Impressions Edition March 2018

Library of Congress Cataloging-in-Publication Data
Names: Gilbert, E. Reid, author.
Title: Stories tell what can't be told: my story, a memoir / E. Reid Gilbert.
Description: Tucson, AZ: A3D Impressions, 2018.
Identifiers: ISBN 978-0-578-20193-1 (pbk.) |978-0-578-19453-0 (ebook) | LCCN 2018935792
Subjects: LCSH Gilbert E. Reid. | Clergy--Biography. | Mimes--Biography. | Authors, American--Biography. | Teachers--Biography. | Actors--Biography. | Theatrical producers and directors--Biography. | Mountain life. | BISAC BIOGRAPHY & AUTOBIOGRAPHY / Personal Memoirs | BIOGRAPHY & AUTOBIOGRAPHY / Entertainment & Performing Arts | BIOGRAPHY & AUTOBIOGRAPHY / Cultural, Ethnic & Regional / General
Classification: LCC PS3604.I43 S76 2018 | DDC 818.5409--dc23

Book design by Richard G. Wamer, JR
Jacket design by Donn Poll
Edited by Dina Renee Delaney

Library of Congress Control Number: 2018935792

ISBN: 978-0-578-20193-1
ISBN: 978-0-578-19453-0 (eBook)

1 2 3 4 5 6 7 8 9 10

Dedication

This book is dedicated to all those along the way, who contributed to my story with encouragement, challenges and friendship.

Of special note:

Robert and Derry Graves for their professional collaboration by inviting me into their Uplands Arts Council program, which has guided me in my subsequent educational and cultural pursuits.

Dr. Dean Connors, who provided physical facilities for Valley Studio and assistance in the leadership of the Wisconsin Mime Theatre and School. Valley Studio would never have happened had it not been for the generosity of Dr. Connors.

Robert and Derry Graves, Founders of the Uplands Arts Council

Dr. Dean Connors

CONTENTS

Part I: Kin 1

From the Virginia Hills to the North Carolina Mills 3
Mamma's Life on the Farm 11
Tari Lynn Gilbert 23
Adrienne Lee Gilbert 31
Karen Ann Gilbert 39
Smokey 47
Aunt Bettie Light 55
The Evil Weed 61
Primitive Baptists 69
Uncle Sammy Jane 77
Great Grandma Clarissa Jane Brinkley 83

Part II: My Mentors 89

The Reverend Ralph Reed 91
The Legacy of Richard Chase 97
Professor Robert Seaver 101
Charles Weidman 104
Etienne Decroux 109
Professor Scott 113
Sidayo Kita 119

Part III: Other Folks Along the Way 123

It's a Small World 125
Sister Willie Mae Tyger 133
Edna and Augie 139
Verna Mae Slone 145
Red Creek Friends: Stoneledge 149
But for the Grace 159
Harry Nohr 163
Herbert Fritz 165
Governor Lee Dreyfus 167
Connectedness 173

Part IV: Education 183

Fudging the Fudge or The Beginning of My
Educational Journey 185
Senator Clyde R. Hooey 191
Warming up My College Dorm Room 193
Brother Joe and Sister Lucy 197
Lessons from Shapechangers 201
I Am a Teacher: I Do Not Teach 205
Extracurricular 211
Transcending Technique 215
Signposts Along the Way: Children's Lessons for Adults 219

Part V: The Church 237

My Methodist Roots and My Methodist Disconnect 239
My Black Heart or Growing Up White 245
Ribside of the Religious Life 257
Road to Salvation 265

Contents

Part VI: The Theatre 269

My Life of Mime 271
National Mime Week 279
Performing for Benefits or Benefits for Whom 283
Blossom and Beethoven 287
A Sacred Valley 293
Witwen 299
USA Moon Landing on the Gard Theatre Stage 303
Insufficient Evidence 305
The Old Timer 313
Tucker Tales 317
Valley Ridge Theatre 323
Why the Gathering 327

Chronology 331
Photographs 333

Stories Tell
What Can't be Told:
My Story

FOREWORD

A Native American storyteller said, "Stories tell what can't be told, and the important things we leave to silence." These tales seem to fit that description. They don't adequately tell of all the events and people in my life, and I must admit that there are many stories left untold. Perhaps a silence would be appropriate at the end of the telling/reading.

In biblical times when the disciples of Jesus would ask for a theological answer to a perplexing issue, he would answer with a parable. Even though many folks think that storytelling is for the children's hour, we continue to exchange information, feelings, gossip with stories, even as adults.

Stories are shared in so many ways. Georgia O'Keeffe was noted to have said, "I'd love to tell the story of the beauty of these mountains, but I don't have the words. I do have the paint." I have encouraged young people to tell their stories in whatever medium is most appropriate. Of course, I've been known to tell a "tale or two" in the silent communication of pantomime.

This volume is a collection of my stories after the publication of those stories of my earlier life, as recorded in *The Twelve Houses of My Childhood*. There is some repetition in these stories. However, as it's intended for each story to stand on its own, there may be some important shared elements from another story.

The stories are not arranged in chronological order, and are not meant to be a complete autobiography. They are loosely divided into six sections, which I hope will help the reader to see somewhat of a pattern within each Part: Part I. KIN, Part II. MENTORS, Part III. OTHER FOLKS, Part IV. EDUCATION, Part V. CHURCH, Part VI. THEATRE.

Foreward

These various stories are like pieces for a patchwork quilt, more precisely a crazy quilt, made of fabric of different sizes, shapes, colors, and textures. Certainly not a traditionally designed quilt, but hopefully when stitched together, becomes a useful item, perhaps appreciated on a bleak midwinter evening.

PART I
KIN

A Native American storyteller said,
"Home is where your story begins."
Thus, Part One of these tales begins with kinfolks.

FROM THE VIRGINIA HILLS TO THE NORTH CAROLINA MILLS

The "War to end all wars" was recently over, and mountain folk began looking beyond the boundaries of the family farm for a livelihood. My grandparents, Elder Noel B. Gilbert with wife, Nancy Sue Fulcher Gilbert and children in 1919 headed south to Winston-Salem for the promise of employment in the mills there.

My dad, Peter Reid Gilbert, (age 11) and his younger brother, John (9), had stayed at the home place to raise a crop of tobacco and corn. They slept in the old log house (the sleeping house), which faced another mirror image house (the eating house).

As they were the only ones left there that summer, they ate at Uncle Lemly and Aunt Alice's, just on the other side of the pasture field. Uncle Lemly was Grandpa Noel's twin brother—both were Primitive Baptist preachers—and Aunt Alice was Grandma Nancy Sue's younger sister. Daddy and his siblings were double first cousins of Uncle Lemly and Aunt Alice's children. Daddy's three older brothers and an older sister had already settled in with "public work" in the mills of Winston-Salem. They called it "public work" because it was different from their "private" work on the farm.

The trip to Winston took two days by wagon and buggy. On their first trek across the state line they stopped at Nancy and Branscombe Young's farm right outside Danbury. Nancy was the daughter of Uncle Lemly and Aunt Alice. Later, Grandpa bought a car, and the trip could be cut in more than half, if they didn't get stuck in the ruts in bad weather.

It was after World War I, when the general migration began from the hill farms, as they were no longer competitive with the Midwestern farms which had begun to mechanize for greater efficiency in the farming process. Those tractors would have been useless on the rocky hillsides, not being able to remain stable on the slopes. They would have worked fine in the bottom fields, which were too small to afford the cost of expensive machinery.

Winston beckoned the hill families for labor in Hanes Hosiery, PH Hanes Underwear (the old fashioned BVDs), RJ Reynolds Tobacco (Camel Cigarettes), BF Huntley Furniture, etc. The three Winston high schools were even named after the entrepreneurial industrialists: Hanes, Gray and Reynolds.

Daddy had finished the seventh grade in the old two-room Gilbert School outside Stuart, Virginia. When his family got to Winston, both he and John enrolled in Fairview Elementary School on N. Liberty Street. John later went on to finish high school, but the city kids teased Daddy about the way he talked with his Appalachian Mountain twang. Well, he couldn't stand being made fun of, so he just up and quit. His parents allowed him to quit, as mountain folk so honored individualism that they even gave children the opportunity to make their own choices about school, work, church, etc.

He worked for a while at BF Huntley's, lifting heavy pieces of furniture. Then he worked at PH Hanes, ironing the BVDs with a heavy iron, which caused a hump on his back between his young shoulders. That hump stayed with him for the rest of his life.

Because he was younger, he wasn't given the same pay as the older fellows, so he protested, and when his supervisors wouldn't raise his pay to the same level of his co-workers, he again quit—this time quitting a job instead of a school. In 1925 when he was sixteen, he started work at Hanes Hosiery, where he worked until his retirement at the age of sixty-five.

By the time Daddy was twenty, he was married, and his first child, Della Sue, my older sister, was born. I was born eighteen months later. Daddy always felt intellectually inadequate because of his limited educational background. He did go back to school [night school] when I was eight.

He knew he could excel in something, so he put all his effort into his work at the mill, from knitter to fixer to assistant foreman to foreman. He was the one chosen to introduce Gordon Hanes, Mr. Jim Hanes's son, to the intricacies of the knitting machines. Gordon was, of course, expected to take over the mill when Mr. Jim would retire, as all of the mills were still family affairs. By the time Gordon joined the firm the stockings were no longer using silk thread, but the new synthetic nylon thread which gave the new stockings the name, "nylons."

Daddy was always willing to do whatever task was required of him, including the shift where he was needed. He worked most of his time on the second shift, often called the "swing shift," as it was the "swing" between the day shift and the night shift, called the "graveyard shift." He actually preferred the graveyard shift, as it gave him the opportunity to use his daylight hours however he pleased. This was useful, as we raised some pigs and always had a large garden and corn and hayfields for the livestock, including the horse and cow. Of course, we also had to have wood for cooking and heating the house.

When I was about ten, Daddy had so many boils on his arms that we had a shared wood chopping, a gathering of men to saw, chop and gather in the wood for a family who had some illness. This was a whole lot like wheat-thrashings, hog-killings and barn-raisings, when farm neighbors would get together to help each other in chores that needed more than one person or one family. This also seemed to make the work easier and more festive, like the quilting bees and corn shuckings. The mountain folk brought this kind of communal effort to their new homes and their camaraderie in the mills.

I might note that one of Daddy's co-workers suggested that what he needed for his boils was an old remedy from the co-worker's grandmother. He was to gather a quart of dried cockleburs and boil them to make a quart of cocklebur tea. Then he was to strain it through some cotton fabric, like a milk strainer, and drink it as quickly as he could. Daddy followed the instructions implicitly.

Although at first he was jubous (dubious) about it, he never had another boil the rest of his life, even though his previous life had been plagued by boils. People were used to sharing work, remedies and ideas.

The value of sharing was also accepted by the mill owners, as they had, in many instances, come from the same cultural background as the mill hands. R. J. Reynolds had grown up on a tobacco farm not far from Daddy's home place in Patrick County.

James Hanes was the founder and president of Hanes Hosiery Mill. Everyone in the mill and elsewhere always affectionately called him "Mr. Jim." He had built a gymnasium and a baseball field for his employees. A latter-day critic may charge this attitude as "paternalistic," and one must admit that Mr. Jim did treat his employees rather fatherly as a large, extended family. When the unions tried to organize at Hanes Hosiery, Daddy said, "Nauw, I can't walk out with the union. I just can't do that to Mr. Jim."

During the depression, things were not going well at the mill, as the hosiery orders had slackened considerably. Mr. Jim called all the workers together. Daddy said Mr. Jim had tears in his eyes, as he laid out the situation that the mill was in—the same condition that Daddy and all the rest of the employees were in. Mr. Jim explained that business had slowed down so drastically that, in order for the mill to survive, either some folks had to be laid off or wages would have to be cut. He said that he just couldn't make that decision alone—asking the employees to let him know what course they preferred. No one wanted to be laid off, and they didn't want to see anyone else laid off, so they chose to have their wages reduced.

This extended family attitude persisted as long as Mr. Jim was at the helm. He was not only merely in charge of the factory operations and business; he was also available to talk with any of his employees about anything that bothered them or whatever was on their mind. This was what he called his "open door policy." His office door was always open and his shoulder always available for crying, personal problems or family celebrations. He—without fail—acknowledged the birth of a new baby or death in any of the families.

Actually, in 1936, my folks had built a new four-room house, where we lived for less than a year, when Daddy was laid off at the mill, due to the worsening of the depression. The "little white house" was lost to bankruptcy, and we had to move to Virginia to live with Uncle Bob, Mamma's bachelor brother. After about six months, Daddy returned to Winston to his old job at Hanes, as the depression was easing up a bit.

When we settled on Baux Mountain Road in 1939, Daddy loved to go frog gigging and turtle hunting. The woods and creeks were close by.

One Saturday night he caught several bullfrogs, and as it was so late, he didn't clean them. He simply put them in the refrigerator. The next morning when Mamma started breakfast she opened the fridge and all those frogs jumped out at her, croaking like crazy. She fainted and woke up under the wood range.

On another occasion Daddy had set out a turtle trap in Old Field Creek. One Sunday after church and Sunday school, he decided to check his trap. He said to my brother, "Ott do you wanna go with me to check the turtle trap?" Ott, of course, agreed and set off with Daddy across a freshly plowed field. Daddy was hurrying along, as he didn't want anyone to see him checking turtle traps on a Sunday. It wasn't a venal sin, but on Baux Mountain it would cause a great deal of talk about the Sunday doings of their Sunday school superintendent.

Suddenly Daddy heard Ott behind him making a lot of noise, grunting and groaning. He turned around to see what the matter was. "What's wrong, Son?"

"Daddy it's awful hard tryin' to step in your foot prints." Not only had Daddy been moving fast, he had also been taking long steps.

At Sunday school the next week, Daddy confessed his waywardness at checking turtle traps on the Sabbath. Then he admonished, not only himself, but also the other grownups. "Be careful where you're walkin'. You might find a tyke tryin' to follow, an' you wouldn't wanna be leadin' him down the wrong road."

When I was in college, Daddy served as local preacher in three mountain Methodist Churches in Stokes County, NC and Patrick

County, VA (Hunter's Chapel, Carter's Chapel and Chestnut Grove). Even while working forty hours a week he'd spend the weekends at those churches, particularly visiting the shut-ins. One Christmas time when I was home, visiting, he asked me to help him deliver Christmas fruit baskets he had bought for some elderly shut-in church members. That weekend we were staying—as he usually did—at the home of Theodore and Bertie Gwynn.

The gift deliveries went fine until we had to wade across a wide creek to complete our mission. Although we had on our rubber boots, it was quite a challenge to avoid the deep water by stepping on the highest rocks. Later he loved to tell of hearing me grunt when I slipped off a rock, and my boots filled with water. He looked back and laughed—not at my misfortune nearly so much as to express his boyish delight at accomplishing a good deed amidst difficult circumstances.

Some years later, on one of my visits with Daddy, he wanted to show me the new Hanes Hosiery Mill, which had moved to new quarters north of town. Even though he had retired by this time, he was as proud of the mill—its products, its equipment, its employees, its new facilities—as though he were still working there or even part owner. After all, he had spent the better part of fifty years there—a part of its extended family. It was a kind of investment of his life. But, of course, Mr. Jim was no longer there, and the business had been sold to Sara Lee, whoever she was.

When we entered the front gate, the guard—although he knew Dad—looked a little apprehensive, as Dad simply told him, "My boy is home from college, and I thought he might probably like to see all the new things we have here now." The watchman gave his okay, so Daddy was showing me all the new machinery and operations, when the plant superintendent saw us. Daddy said, "Hello, Bill (not his real name, just an attempt on my part to protect the not-so-innocent). I'm showin' my boy around the new plant, and all the latest stuff we've got in...."

Bill cut him off short, "Pete, you don't belong in here. You don't work here anymore."

"It's okay, Bill. He's just here for a short while, and I thought he oughta see . . . "

"Pete, listen to what I'm telling you. You're retired now, and we can't have just anybody in here roamin' around. We've got work to do."

I'm sure Daddy thought to himself that he wasn't *just anybody*. "Yeah, I know, Bill, but we surely won't be interfering with any of the work. It'll be okay, Bill."

"No, Pete, it won't be okay. Listen to what I'm tellin' you. We can't let unauthorized personnel in here. Our insurance carriers don't allow it."

Dad looked down at his shoes for a moment, taking in the language of "unauthorized personnel" and "insurance carriers," coming to the realization that the old paternalistic workplace of Mr. Jim's mill was gone.

He then looked directly at Bill, a lifelong acquaintance, saying, "We'll be goin' now, Bill. You have a real good day now, ya' hear!"

I felt terrible for Dad, as I had never seen him so humiliated, and certainly unnecessarily so, I thought. But he held his head high as we headed toward the gate.

He said goodbye to the gate guard, and I think I heard him murmur under his breath, "I wonder if Miss Sara Lee is in her office today, and would care to speak with me."

We left the mill and went to Hill's Barbeque for a spit-cooked, hickory-smoked, pulled-pork barbeque sandwich with baked beans and coleslaw.

Neither of us ever mentioned the incident again.

MAMMA'S LIFE ON THE FARM

Stella Mae, born May 16, 1906, to Winfrey Brinkley and Van Della Mae Edwards Brinkley, was the oldest of eight children—four boys and four girls. Home was in Pine Ridge, a suburb of Mt. Airy, NC, where her daddy worked in a furniture store. Life was rather peaceful there with Stella and her two younger brothers, Bob and Elbert and living rather close to other cousins; children of Mamma Brinkley's (my mother's mother) many brothers and sisters.

Mamma told me that she and Bob and their cousins, after attending a funeral, decided that they ought to have their own funeral; but, without a corpse they thought baby Elbert might be a good candidate—after all, he could fit into the wooden stove-wood box chosen as an appropriate casket.

They found a gully deep enough to save them from having to dig a grave, but by time they'd started throwing some dirt on Uncle Elbert's coffin or had begun the sermons and prayers, Mamma Brinkley discovered them. That night there were several bruised bottoms in the little beds of Stella and Bob and their Edwards cousins.

After Grandpa Winfrey saved enough to buy a farm, the whole family moved to an old plantation in Powhatan County, VA. Great-Uncle Roy, Grandpa's bachelor brother, moved with them to open a general store in the crossroads postoffice of Ballsville.

Grandpa's mother, Clarissa Jane, was quite upset with my grandmother, who was eighteen when she married Grandpa, who was thirty. Great-Grandma was sure that no girl was good enough for either of her two boys, so it was apparent to her that the young Della Mae, usually called "Delly," must have tricked Winfrey into marriage. Uncle Roy never married.

In Mt. Airy and then in Virginia, younger siblings were born a couple of years apart until there were eight in all. Mamma and her younger siblings helped with all the farm and house work and enjoyed playing in the trenches left from the Civil War and amongst the ruins of the slave quarters from so many years earlier.

Mamma was probably Grandpa's favorite, as they shared interests in education and the arts, prompting him to give her a pump organ and a quartered-oak library table. Before Mamma had finished high school, Grandpa had already paid her tuition and room and board at Radford College for her first year in the pursuit of her dream of becoming an elementary school teacher.

However, in May, 1925, Grandpa was bitten by a wood tick and contracted Rocky Mountain spotted fever. On June 15 he passed away. Mamma Brinkley told me that the night before he died he was delirious all night and kept singing "Will There be Any Stars in My Crown?"

While away in college, Mamma felt lonely for home. Although her tuition had already been paid, family funds were low. In a letter home, February 14, 1926, she wrote, "Mamma, the next time you write, if you have it, send me a dollar. You know how much I hate to ask for it."

After her year in college, she left for Winston-Salem to find a job to help Mamma Brinkley with the expenses of raising the younger children, the youngest of whom was only eighteen months old when their daddy had died. Her Uncle Sam found her a job at the Turner White Casket Company where she would sew satin linings into the caskets.

When telling me about her work at Turner White Casket Company, she said, "Every time I sewed linings in a small casket I cried a little. I had hoped to teach the children, but instead, I'm comforting their little bodies."

Her half-aunt, Blanche Edwards, persuaded her one day to walk up to Liberty Street where there was a family who had recently moved from the mountains of Patrick County, Virginia. Well, it so happened that Mamma and Daddy met and were married July 14, 1928. Aunt Blanche had already married Daddy's older brother, Sam. Aunt Blanche then became Mamma's sister-in-law as well as her aunt. Both young couples shared a house for a while.

My sister, Della Sue, was born June 7, 1929—just three weeks before Daddy's twentieth birthday. I was born eighteen months later, November 15, 1930, and my brother, Arthur, was born July 13, 1932. Mamma was kept busy with the cooking and sewing and housework for her small brood. Life wasn't easy; before I was nine we'd moved nine times.

We had lived in a tobacco pack house for one winter while planning in 1936 to build a new house, which was lost when Daddy laid off from his job at the Hanes Hosiery Mill. We then moved down to Mamma's old home place with Uncle Bob. It wasn't a good arrangement, so Daddy went back to Winston to see if he could get his job back, which he did. But we stayed in Virginia until the school year ended for Susie and Uncle Jack.

We moved back to E. 24nd St. in Winston for a few months before moving in with Mr. Styers and his son, Percy. Mrs. Styers had died the year before, leaving her helpless husband and son without a cook/housekeeper. Mamma was to fill the vacant employer position in the Styers' household in lieu of rent. This didn't work out, because of the way Mamma and we kids were treated, so we moved again right after school started and directly across the road from the schoolhouse, which was to be my school for the next eight years, even with two more moves within the same school district.

The next year, we moved up the road about a half mile, where we stayed for two years, before we moved farther out in the country to a Baux Mountain farm.

In each of these homes, from the time she was married in 1928 until in 1939 when we moved to Baux Mountain, Mamma's responsibilities of birthing and caring for three children; cooking for her own family as well as, at times, other hungry mouths (Uncle Bob, Mr. Styers, Percy and, quite often, younger siblings who lived with us from time to time); cleaning house and doing all the laundry—by hand—was a tiresome burden.

However, none of those households presented all the challenges she would face at Baux Mountain. The 25-acre place was hardly a farm, as it had no outbuildings, such as barns, pig sties or chicken houses. There was, however, an outhouse, built earlier by WPA workers with German siding boards and a concrete base and seat. It even had a coat of white paint, and the old, drafty six-room farmhouse had never been painted, presenting a rather somber, dull exterior.

There was no electricity. The cooking had to be done on an old wood range, and the only heat facilities were fireplaces in each room. Of course, the fuel to be used was wood, which had to be cut from the trees on the place. Lamp oil was the fuel for the lamps, which had to be cleaned each week. One lamp, called an Aladdin lamp, had to be specially prepared in order to have enough light for reading.

Some of these inconveniences were also in a few of the earlier homes, but this was the first place with no well. Water had to be fetched from a spring 50 yards down a steep slope. This being the source of water, Mamma chose to do the laundry down near the spring. I was in the third grade and could help dip the water from the spring and carry it in buckets to the wash tub, the rinse tub, the bluing tub and the big iron pot where the clothes were boiled. She also used a dishpan to starch the collars of the Sunday shirts.

In addition to fetching the water, Susie and I would help Mamma by stirring the boiling clothes in the iron pot with a long stick. The only other utensil available for such a laundry setup was the washboard, which Mamma used for scrubbing down each article of clothing with a big bar of Octagon soap. She had to wring out the clothes by hand, as she didn't have a wringer—even a hand-cranked one.

We would then carry all that laundry up the hill for Mamma to pin them on the clothesline right behind the house. If it were a cold day, everything would be frozen stiff, and the sheets were like large wooden boards.

Of course, the ironing process was just as antiquated, as she had to use old sadirons which were flatirons needing to be heated on the wood range or propped up in front of the fireplace, in order for it to get hot enough to press each article of laundry, even the sheets and BVDs.

She wouldn't let me or Susie help with keeping the irons hot, because she was afraid we'd burn our hands, as the whole iron, including the handle, would get extremely hot.

Once, when we were at the spring with the laundry, I heard Mamma say that she felt sometimes just like lying at the spring with her head in the water, just to pass away peacefully, as life was sometimes just too hard.

The old house was so drafty that snow would blow in through the cracks. My fourth-grade teacher told us that we needed to keep our windows open at night for the fresh air. I said, "Miss Harris, we don't need to do that at our house, because the wind blows the fresh air in through the cracks."

I told Mamma this, as I was kind of proud of our special house which had automatic air fresheners. She was terribly embarrassed as she tried so hard to maintain a sense of pride.

Daddy decided to tear the old house down, use the scrap lumber and recycled nails to build a smaller house at the edge of the yard, saving a spot in the middle of the yard for a new house. We even began digging by hand a basement for the future house.

However, World War II was on, and everything within the country had to be contributed to the war cause—no lumber, no nails, and no paint. Everything was rationed, and Mamma had to plead with the authorities for extra sugar for her jams and jellies and the curing of the hams.

So Mamma now had to deal with a three-room-cobbled-together house, a new baby, a yard full of used lumber and a hole in the ground awaiting a new house, which had to be postponed until the war was over. There was no lawnmower, so we had to stake the cow in the yard to serve as an organic grass cutter. Mamma would have me cut the grass around the walkway stepping stones with an old pair of scissors.

Three years later, we did get electricity, a hand-dug well and a kerosene heater for heating the house.

Mamma had to wait until I had left for college in 1949 for a new house, a telephone, a heating oil floor furnace and an electric cook stove. She even got a TV, which she said she could do without.

Throughout all the years of hardship, she was determined to encourage education, books and the arts for her children. Each Mayday she took us to see the outdoor Mayday pageant at Salem College. It was free and gorgeous, with little nymphs in flowing costumes, dancing down the rocky and wooded hillside behind the college dorm.

Whenever we could get a ride to town, she'd take us to the library to borrow books. She even saw an advertisement for printed summaries of the great literary classics for the reduced price of only 5 cents each. She ordered a dollar's worth. When the twenty books came they really were reduced—to a folded, four-page 3 X 3 card.

She would often comment of the painful necessity of the mamma birds having to push the fledglings out of the nest, but as painful as it was for her when it was her time to push she was up to the task in her quiet manner by gently pushing.

Della Sue was the first to depart for higher learning as a nurse at the Presbyterian Hospital in Charlotte. After several months, Susie came home, physically ill from some misunderstanding with her teachers. Mamma put her on the Greyhound bus to return to school, but Susie started crying again, so Mamma bought herself a ticket and accompanied her fledgling back to Charlotte, to find out what was the problem—it was simply that another Miss Gilbert, a cousin, earned several demerits, but they were put on Susie's record, and she was always careful to do what was right and what was expected of her. Years later, she said that that was the best thing Mamma ever did for her.

This story could be endless, relating the troubles of Mamma's life as well as her joys and delights in the beauty of her flowers and the autumn leaves—even the beauty of her cooking and needlework. However, her later life was easier though without the joy of having all of her children and grand-children close by.

Anyone, knowing Mamma, would never consider her a comedian. Whenever she would tell a joke or a funny story, it would always fall flat. All the essential elements of the story would be there, but she would either invert the punch line or miss the comic timing.

She would say, "When Pete (my dad) told the story, everyone laughed."

Someone would usually say, "Stella, it is a funny story." But the intellectual assessment of the joke never sufficed for the absence of laughter, itself.

People responded to her serious mien with an equal amount of seriousness. However, her demeanor would at times become comic, because she would be so terribly serious. Although she was not a bumbler like Barney Fife, she would be as serious as he in assessing a situation or responding to a question.

The first occurrence I readily recall of the comedy of her seriousness was when I was ten years old and waking up from an anesthetic sleep after an appendectomy. It was in the terribly hot, muggy dog days of late July in the old City Hospital in Winston-Salem. In 1940, air-conditioning was unheard of, even in the hospitals.

That was the week also of our annual summer church revival, during which there was some powerful preaching about sin and repentance, heaven and hell.

The ether-induced sleep was like no other experience I had ever undergone before. Shortly after the anesthetist placed the mask over my nose, I began to drift up off the table, witnessing all the activity below. It seemed like only minutes before I started waking up in a hospital bed with my parents and siblings standing around—everyone looking very serious and very hot.

The whole event was so strange, that I asked Mamma, "Mamma, have I died and gone to heaven?"

She, of course, was trying to be reassuring when she answered with an ominous question: "Do you think it's going to be this hot in heaven?"

This really scared me to death for sure. I had landed in the wrong place!

I quickly reassured myself. If I have died, I certainly wouldn't find Mamma down in the devil's netherworld.

When I was a student at Brevard College, I was a cheerleader for the football team. I played basketball, but I was too scrawny for football. Mamma and my little sister, Evelyn, came one weekend on the Greyhound Bus to visit. Mamma liked nothing better than getting on a Greyhound bus and riding to wherever.

On Saturday evening there was a football game, and Mamma had never been to a football game before. She and Evelyn sat in the stands with Mrs. Raines, my dorm mother.

It was cold and rainy, and even into the third quarter neither team had been able to score. Our team hadn't won any game the whole season, anyway. There had been several good plays on both sides and several near misses and some impressive kicks. Of course, we cheerleaders had led lots of cheers when anything seemed to be promising.

In the midst of all of the commotion, Mamma had been trying to figure out exactly what was going on, so she yelled down at me, "Reid, what's the score?"

I was terribly embarrassed, wondering how to yell back at her and admit we hadn't scored and implying that Mamma didn't know anything about the game. But I did yell back at her, "Mamma, nobody's scored yet."

With that bit of information, still attempting to make some sense out of it all, she yelled back, "Well, what's everybody yelling about?"

I had to wait until later to explain the game to her.

Her seriousness was also exhibited in a letter to me a couple of years later. Apparently she had encountered a former neighbor while shopping downtown. The neighbor started telling Mamma about her delight in her new evangelical church. She related that she wasn't really "saved" when she was a member of the Methodist church. In the letter Mamma related more details of the self-righteous attitude of the neighbor, and as I read between the lines I could tell that Mamma was becoming increasingly offended. She ended the letter by stating that "All that may very well be true, but at least, thank God, we Methodists are humble."

Mamma was proud of her Methodist humility, and I don't know of anyone else who could more justly lay claim to that assertion.

Several years later in 1957, Mamma, Daddy, my brother Ott and my little sister Evelyn drove to South Bend, Indiana for my wedding. None of them had ever been north of the Mason-Dixon Line before, so Mamma, I'm sure, was prepared—without pre-judgment—for anything.

Suspecting that alcohol might be served, Mamma peeked at the list of things to be bought for the reception and saw "two pints of half and half." She asked Evelyn, who was fifteen at the time, "Evelyn, what is half and half?" I suppose she figured that her teenage daughter was more worldly-wise than herself. It should be noted that at that time in the South one would buy either milk or cream but not a deliberate mixture of the two.

Evelyn answered, "Mamma I don't know what half and half is."

Mamma pondered for a moment—then in a stern attempt to protect her young daughter—she said, "Well, whatever it is, don't you touch it!"

A southern matron must be ever wary of pitfalls awaiting her offspring when traveling in a foreign land.

The last Greyhound bus ride Mamma ever took was to visit me and my family for the Christmas of 1968. She said that she had such a wonderful time with her three small granddaughters that she was going to take the Greyhound bus every year to spend Christmas with us no matter where we might be living, even in India.

On June 15, 1969, on the forty-fifth anniversary of the death of her beloved father, Mamma died in an automobile accident.

What does one do to memorialize the life of one so significant in ones' own life? Nothing would be adequate, but I wrote her a poem, planted irises around her gravestone and contributed a scholarship in her name at Brevard College to assist a young student who would be interested in studying to be a teacher—a dream, Mamma was never able to fulfill in her lifetime.

Hopefully, Laura Barr, the first recipient of the Stella Mae Brinkley Gilbert Scholarship will be able to fulfill her own youthful dreams of education and art.

The Wonder
June 15, 1969

The wonder
The wonder
Always the wonder
Of a flower
Of a heart

Grief,
It rubs the soul raw
Then bathes it clean.

I picked two wildflowers
Today, Mamma, and stuck them in my overalls bib
For you.
You would have planted them
    And nurtured them to grow.

You had a language, I think

That we didn't know,
But it coaxed things to live
    Children to blossom
    And Bulbs to burst open
        Reaching for the sky
        Where they unfolded
           In a wonder
              Of Color
              Of form
              Of beauty.

Today, Mamma
We seek that beauty –
Your beauty
In the world
To carry in our hearts.

Your devoted son

TARI LYNN GILBERT

After Luan Miller and I were married in December 1957 at the South Bend, IN First Methodist Church, where I had been the Associate Minister, we moved to Paterson, NJ, where I was to be the new Minister at the Vreeland Avenue Methodist Church and would attend classes in NYC. Luan got a position with the local YWCA.

About a year later Luan, not feeling well, went to see Dr. Helga Vogel, who had been highly recommended by some of our new church members. Luan said, "Dr. Vogel, I think I have some kind of bug and probably need some medication."

After a thorough examination Dr. Vogel said in her strong, German accent, "Vhat you haf, is bigger dan a bug, but I vill prescribe something for your morning sickness." Although we were not prepared for this news, we were overjoyed at the prospect of our first "blessed event."

Things went fairly smoothly for the next several months, while Luan's situation was expanding. Then on the morning of May 29, 1958 —also the birthday of JFK—there was excessive movement of the bug. We met Dr. Vogel at the St. Joseph Hospital, and I waited in the fathers' waiting room for news of the arrival of our little bugger.

After my wait, which seemed like days, I was told I could go see my new daughter through the picture window of the maternity ward. I inquired as to her wellbeing, particularly if she had ten fingers and ten toes. I was told that everything was in place. Only somewhat later were we to find out differently.

As I hurried down the hall, which seemed to be a mile long, I overheard several whispered questions, "Have you seen the orange haired baby down there in the baby room?" Most of the babies there were children of African Americans or Latinos, so I just assumed that any baby with light colored hair would probably be an oddity. However, when Tari Lynn was held up to see me through the glass, I saw for myself that she did, indeed, have orange hair and even orange cradle cap. Perhaps we were prescient as we had already chosen the name Tari for her, which in Hindi—unbeknownst to us—meant "little star." My mother's name was Stella, which also meant "star." Luan's mother's name was "Clara", another rending of "bright star". Tari was already the star of that wing of the hospital, thus assuring us that she would continue to excel in some place in her galaxy. Her second name, Lynn, sounded just right with Tari, and her surname had already been chosen by some ancestor.

After we brought her home, she continued to shine with her pleasant smile and calm demeanor, except at bedtime, when she shone in another way by practicing to be an opera singer. The opera would have continued for hours if we hadn't gone and fetched her to our bed. When we discussed this with Dr. Vogel, she advised us strongly to leave the baby in her bed until she would quit crying. I told the doctor that it was nerve wracking to listen to the tragic wailing of our baby every night, but the doctor assured us that after the first night of about two hours of crying, it would diminish a bit each night until she would quit crying in about five nights. She was right; after that, little Tari would go to sleep immediately after being put into her bed.

Just before we were to move to Kentucky where I would be teaching at Union College, Dr. Vogel had some bad news for us. She laid Tari on her tummy and stretched her legs, showing that the wrinkles in the backs of her legs weren't aligned. The diagnosis was congenital displacia, which meant that one hip wasn't fitting properly into the hip socket. She told us that when we got to Kentucky we should get medical attention immediately, otherwise Tari would have one leg shorter than the other all of her life and would have to wear corrective shoes.

We followed the doctor's advice and was referred to the Shriners' Children's Hospital in Louisville, which was 168 miles from our home in Barbourville. The outstanding doctor in Louisville wanted to observe Tari for a few days before we would take her back home. We were certainly reluctant to leave our baby that far away from home, but we called every day, receiving reassurance that she was a model patient and that things were going well, but they would like to observe her for another day. After two full weeks of terrible anxiety and loneliness for our baby, we were determined to go to Louisville to bring her back home, even if we had to beg, borrow or steal to pay for her local medical care. The Shriners' hospital didn't charge anything, and we were well below the poverty line, as I was making only $3600 annual salary.

When we saw her in the hospital in her little bed she looked so small. She greeted us with a smile, and we were thrilled but devastated when it was obvious that she didn't recognize us. In order for them to dismiss her in our care, we had to sign all kinds of release papers, relieving them of any responsibility for her, then current or future, condition. That was okay, we were heading home with our orange haired baby girl.

Years later she would return to hospitals, clinics and medical care, except then she would be the provider, rather than the recipient, of health care.

Fortunately, the local doctor knew what to do for Tari. He put her in a cast from her waist to her feet in a wide stance to hold her hips properly into the hip sockets. The cast had an opening for us to diaper her. She could only lie on her stomach or on her back, in which position she would look at books and magazines, never tearing a single page. I made her a little swing of heavy cotton ticking, which she could straddle like on a bicycle seat.

After about five months of casts and seven months of a metal brace between her shoes, still holding her hips into place, she learned to crawl and then to walk, making up for lost time. When Adrienne was born, Tari would walk to the baby crib and throw in a magazine, declaring, "Baby wants maggies." She seemed to be convinced that her new baby sister loved maggies as much as she did.

Her legs mended quite well and later, as a teenager, participated both in modern dance and mime.

After Kentucky, we moved to Belleville, WI where I was to be the pastor of Grace Methodist Church and attend graduate classes at UW. Tari continued her interest in books, impatiently waiting to start kindergarten across the street from the parsonage. One Sunday after church when she was five, she asked me a very serious question. I was surprised at the complexity of the question, wondering whether I should give her just a short pat answer or explain the answer in detail. I decided to give her the complete answer; after all she was my first-born. She did realize how much I used stories to make a point in my sermons, so when I finished the complicated answer she asked, "Now Daddy, are you telling the truth or are you preaching now?"

The next Sunday I had to relate that episode to the congregation who gleefully chortling, looked admiringly at the bright red hair (not orange now) glistening in the second pew. I think they saw a golden halo of wisdom.

The church had a new basement, which Tari enjoyed, inspiring her to write one of her early poems:

> Church Basement
> I can run and run down there.
> I can even curl my hair.
> I can get a drink
> From a little sink
> And flash my underwear.

She would occasionally request that we let her go "barefoot all over." Her best poem at that early age was:

> Window Shopping
> I took
> A look.

In 1964 when I had an assignment to study Japanese Noh Theatre in New York.

While I was in rehearsal, Luan took the girls every day to the Museum of Natural History or the Central park sculpture garden of Hans Christian Anderson and Alice in Wonderland. When I had a day off the whole family would go to see other places. On our visit to St. Paul's Cathedral on Fifth Avenue, we were all awestruck. Tari quickly assessed the ambience, noticing particularly the nuns, dressed like penguins, silently bowing at each altar arranged around the walls. She immediately went to the nearest altar on the south side of the cathedral and there she knelt with clasped hands as though in prayer. She then proceeded to go to each altar—probably a dozen—saying her novenas or whatever it is that nuns do at these stations. After observing Tari's worshipful activities for a while, Luan looked at me and said, "My heavens! We're raising a Catholic nun."

In 1965 we left Belleville for a year's Fulbright assignment in India. We enrolled Tari and Adrienne in Blue Bells School in Jor Bagh, a subdivision about three miles from where we lived in Nizamuddin East. Quite often we had neighbors, with the Ford Foundation, who gave us a ride to the girls' school, but one day I had to go pick up Tari on my bicycle, my only vehicle. On that particular day Adrienne had not gone to school. I could put both girls on the bike; one behind and one on a little saddle attached to the frame just in front of my seat. As Tari was my only passenger that day, she sat on the little seat in front of me,

When we were about halfway home Tari thought she ought to get her legs out of my way, so that I could pedal more efficiently, she stretched her feet up toward the front fender, which she couldn't quite reach. Her foot instead went into the spokes of the wheel, which brought the bike to an abrupt halt, and as it was the front wheel, it locked, throwing the back part, including Tari and myself, over the handlebars. I realized that I was about to land on top of her, so I stretched my arms straight in front of me and locked my elbows, so that I would not crush her by landing on her.

People gathered about us immediately to give us some assistance. It became apparent immediately to me that my arms had sustained injuries; both elbows were broken—severely impacted. I had to have both arms in slings for several days.

Although Tari felt terrible for having caused the accident, her intentions were good. It was a good thing that she was wearing her heavy shoes that day; if she had been wearing her sandals, her foot would have been seriously injured.

When we returned from India, we moved to Jackson, TN where I would be teaching at Lambuth College. In the summers we went to Wisconsin to work with the Uplands Arts Council. We lived in an old farm house, aptly called "Stonedge." Next to the chicken house was a patch of stinging nettles. Tari barely walked into the edge of the nettles and was immediately attacked by the stingers. She started screaming, which was unusual for her to express such pain or fear. I went running out, picked her up, stripped her of all her clothes—she was then barefoot all over—and put her in the bath tub with cool water and a whole box of baking soda. This treatment, also with calamine lotion, seemed to soothe her skin and allay her fears. We were reminded of how sensitive her fair skin was to any kind of irritation.

One Sunday afternoon when Tari was eleven we were at Tower Hill State Park, she was stung on her ankle by a bee. Her ankle immediately became inflamed, and she seemed to have trouble breathing. We found a phone and called Dr. Kempthorne, but he was on a call for someone at Taliesin. We then called another doctor, who had convinced many people in two counties that he had saved them from the throes of the grim reaper. He told us to come directly to his house. As she was lying on a couch, and he was giving her a shot of antihistamine, he looked seriously at me, as he sorrowfully shook his head. It scared me to death. He called for an ambulance, and as she and Luan were leaving in the ambulance, he attempted to console me. In his eastern European accent he said, "It would be too bad to lose the life of an unnecessary child." His syntax was a little awkward, but his intentions were good, and his medical expertise was life-saving. After that we called her our "unnecessary child."

Which reminds me what Tari told me several years later. She said that I had convinced her she was going to hell. I was horrified. "What do you mean? I never preached hellfire and damnation."

"Don't you know what your favorite saying was?"

"I guess I don't remember."

"You said that the road to hell is paved with good intentions, and I have had a lot of good intentions; also a few bad ones. But it didn't matter what my intentions were, I was going to hell."

I hope I have disabused her of the notion of her going to hell, as she has some of the best intentions I have ever encountered, exemplifying the fruits of good intentions, focused endeavors and consummate skills. Anyone who has ever met her, particularly those who have worked with her, would attest to the compassionate presence she brings not only to her bedside manners but also to her everyday encounters with people.

I am proud to be her daddy.

ADRIENNE LEE GILBERT

In September 1960, Luan, Tari and I had moved from the old, drafty house on School Street in Barbourville to a cute pine paneled garage apartment on College Street.

We had felt we were moving up, as we were renting from Mr. and Mrs. Viall, right across the street from the College, which had now raised my salary from the initial $3600 per annum to $4200.

We were all getting ready for a new arrival, just prior to Christmas. We had arranged for Mrs. Viall to baby sit with Tari, who was then eighteen months old. Luan woke up early on December 4 with signals that our Christmas package was about to be delivered.

I ran to wake up Mrs. Viall, while Luan finished packing her bag for London (KY) and St. Mary's Hospital. I was in such a hurry, rushing to the car and starting it, that Mrs. Viall was afraid that I was going to take off across the mountain without Luan. Even though I was an absent-minded professor, I was not quite that absent-minded.

We flew from ridge top to hill crest in the '57 Dodge that Luan and I had courted in a few years earlier. Although we were both anxious to greet the Christmas package ASAP, we wanted to make sure that we got to Dr. Santa Claus in time for him to make the delivery. We got there with some time to spare, but I had to return to Barbourville to look after Tari. By the time I got back home there was a telephone call from the hospital announcing that the package had been delivered with all parts intact—a new baby daughter.

My next task was to call the grandmothers; Grandma Gilbert in NC and Grandma Miller—call her anything but never "Granny"—in WI to tell them that Adrienne Lee Gilbert had arrived in perfect condition. We had selected the name, "Adrienne," which was the name of a famous French actress. I'm not sure that we then thought our Adrienne might be a performer, but we did like the sound of that name, so we attached "Lee" onto that.

All of my daughters were, of course, beautiful; one a redhead, one a brunette; not knowing at that time who might greet us farther down the road. However, Adrienne, my brunette, second daughter, was born without the usual bright pink, wrinkled skin. When she was old enough to sit up, we had a professional picture of her to send to the relatives. The 8 x 10 picture displayed her dark hair and skin and piercing blue eyes quite beautifully. When Grandma Gilbert showed that picture to a neighbor, Madie Tuttle, in NC, the neighbor said, "Well, Reid's wife must have jumped the fence for that one." Mamma was furious, but as usual, would never say anything directly to the person offending her. She might think of a retort later, but it would usually be too late to be effective.

It would be years later when Adrienne was a teenager that we could tell from an old photograph that Adrienne looked just like Grandma Miller when she was a teenager.

It soon became evident that Adrienne would be a leader in some way. Quite often she would lead her sisters in games, sometimes mischievous pranks. When I would threaten to whip her and her sisters, I would send them for a switch adequate for the job. I think she was the one who urged them to dawdle long enough for me to forget what I was going punish them for. I feel that they took undue advantage of my situation of being an "absent-minded professor."

In 1964, when I was studying and rehearsing a Japanese Noh play in New York, Luan and the girls spent the days in the Natural History Museum. We had planned one day, when I would have a day off, to have a picnic in Central Park, which was only half a block away. Unfortunately, it was raining that day, so we had to have our picnic in the apartment. Adrienne and her sisters laid out a picnic cloth on the floor. When we started eating, Adrienne started a picnicking song; "Here we go a picnicking, a picnicking, a picnicking, Here we go a picnicking. Where? In our apartment!"

The apartment was quite small, so we had the three girls sleep in the full-sized bed in the bedroom, and Luan and I slept on an oversized couch, much too small, in the living room. One night, toward morning, Luan must have had a nightmare, as she thrashed around, pushing me out of bed. As the night was nearly over I went and crawled in with the girls. They woke up and asked me what was happening. I said that their mom had "kicked me out of bed."

Adrienne immediately commandeered the troops, marching into the living room to push their mother out of bed. The startled Luan then asked what was happening. Adrienne announced that punishment had to be administered—I'm not sure she used those exact words. It seems quite often that the middle child in a family develops a keen sense of justice—perhaps because they're sandwiched between two hostile forces.

When we left NY in November, Adrienne led us back to the Hans Christian Anderson Statues to say goodbye to the storyteller and to Alice.

Only a few months later we were back in New York catching a ship for India. We would have chosen to fly, but Dr. Olive Reddick—an old missionary spinster—was convinced that foreign travel should only be undertaken by ship. She hadn't reckoned with three little girls. Actually, they were all three wonderful seafarers.

However, when we had embarked on the USS Constitution, and were leaving the NY harbor, Tari, Adrienne and Karen in their blue denim jumpers stood on the aft deck of the ship waving, "Goodbye, Lady!" to the Statue of Liberty as they had told goodbye to Alice such a short time earlier. Adrienne seemed always to be the anchor or fulcrum between the taller, older Tari and the shorter, younger Karen. As they stood there waving so innocently, yet excitedly, at the beginning of a wonderful adventure, I wondered silently to myself, "If something terrible happens to my marvelous daughters, I'll just kill myself."

We had several exotic ports of call; the Azores, Morocco, Gibraltar —where we saw troops of monkeys, and Naples, Italy where we disembarked to catch a train for Marseilles, France, where we then boarded another ship—a French one this time—the Laos. We passed close by the Etna Volcano and could see the flames shooting out the top. We stopped at Alexandria, Egypt prior to traveling through the Suez Canal, where Adrienne spotted a ship going in the opposite direction, and it looked as though it was driving through the sand, as we could not see the water in that channel.

Two more stops before Bombay were Aden, Yemen and Karachi, Pakistan. Sharing our table at meals was an Indian family, who spoke no English. They included a worried looking wife/mother, a large husband/father, an eight year old son/brother and a five year old fussy daughter/sister, Florence, who quite frequently would howl if she disapproved of certain foods or situations. Every time that Adrienne would start to complain about something, Luan or I would simply look at her and call her "Florence", which was sufficient to deter any further fussiness. She and her sisters had been appalled to observe Florence's tantrums.

After a week in Bombay we took a long train trip to New Delhi, which would be our new home for the next year. It was in India where Adrienne began to expand the leadership abilities, she had exhibited earlier. Every morning in our beautiful apartment, upstairs over the Mehta's, our landlords, Adrienne seemed to take the responsibility of getting everyone organized. Tari was usually simply reading a book. Karen was happily greeting the morning with a big smile as befitting a nearly three-year old. Adrienne, while kind of floating between her sisters, was attempting to make some sense of it all.

We enrolled Adrienne and Tari in Bluebells School, which was a couple of miles from our apartment. Usually I took both Adrienne and Tari on my bike to school, but Adrienne was not with us the day that Tari and I had our bike accident. She and her sisters did think it was great fun to feed Daddy, as I had both arms in slings for my broken elbows to heal.

When the whole family was attending a conference for Fulbright families at a splendiferous resort, Luan and I were having tea with the other adults when we were all alarmed to hear a big splash, accompanied by a great deal of laughter and a scream from Adrienne. We went running to discover Adrienne—covered with lily pads and lotus blossoms—pulling herself out of a lily pond. Her pretty blue dress was drenched, as was her hair, which Luan had fixed up so prettily that morning. We discovered that Adrienne—testing her leadership abilities—had coaxed the younger children to listen to her and watch her as she demonstrated how to dive into water, trying to impress them by standing on the edge of the pool, clasping her hands together and leaning toward the water. She leaned over a little too far, failing to test also her balancing ability. Even though she was so thoroughly humiliated, she simply used this negative lesson to understand how far she could risk her leadership capabilities thereafter.

Not only was she destined to be a leader, she also began a performance career quite early. A wonderful example of that was on an occasion just after we had returned from India. Luan had dressed all the girls in lovely, frilly dresses for a lunch out at the Pancake House on South Park Street in Madison Shortly after we had sat down to order the meal, Adrienne announced that she had to use the restroom. Of course, Luan had to take her. She seemed to sashay all the way through the restaurant to the restroom, then sashay all the way back. She did have on a beautiful little dress, which she was anxious for everyone to see.

In about fifteen minutes she said that she had to go again. As she followed her mother to the restroom, she didn't seem to be in a hurry. Again she danced her way through the restaurant, both going and coming. When we were about half way through the meal, she had to march again. Luan was getting a little upset, but she knew that she was the only one to take her. This time, Adrienne led the way. She knew the way by now. On their return, all eyes of the other patrons were on her as she flounced back to the table, while Luan followed with smoke seemingly coming out of her ears, "Three times to the bathroom was certainly unnecessary!", but Adrienne did enjoy the parade.

In 1969 we moved back to Wisconsin from Tennessee, so I could finish the dissertation for my PhD, which I received in January, 1971. The girls' classmates were impressed that their father was now a "doctor." Adrienne assured them that, "Well, he's the kind of doctor that doesn't do you any good."

Later, at Valley Studio, Adrienne amply demonstrated both her leadership and performance abilities. Her best classes there were ballet and period dance, both taught by William Burdick, an old friend of mine, and a former ballet master with the Metropolitan Opera Ballet. William had brought wonderful period costumes with him from New York. When Adrienne and the other dancers performed in those old costumes, they could have elegantly graced a New York stage. Adrienne looked as professional as any of the older dancers, who had studied dance for years.

As a matter of fact, William was so impressed with Adrienne's performance ability that he arranged for her to meet Margaret Craske, Margot Fonteyn's ballet teacher. Although Ms. Craske accepted her as a student, Luan and I were reluctant to let her go at the age of fourteen to the Big Apple.

When she was sixteen and with her new driver's license, she asked me if she and Karen could go for a ride in my Saab. We were at the Studio, and as the roads weren't heavily traveled, I thought it would be okay. It was quite a bit of time before they came back—walking. I asked where my car was. Adrienne explained, that, "Well there was some loose gravel on a little curve up the road, and the car kinda slid a little into the ditch." As Karen couldn't push it out, Adrienne thought I might have to get someone to help get the car out of the ditch and her out of this new jam.

I couldn't determine if she was performing for Karen or trying to exhibit her leadership ability in her negotiations with me. Actually it wasn't very bad, only a slight scratch. I never worried any more about her driving, as she became quite an excellent driver.

She continued her ballet studies and performances in Madison and even went to Paris to experience the French scene. After her formal education was completed she obtained a position with the Wisconsin legislature and there met her future husband, Jesse. I was honored to assist in officiating at their wedding. Since then she has amply demonstrated to all of us and the whole state of Wisconsin her leadership abilities in the hallowed halls of the state capitol.

She has continued writing the rest of her story with Jesse and their two soccer player sons.

KAREN ANN GILBERT

When Luan, Tari, Adrienne and I moved to Belleville, Wisconsin in 1962 we were fortunate to find housing in the parsonage of Grace Methodist Church, where I had been appointed as the pastor, while in graduate school at the University of Wisconsin. As we already had two daughters, everyone thought that the next baby, expected in September, would be a boy.

On September 26, our third daughter, Karen Ann, was born. The naming of our daughters seemed to become more mainstream as each new one was born. Karen was blonde, contributing significantly to the diversity of hair colors of her sisters; Tari the redhead and Adrienne the brunette. She was born at St. Joseph's Catholic Hospital in Monroe, about twenty-five miles from Belleville. We were delighted to have another perfect baby girl, daughters of a Methodist minister; each born in separate states in Roman Catholic hospitals.

Based on everyone's assumption that our next child would be a boy, when I introduced myself and my family to the Grace Methodist Church family in June, I, facetiously, announced that we were expecting our first boy in September. I had not thought anymore about this prediction until a couple of weeks after Karen's birth. I was in the Belleville Post Office, when I was confronted by a ninety-year-old grim-faced church member—one who never came to church because of his hearing problem. He quite seriously approached me saying, "I don't think it's right for a minister to lie."

Stunned, I asked, "What are you referring to, Mr. Argue?" His last name was Argue, and I had already been told that the name suited him just fine, as he could be rudely contentious, enjoying a bout of argumentation.

"I understand that you announced in the pulpit that you and your wife were going to have a baby boy, and since your new baby is a girl, I consider your announcement a lie," as he laughed heartily at his own joke. Realizing he was just having fun at my expense, I enjoyed it too.

Thirty-seven years later when Karen gave birth to her only son, she named him Theo, unaware, I suppose, that Mr. Argue's first name was Theo.

At a very early age, Karen showed promise as the "hostess with the mostest." When she was about two years old, the Methodist District Superintendent had a quarterly conference at the church and afterward came over to visit my family. Soon after we had been seated, Karen disappeared into the kitchen. She returned soon, holding a tray with three glasses of water, which she graciously offered the three adults: her mother, the district superintendent and me. Although the water was warm, we felt we had to drink all of it as a show of appreciation for Karen's thoughtfulness. The DS, who was ostensibly my boss, was duly impressed with Karen's hospitality.

She also expected others to share with her. In the fall of 1964 when we were in New York, we spent every weekend in New Jersey with Joyce Stansell and Stanley Godfrey, friends of ours from the time Luan and I had formerly lived in NJ. Joyce and Stanley, who were professional performers and had performed with Yul Brynner on Broadway, were impressed with all our daughters, but Stanley was particularly enthralled with Karen's good-humored assertiveness.

When we would all be at the dinner table, Karen, then barely two, would stand, rather than sit, in her chair and survey everyone else's plate, to see if there was something there she would like. If so, she would simply reach across to purloin the delectable item for herself. She seemed to be particularly fond of Stanley's ice cream. Luan and I tried to correct this behavior, but Stanley, although on the surface he seemed to dislike children, was quite favorably impressed with Karen's candor.

My Asian Theatre professor, A. C. Scott, was also a recipient of Karen's good humor. When he would visit us, and we were sitting in the living room, Karen would walk toward him until he reached out for her. She would then turn laughingly away. I don't know why he seemed to get such a joy out of her flirtation, as he was a rather stern Briton.

A couple of years later, Stanley and Joyce told us that they had adopted two children from Bolivia. They said they had thought a lot about our children and were so influenced by their personalities that they thought they would like to have children of their own. I should have told them that no one could ever have daughters as perfect as ours.

In July 1965 we moved to India for a year. After traveling by ship and by train for more than a month and finally settling into our apartment in Nizamudin East in New Delhi, Karen said, "Let's go see Grandma," not realizing that Grandma was half way around the globe. I told this to Professor Scott, who loved to hear anything about Karen. He said that children had a wonderful sense of Zen with no regard for space or time—everything is immediate and close at hand.

A couple of months after we arrived in India, Karen celebrated her third birthday. The Mehtas, the landlords who lived downstairs, had a little girl, Minoo, the same age as Karen. As neither one of them knew the other's language—Minoo of course spoke Hindi—they developed their own language. Karen told us that the Indian word for train was Gooshgoo. Minoo told her parents that the American word for train was Gooshgoo. I don't know what further contributions they made to the vocabulary of their new language.

Although Karen played in the dirt in the front yard with Minoo and often ate unwashed grapes, both activities were strictly taboo. We were told, officially and quite adamantly, never to put our hands or feet in or on the soil or eat anything that was either unwashed, unpeeled or uncooked. In spite of these dire warnings, Karen was the only one in the family who was never sick in India. The rest of us, on a regular basis, had to take "samples" to Dr. Dorothy Chaakra for antibiotics for our sieges of diarrhea.

Karen again paid particular attention to her food; this time her aversion to Indian food. She would never complain that she didn't like it;

she would simply smilingly push her unwanted food under her place mat. At the end of most meals her plate was fairly toppling on a mound of undesired food. Our Muslim cook, Khan, would say mournfully, "Ooh, Baby doesn't like Khan's cooking." We would assure him that his cooking was fine . . . which it really was.

Every morning, as everyone else was grumpily waking up, Karen would bound out of bed to greet the day, saying with her body language, "Hello world! Are you ready for me?"

Whenever I would walk down the neighborhood street with Karen, a rather large aggressive Indian woman would come out to urge me to bring "your baby to play with my baby boy." I don't know if this was an attempt to begin marriage negotiations, as marriages can be arranged quite early in India. The neighbor exhibited her great fondness for Karen by pinching her cheeks. Karen soon learned to hide her face when she would see an Indian woman coming toward her with hands pointing toward her cheeks.

Moving back to the States, we enrolled Karen in a preschool in Jackson, TN, where I was teaching at Lambuth College. Her teacher was Ms. Dot. One day after school Karen gave us a beautiful performance impression of Ms. Dot: "Ooh, Karen what a beautiful little coat you have," as Karen stooped down to baby talk with an imaginary child. I was sure she would grow up to be an actress.

While still in pre-school, she developed a strong yen for a pair of white go-go boots. When she asked me if I would buy them for her, I told her that there were other things we needed much more than go-go boots. Without saying anything further, she calmly went upstairs to the attic bedroom, which she shared with her sisters. When she came down with a small white suitcase, she sat on the bottom step and asked me if I would miss her. I sat beside her to ask where she was going. She said she was running away from home because I wouldn't buy her any white go-go boots.

Again she asked, "Will you miss me when I'm gone?"

I assured her that I would miss her terribly and hoped that she wouldn't go. It was evident that she was determined on her mission. I then asked her what her plan of escape was.

She said that she was going across campus to spend the night at the Whiteheads, where she had a friend about her age, and that the next day she would go to Grandma's in Wisconsin. She was still being rather Zen, not realizing that Grandma Miller lived about five hundred miles away.

We talked a little while longer, and she thought she'd wait until morning to start her trip. I told her, "I think that's a grand idea."

By the next day, we had other things on our minds, so pushed the go-go boots to the bottom of our agendas. Many years later, only a few years ago, I saw a white pair of go-go boots in a thrift store and bought them. When I presented them to Karen, she didn't show much sign of appreciation.

When Luan or I would take Karen shopping with us, she had an amazing ability for her little hands to reach quickly for something that struck her fancy. However, if we scolded her, "Karen leave your hands off those things," she would cower as she put her arms over her head, as though to fend off any blows which her parents might inflict upon her.

Then in a whimpering voice she would say, "Okay, Daddy, I won't do it again."

If anyone else would be watching this little charade—acting performance of hers—we would have difficulty explaining that we never whipped her for anything, only to be confronted with belligerent stares toward us and sympathetic, smiling glances toward that poor little abused child. We had to be extremely careful how we would attempt to correct her in public, or her acting ability could be the cause for humiliation on our part.

Karen loved all the pets we had. Just before we left Tennessee someone gave us a beagle pup, which we named Aacha—in Hindi meaning *OK*—but Aacha kept running away when we brought him to Wisconsin. When we were at Valley Studio, Aacha left one day, so we put out an APB. We heard that a nearby neighbor had Aacha. Karen was so excited, but when we got to the farmer's home we discovered it wasn't our puppy. Karen tearfully said, "That's not Aacha." I heard of another beagle which had been found. I didn't tell the girls, as I was afraid they'd just be disappointed again. It was Aacha, and when I brought him home, Karen was certainly excited: "It's really Aacha."

When we moved over to Plain, Aacha kept running away to a neighboring farm over the ridge. He seemed to like all the farm animals there, so we decided it'd be best just to let him stay at the home he'd chosen.

Shortly after that we got a black lab pup, which Karen and her sisters named Smokey. That Halloween (1969) a small kitten found us, so the girls named her "Trick or Treat." She had kittens before we moved to Madison, but she and the kittens all died. Smokey was with us all the way—several years later—to WV.

The first pet that was Karen's alone—when she was a teenager—was a black Persian cat which she named "Nigel;" an apt name for a black cat. Nigel somehow sensed that I wasn't a cat person, but we had a healthy respect for each other, particularly after our ride to West Virginia.

Karen moved with me to WV in my VW Rabbit. Nigel was ensconced in a box in the back seat. I had told Karen that I couldn't risk having Nigel crawling and bounding all over the car while I was driving. She agreed to keep him in the box. By the time we had reached the Wisconsin state line, Nigel had begun crying . . . almost sobbing . . . by calling, "Mamma!, Mamma!, Mamma!" which freaked me out. I told Karen she could let him out of the box, but if he got underfoot she'd have to put him back in. She agreed to this caveat.

Everything went just fine until we reached the twisting roads of WV. As I had learned to drive in North Carolina on such curvy roads, I have always been inspired to speed up just a little in the center of the curve. (Flatlanders tend to brake in the middle of the curve, which is absolutely the worst thing to do, even on a dry road.)

Nigel was sitting on Karen's lap and had been behaving quite well; no yelling and no crawling under my feet. However, when I started speeding up—just a little—in the curves, he stared at me and put his right front paw on my arm, as he pressed down on it while continuing to focus on my eyes. Sensing that he was telling me that he did not approve of my mode of driving in these mountains to which he was unaccustomed, I looked at Karen and then at Nigel, saying, "All right Nigel I'll slow down, if it will make you feel any better."

He seemed to relax, and Karen just smiled.

We got along fine in West Virginia, and even in Ohio where we lived for a while. Sometime after that, when Nigel and Karen had moved back to Wisconsin, Karen called to tell me that Nigel had died. She and I shared a quiet cry over the phone.

Before we moved to West Virginia, Karen had been the company manager of the production I directed of *Grease* at the civic center in Madison. Then when we moved to West Virginia, she was the company manager of the ten weeks of performances I directed for the Mountain State Players.

Karen lived with me for a while in Columbus, Ohio where I was on the OSU faculty. In 1982 she moved back to Madison, where she has continued to write her family and professional story, by living it.

Her theatre career has been put on hold! . . . at least for the time being.

SMOKEY

"Daddy, he looks like a little bear."
"He looks like Smokey Bear."
"Why don't we name him that?"
"He'll feel silly being called. 'Bear'."
"Don't you be silly. I meant 'Smokey'."
"Yeah, let's name him Smokey."

It was impossible to know which of my three daughters (Tari, Adrienne or Karen) blurted out which point of that discussion, but they all readily agreed that they had found a proper name.

He did look a whole lot like a little Smokey the Bear with his long black hair, except for a little white marking on his chest. When he romped, which was constantly, he looked like an unpredictable black furry football.

The O'Brien's, who were living in a Robert Graves rehabbed barn, where the American Players Theatre is now housed, had rescued a pregnant mixed-black lab. She had probably been abandoned out in the country by some city folk, who no longer wanted her, particularly now that she was about to "find" pups.

I can't understand why people think it is more humane to dump an unwanted pet out in the country, rather than simply finding a new home for them or euthanizing them. She "found" eight, as I recall, and John, the youngest O'Brien son, seemed to be in charge of finding homes for the foundlings. He had already picked out the one he wanted to keep—the largest male of the litter.

Smokey was the smallest, but also the friskiest. When we took him home to the old farmhouse we were renting right outside Plain, Wisconsin, he had the whole place to roam. We walked with him out to the pasture where he discovered the small clear running stream. He would run through the water then turn around to run through it again, with his big paws splashing the water higher than his head. Even though he was the runt of the litter, I knew that his large paws meant that he would probably grow up to be a rather large adult.

Of course, we hadn't taken him from his mother until he was eight weeks old, when he was weaned. After several more weeks at our place, Smokey was visited by John, who came over to see how the new pup was doing and was duly amazed at his progress. The pup that John had kept was now not as large as Smokey and hadn't yet learned to lift his leg—as Smokey had aptly demonstrated—when he needed to pee. John was dismayed that he had chosen the wrong dog, but the deed was done. *Smokey was at home with his new adoptive family.*

The new family member was to be an outside dog, so I fixed a nice warm bed for him in a large doghouse, which Junior Bindl, our landlord, had built next to the farmhouse. The pup seemed to be quite content with his upscale digs. When he was about three months old he experienced his first snowfall, which delighted him, as he tried to catch the large snowflakes in his mouth. When the snow had accumulated a couple of inches on the ground, he would stick his nose under it then toss the flakes into the air. He didn't seem to tire of this little game.

At the age of six months he had wandered all the way up to the neighbors, who lived at the end of the road. They had a male German Shepherd, approximately the same age. The two adolescent males became such great pals that we were afraid he might abandon us and take up residence there.

Smokey would always come back home after his neighborhood visit, particularly at chow time. He always maintained a healthy appetite.

He grew up to be a sixty-pound friendly adult, who still loved to romp with other dogs and was equally friendly with people. He exhibited his joy by wagging his enormous tail—not such a long tail, just a thick, strong one. I even accused him of being part kangaroo. That was when I moved him to Valley Studio where I had a mime theatre school. There he had numerous opportunities to interact with many people and occasionally other dogs in addition to Thistle, a collie who already lived there.

It was the experience with another dog that proved to be his undoing. On a Sunday afternoon, a prospective student and her family and dog were visiting. Their dog, a standard poodle about the size of Smokey, was being walked by one of the girls of the visiting family. Smokey, always the curious and friendly one, and the canine visitor were getting to know each other by sniffing each other's rear ends. The girl, holding the visiting dog's leash, kicked Smokey in his butt when he was becoming acquainted with his guest.

He immediately panicked and clamped his jaws onto the other dog's neck and wouldn't let go. Both dogs started what seemed to be a macabre dance with the poodle swirling, Smokey hanging on, as the girl started beating him with her purse. Karen, my youngest daughter, saw all this and started crying, saying, "She's beating my dog. She's beating my dog."

Smokey wouldn't unclamp his jaws until I joined the whirling dervishes to blow in his ear, causing him to open his mouth. As a young boy I had learned that in order to make a dog release whatever he was holding in his mouth, you needed to blow in his ear, which I suppose created some pressure in his head. This was necessary when the hunting dog would get to the downed game before the hunter got there.

The dog, usually a hound, felt that the rabbit belonged to him after all the tracking and running he had been doing to jump and chase the prey . . . and then to claim the prize.

Everyone, including the dogs, were exhausted, exasperated and angry by this time. The girl put the poodle back into the car, while Karen and I hugged and consoled Smokey and each other.

After that, Smokey would panic every time he saw another dog, but instead of running away, he would run toward it. Maybe he understood that the best defense is an aggressive offense. Before the purse-beating incident he had loved to play with other dogs. Thistle had certainly never been a threat to him. He seemed to fear that any new dog would somehow cause him to get a beating with a heavy purse.

One of the young students, studying dance, was Eve Wright. Her mother, Iovanna Wright, Frank Lloyd Wright's daughter, brought Eve every morning for ballet class. Iovanna would also bring her French poodle, Pretty Boy, and sometimes let him play in the front yard. Several people cautioned her not to do that, as Smokey might attack him, even though he had not had another fighting encounter since the visiting standard poodle. Iovanna seemed always to be in her own little world. Ignoring this timely advice, one morning she let Pretty Boy out to play.

Unfortunately, Smokey left his usual environment behind the office and upon seeing Pretty Boy, immediately ran to greet him. The poodle didn't have a chance, being so much smaller, but quite yippy. Smokey grabbed the little dog at the shoulders, shaking him vigorously no more than three times, apparently breaking his neck. He then brought him to Iovanna, laying him at her feet. She, of course being justifiably distraught, picked up the lifeless body to carry him back to Taliesin for a burial.

I wrote Iovanna and Mrs. Wright a long letter, extending my regret and apology for the unfortunate incident, also relating my earlier reluctance to intrude myself into the prestigious Taliesin community and expressing the irony of the occurrence to prompt that communication. I offered to buy another French poodle for Iovanna, but someone from Taliesin assured me that Pretty Boy couldn't be replaced, which I certainly understood.

I moved over the ridge behind the Studio to an old farm house where a bachelor farmer, Leslie Richardson, had died a few months earlier. He and his spinster sister, Lola, had lived there for decades after their folks had passed away. The ancient house had neither running water nor electricity. Smokey would be safe there and so would any dogs visiting the school. Before I had all the furniture put together and in place, I had gone into a back bedroom with an old kerosene lamp. I then heard Smokey start to growl. I called to him, "What's the matter,

Smokey?"—as though I was expecting him to answer me. We did have that kind of relationship.

I knew Leslie had died in that room and thought that perhaps Smokey had been confronted by Leslie's ghost. He continued to growl, so I went into the room where I saw him facing a mirror that I had left on the floor. Of course his image was facing him in the mirror. He hadn't attacked the image. Even though he saw what he thought was another dog, he hadn't smelled a different one. When I laughed at him, he tucked his head and walked into the kitchen. I tried to get him to come back in to look at himself in the mirror, but he was too embarrassed to look again.

There were no more disastrous Smokey incidents at the Richardson home place.

After living there for a while, I moved to West Virginia and thought Smokey would be too shy in this new environment to remember his old habit, as he wouldn't need to protect the Studio territory, but I was proved wrong.

Both Smokey and Karen moved with me to West Virginia. Smokey loved to ride shotgun in the car, always sitting straight up, observing the passing scene, whether other vehicles or the panoramic vistas along the way. He always looked like a wise old man just ready to impart some significant wisdom, but there was also a kind of sadness in his demeanor.

While on tour out of town, I had left Smokey with friends in Elkins, cautioning them in as strong terms as possible, to keep him on a leash whenever they were outside with him. Unfortunately they were careless, letting him run down the street where he encountered another dog. What seemed to drive him the wildest was the incessant yipping of a dog—usually a small one? He again efficiently accomplished what seemed to be his appointed task.

The little dog's mistress was a jeweler in Elkins. As soon as I found out about this latest incident, I called her, offering my condolences and asking what redress I could give. Apparently the careless person who had allowed Smokey to do this, had told her about my background and that Smokey had done this before.

She railed about me being a man of the cloth and keeping such a vicious creature. That was when I assured her that he would never do this again. It would have been useless to tell her that this terrible behavior of his had been prompted by a stupid person's thoughtless behavior, kicking him some years earlier when he was innocently getting acquainted with another dog.

The only way to prevent this behavior of Smokey's from recurring was to put him down. Karen was living with me in Thomas, and was devoted to Smokey as well as to her black cat, Nigel, who had his own story. I told her that June (Junior Streets) and I were going to take Smokey up to the strip mine, where I had often run with him, and I would shoot him there with my .22 rifle.

I would also take a shovel for burial. She knew how difficult that would be for me, as she knew that as a country boy on the farm I had never killed a rabbit while hunting or even a chicken for Sunday dinner.

She knew that Smokey had to be put down, not as a punishment of execution, but as an assurance he would never kill another little dog. She urged me to take him to the vet to have him euthanized, but I said that he was always so frightened at the vet's with those slippery stainless steel tables, just as he always hid in some small dark place, whenever there was a thunderstorm. I explained that this was between me and Smokey, and that June, also being a mountain man, understood what I had to do.

When we got to the strip mine, I talked with Smokey a little, telling him that what I was about to do had to be done—not out of retribution or punishment—and that I loved him as much as ever. He looked at me with those wise, sad eyes. Standing about eight feet from each other, looking directly into each other's eyes, I loaded the rifle. He stood still before I pulled the trigger.

When I fired, he slumped into a sitting position with a small trickle of blood streaming down his face from between his eyes. We continued to look at each other, while I put another cartridge into place. He then gave three strong thumps with his kangaroo tail, seemingly to assure me that he understood and that everything was all right between us.

This was always his signal to me—three slaps on the ground with his tail—that everything was as it should be. I shot one more time, and he went down. I put aside the rifle and held him in my arms, while rocking him and crying.

June, standing close by, without saying a word, put a hand on my shoulder, patted Smokey's head and picked up the shovel to find an appropriate burial spot. I dug and wept and wept and dug.

Upon calling the jewelry lady, I told her what I had done, thus assuring her that Smokey would never be the cause again of another dog's death. Her response was quite unexpected. "I wish you would have hanged him, so I could have been there to witness him grasp for his last gasps of breath. That would have delighted me."

I could not imagine that anyone in the world would have enjoyed such a scene of anguish and suffering. Possibly she felt that her suffering and that of her little dog's would have been relieved, perhaps balanced, with Smokey's anguish, if his demise had been slow and painful from the end of a hangman's rope.

All I have of Smokey, aside from the joyous and sad memories, is a picture of him looking out from a small picture frame—the look of wisdom still emanating from his sympathetic eyes—eyes not fully understanding the ramifications of what he had done, but completely understanding what I had to do.

Although I have rescued a couple of abandoned dogs since then, Smokey will always be with me, particularly on a misty morning while traipsing across the high meadow of my West Virginia farm or while meditating in a spruce grove overlooking the Dry Fork River.

AUNT BETTIE LIGHT

Aunt Bettie was born in 1860, the daughter of Lorenzo Dowell Gilbert and Sarah Cassell. She lived until she was ninety-one, giving me an opportunity to visit with her quite often.

Actually Aunt Bettie, whom all of the children adored, was not our aunt. Rather she was Grandpa Noel Gilbert's first cousin. We probably called her "Aunt Bettie" because we saw her so often when we would be visiting sick kin folks. We weren't in the habit of calling cousins, "cousin", but we would have to give some title to older kin, so "Aunt" or "Uncle" seemed appropriate.

At the age of forty-six, she married Henry Clay Light, who was sixty-two. He was a widower with eight children. Aunt Bettie had no children of her own, but raised her stepchildren and cared for her husband until his death in 1917.

When I was born in 1930, Aunt Bettie was 70 years old. Even at that age, after her husband had died and her stepchildren were grown, she would live with various Gilbert families. It wasn't because she needed a place to live; it was because she would be called upon to help out with anyone who was sick or having a baby. She even served as midwife to neighbor women, who weren't kin.

She seemed to stay most often with Uncle Lemly and Aunt Alice, as Aunt Alice was sickly a great deal of the time. Occasionally she would come to Winston and help out Grandma Gilbert at her boarding house. That was when our city cousins would be able to visit with her.

Whenever my siblings and I would see her at any of her places, she would let us stand back-to-back with her to measure how close we were to growing up.

As she had a huge hump on her back, she was no more than four feet eight inches tall. She always seemed as delighted as we were to measure our height since the last time we had seen her.

Even though she had that deformed spine, she told me, "I've never been sick a day in my life . . . not even a headache." As she hadn't had any children, she hadn't had to endure childbirth.

What added to the mystery of her lack of illness, was that I had usually seen her working at manual labor to help the family of some sick relative, sometimes much younger than she. She would milk the cow, fetch water from the spring, split kindling for the cook stove and even chop wood for the fireplace.

No matter what season of the year, she always wore a complete black outfit; long black dress, black stockings and a black bonnet. The visor of her bonnet stuck out nearly eight inches, encircling and shading her wrinkled face. She also wore black galoshes, no matter what the weather. We kids were fascinated by the galoshes, because the snaps were never fastened, so they flopped back and forth whenever she walked. That was particularly bizarre for the city cousins, as they watched her walk on the sidewalk, where galoshes certainly weren't needed.

It seemed strange to me why people who wrote those stories about witches, drew them to look like Aunt Bettie with her black costume and furrowed face. To us children she was a beautiful person.

When I was eleven years old, World War II broke out. Aunt Bettie was eighty-one, so we had a few more years to share war stories. Of course mine were only what I heard on the radio, read in the newspapers and learned from my four uncles who were in military service.

It was amazing that I could talk with someone who had remembered the Civil War, even though she was only five when it ended.

"Aunt Bettie, that war musta been really different from the war goin' on now. They surely didn't have planes and tanks like nowadays."

"Well they got around on horses. Acourse I was only five when it ended, but I do remember Papa goin' away."

"Was there any of the war near where you were livin' there in Virginia?"

"I didn't see any of the war, but I did see some Yankee soldiers."

"Really?"

"I remember those soldiers jumping the rail fences with their horses, when they'd come 'round botherin' us 'bout somethin' to eat."

"Did you oblige them?"

"Mamma said, 'We can't let nobody go hungry if we can help it.'"

"Do you remember anything else about them?"

"When Papa had come back from the war. Once when one of them jumped our fence, Papa went out there and found this little blue china cup (showing me the cup). You can see the handle is broke, but I don't know if it broke when it hit the ground or it was already broke. He'd probably stolen it from one of those big houses from down near Richmond."

"So your daddy came back from the war before it was over?"

"Yeah his arm was shot in Gettysburg, Pennsylvania where he was captured. They then sent him somewhere in New York State. Would you like to see some of my letters from back then?"

"That'd be wonderful."

"It seems that Papa didn't always follow orders. He said that it wasn't really our war here in the mountains. It was for all those flatland plantation owners. It seemed to him that they had to fight for the property of those planters. You know that at that time the colored folks, who were slaves, were considered as property?"

"I think I knew that."

"They called Papa 'Dow' back then."

She handed me the letter.

> Chester Station   July 20th 1864
> Dear Dow
>   I received a copy of the extension (sic) of your furlough about the 15th of June. I approved it and it went back I supposed to the board and you have been absent without leave ever since your furlough expired. It is now the 20th of July. I have not reported you absent without leave yet but I shall

now have to do it if you do not have your furlough legally extended. I do not want to report you absent without leave nor none of the rest of the boys. Neither do I intend to if I can get over it in obedience to an order issued a short time since I will be bound to report you and all of the balance of the company absent without leave unless you have your furlough legally extended. I will put it off as long as I can.
(The rest of the letter contained greetings for folks back home.)

"Aunt Bettie, it seems that a lot of boys from the mountains didn't want to fight in that war."

"Yes, and I found out years later that counties in the Virginia mountains farther west from us, left the state when Virginia pulled out of the nation.

I also found out in school that that was the time when West Virginia became a state, composed of the rebellious counties of the "Old Virginia Commonwealth".

"Here's another letter from Lt. Flint Aistrop."

July 24th 1864

Dow I have been working to see if I could get over reporting you absent without leave and I find that I will be obliged to do it unless you have your furlough legally extended.
(Again there were greetings and questions about folks back home.)

"I guess he must have gone back if he got shot later."

"Yes, I think he and Lt. Aistrop were good friends, and Papa didn't want to get him in trouble, simply 'cause he, hisself didn't like the war."

"What did he do when he got back home?"

"Oh he kept on farmin' . . . An' sometime after the war he started preachin.'"

"Preachin'?"

"Yeah, in the Primitive Baptist Church."

"Like Grandpa an' Uncle Lemly?"

"Well, yes, but they weren't born 'till after he took up preachin'."

I still had my eye on that little blue china cup. It would be a special thing to have a relic like that from the Civil War and especially since Aunt Bettie had saved it. "Aunt Bettie, do you suppose you could leave that blue china cup to me?"

"If you care for that cup, I'll be sure you get it."

Unfortunately for me, that didn't happen. Cousin Denny Gilbert got the cup, but I did get her valise, which held some of her other worldly goods, including her reading glasses without the cup or any letters.

She told me about the old Gilbert graveyard where her Granddaddy, my great-great granddaddy, was buried. She said, "I had a little brother, named David, who was born a short time after me. He didn't live very long. He's also buried in the old cemetery which is right up the hill from the old spring."

The last time I saw Aunt Bettie was when I visited her with Daddy when she was living with one of her stepchildren. She was ninety-one years old and died shortly thereafter.

I feel that she died not so much from a specific ailment but from distress that she was no longer able to take care of folks who needed her help.

THE EVIL WEED

Tobacco—the evil weed—played an important part in my early life, from the time of working in the tobacco fields in my teens until attending college at a university built with a tobacco fortune.

I grew up in tobacco country, Forsyth County, NC. In my early life my father used tobacco in all forms; dipping snuff, chewing tobacco, and smoking pipes, cigars and cigarettes. At the age of fifty, considering what a nasty habit it was, he just decided to quit and did. He never had any sympathy with anyone who claimed that they had tried to quit, but couldn't. My brother, Ott, couldn't quit and died of emphysema. He was still smoking while on oxygen.

When I was a youngster—no child labor laws then—every summer I would "hire out" to local tobacco farmers for fifty cents a day. The grown men with families were paid $5. I thought that was unfair, but I did realize that they needed the money much more than I did, even though we did about the same work. I was once paid for several days' work in silver dollars. Mamma insisted that I put them in the bank. I was afraid they wouldn't give them back to me—and they didn't. They gave me paper money instead. I haven't trusted banks since.

A tobacco crop takes about 13 months from the time the plant bed is prepared to the time it is all sold at auction in the Winston Salem tobacco warehouses. I never worked with planting the seeds in the plant beds, which were put in a newground; newground is reclaimed ground that has been cleared of trees, stumps, rocks and roots, but is rich loamy soil, having been a woodlands soil for many years. The seeds are sown in early spring and covered with a cloth to protect against frosts.

The kind of tobacco we planted was flue-cured, which took a great deal more hand labor than the air-cured variety. I once counted how many times each individual leaf is handled by hand; it's thirteen times.

We transplanted the seedlings in late May with a hand planter; one fellow handling the planter with water in it and the other fellow throwing the plant into the chute. It would take about four hours for two fellows to plant an acre.

As the plants grew, they would need to be cultivated, hoed, weeded, topped, suckered and wormed before it was time for harvest. A few really healthy plants weren't topped, but were allowed to go to seed to save the seeds for planting the next year.

Worming was a nasty job, as the green worms were about four inches long with a bent horn at the rear end. If we didn't take the worms off they'd eat big holes in the leaves, thus rendering them unfit for market. Ordinarily we'd just pull the worm off the leaf and throw it on the ground before stepping on it or smashing it with a clod of the red clay dirt.

One of the boys loved to show off during the worming process when he'd take one of the fat worms—make sure he had our attention—then bite off the worm's head, releasing all the black innards of the juicy green worm.

The harvesting is called "priming," and happened about the same time the rest of the crops were "laid by". Two or three of the bottom leaves, which were beginning to yellow—in prime—were snapped off. The leaves were put under the arm of the worker until an arm load was pulled, then they'd be taken to a slide (sled) hitched to a mule, which pulled the load to a barn. There the leaves were strung on four-foot-long sticks to be placed on poles, traversing the length of the barn, which would hold about 600 to 800 sticks.

Two people would bunch the leaves, by the stems, in handfuls of three or four leaves. They then handed them to a person, the stringer, who'd tie them onto the sticks. I became a pretty good stringer. One handful was looped on the near side of the stick, then the next bunch was looped in the string and twisted over to the other side. There would always be someone checking the tautness of the strung tobacco, particularly if you were just a beginner.

One older fellow, Mr. Lon Ward, loved to check on the younger guys. He also chewed home-twisted tobacco, which was simply tobacco leaves twisted into a rope-like loop and provided readymade chewing stock. When I wasn't paying particular attention to him, he'd yell, "Reid, catch!" Then he'd throw that "chaw" of wet tobacco toward me, and what could I do but catch it? Unfortunately, it happened more than once.

The workers had to wear long sleeves and hats to cover as much of the body as possible, even in the hot "dog days". Even though the leaves were green they carried a residue of black tar, which exuded itself over any surface, which it might touch, particularly on hairy surfaces like arms and heads.

After hanging in the barn for a couple of days, the leaves came "in order," which meant that it'd be time to put a fire in the flue—thus "flue-cured" tobacco.

The firing took a couple of days and nights, which meant that someone had to stay close by and check the temperature inside the barn from time to time. The overnight firing was usually left to one of the boys, and that was a "fitten'" time for other boys in the neighborhood to stay as well; roastin' field corn on the flue, raidin' the melon patch or even the 'mater patch for those itty bitty 'maters, which we called "tommy-toes."

Before we'd all fall asleep on the worn-out, patchwork quilts, we might play some cards, "rassle" with each other or take turns jumpin' on the jumpboard. That was a contraption composed of a wide oak board laid over a piece of firewood, making a kind of low seesaw, except instead of sitting on it, one fellow stood on one end and another fellow jumped onto the other extended end. They could keep on doing this until one fell off.

Sometimes you might hear children jumping on a jumpboard with their hard heeled boots, and the sound ringing all the way down the "holler" on a crisp wintry evening. The steady rhythm was somewhat like a shared heart beat

The jumpboard was the same kind of thing you might see in a carnival where one person is standing on the board and another person from a high perch jumps down on it, sending the first person up in the air in a "somerset," landing in a "settin'" chair on a third person's head. Except they didn't use a piece of stovewood for the fulcrum, as we did.

When the flue fires seemed to be banked adequately for a couple of hours, we might even take a little time to go off with the dogs for 'possum or coon hunting. For some reason, I was always the one appointed to climb the tree for the 'possum. It was somewhat chancy climbing the tree, but it was particularly tricky climbing back down, holding on to branches with one hand and holding onto a big snarly possum with the other. Even I had better sense than to go climbing a tree for a coon, which could tear up a big pack of coon hounds.

Sometimes we'd just sit, maybe even while still at the barn, and listen to the dogs. It was a kind of symphony of hound sounds wafting over the ridges. Some of the boys knew the sound of each dog's vocal instrument, specially their own. J.D Perrell would say, "Now that's Ol' Queenie. Ain't she got a pretty mouth on her?" This, of course, was also a good time to brag about your own dogs and lay off on the others, such as "I believe, he's lyin' now. He's back trackin'" or "That Ol' Blue of your'n has jumped a rabbit. You know a hound what runs a rabbit at night ain't worth shootin'."

That might provoke some more scuffling around. Our dogs were our "power points" in my day and time, and as they would provide some pride for us, we might be called upon to defend their honor.

Sometimes tobacco curing time would also be a good time for all the neighbors to get together for a chicken stew at whatever tobacco barn was currently being fired. Everyone had plenty of chickens, whole milk and fresh butter to share. The big stewpot was a twenty gallon black iron pot used at hog killing time for rendering the lard. A half-dozen chickens were boiled in water along with some onions before the milk and butter were to be included. Of course, the right amount of salt and pepper were also put in. Everyone was of the opinion that the stew would taste a little better with a squirrel or two included.

At one of the chicken stews, Daddy was tendin' the pot, and it looked as though it was about to boil over. Mrs. Starbuck, a sharecropper wife well versed in superstitions of all kinds, yelled, "Mr. Pete, you better rub your stomach."

"What for, Mrs. Starbuck?"

"To keep it from aboilin' over."

"Aw that won't keep it from boilin' over."

"Rub your stomach!"

Daddy obliged by lifting his shirt front and rubbing his stomach.

After a couple of minutes the stew calmed down, and Mrs. Starbuck triumphantly declared, "See what I told ye. Hit didn't boil over now, did it?"

Daddy just grinned and kept on stirring.

After the tobacco was cured and taken to the pack house to be stripped—the stems stripped out of the middle of the leaf—they were bunched again into "hands" and made ready for market where each farmer's crop would be auctioned off.

In order to be stripped, several sticks of tobacco were taken to the basement which had natural clay floor and walls. The exposed clay provided enough moisture to dampen the dry leaves for the stripping process. Without the moisture, the leaves would crumble into dust when handled by hand. From the time the plant beds were prepared until the stripping was finished, about thirteen months would have elapsed until the last of the crop was sold.

Some neighbors, the Wards, had fourteen barns of tobacco in their pack house, ready to be stripped, when lightning struck the pack house and burned it down. It was nearly their whole crop. One of their log barns also burned that summer when a dry leaf of tobacco fell on the metal flue and started burning, setting all the other tobacco on fire.

Somehow with the help of extended families and neighbors, such catastrophes were quietly dealt with.

After my teen years working in the tobacco fields I was off to college, working at various jobs to pay for my studies. Between my junior and senior years at Duke, I was lucky to get a job at RJ Reynolds Tobacco Company, inspecting cigarettes at $1.10 an hour. It was night work, nine hours each night. I picked up 1300 loose cigarettes every minute, as they came off the conveyor belt. I had to put adhesive tape over the ends of my fingernails to prevent the conveyor belt from grinding them down to the flesh.

Of course there was a lot of tobacco dust and smell in the factory, but no one was allowed to smoke inside. Perhaps the smoke from the smokers might have damaged the unsmoked tobacco before being processed into cigarettes. Everyone claimed that because of the pervading tobacco smell they had to use tobacco in some form, so there was a spittoon at each machine for the men to spit their tobacco juice and the women to dispose of their snuff drippin's.

One evening another college fellow came over to my machine, trying to persuade me to chew a plug of his Brown Mule Chewing Tobacco.

I desisted by saying, "I've tried that stuff, and I don't care for it." He persisted until I took a small chunk, chawed down on it a couple of times, grimaced and spit it out.

My little performance caused him to laugh heartedly, and while doing so he swallowed his cud. His face turned green, as he ran toward the head, unloading on the way. He did get to go home early.

Once when visiting the Reynolds's home office, I became aware of the pervasive advertising of their product. I was already aware of the worldwide promotion, but I had been unaware of their planning for the future of their sales.

In the office I saw several framed pictures of a series of advertising posters, representing a period of time. In the first one of the series the subject was a beautiful young woman with a cigarette included, but some distance from her. Another poster, produced much later, showed another woman, but with the cigarette closer to her. A still later one showed the subject holding the cigarette between her fingers. The final one showed her enjoying her smoke.

After that summer, I never worked again in the tobacco fields or factory, but I have continued an interest in the effects of the habitual use of the weed on the lungs of friends and members of my family. Even though my brother was obliged to carry oxygen with him everywhere because of his emphysema, he had to have his cigarettes right up to the finish.

I've seen some unusual sights in my time—long tail boats on the Bangkok canals, Mummers' Plays in English towns, snowstorms in West Virginia, elephants and camels on the streets of New Delhi—but the oddest phenomenon I have seen is a supposedly rational human being sticking a white cylinder in his mouth, setting the end of it afire, taking a deep breath through it, while pulling the smoke into the lungs before blowing it out through his mouth or even out his nose.

I stand corrected! Even more odd is to see a human being put a wad of dark looking stuff in its mouth, chew on it awhile then periodically spit brown saliva out on the ground or into a tin can, carried around for the daily ritual.

If his smoking addiction has already cost him his larynx, you may see him stick the cigarette to his throat, blowing smoke rings out of the hole left by the surgeon.

They call North Carolina the Tar Heel State . . . some say because of the tar made from the pine trees in eastern NC. Others say it's the name given the NC soldiers in the Revolutionary War for sticking to their guns—refusing to retreat—as though their heels were stuck in tar.

I propose that the real answer is that the tar in all that tobacco, whether still green in the fields or in the finished residue in the lungs, covers the exteriors and fills the interiors of each of its victims, all the way down to their red clay heels.

Thus the TAR HEELS!

PRIMITIVE BAPTISTS

Grandpa Noel Byron Gilbert was an elder in the Primitive Baptist Church. His twin brother, Great-uncle Lemly Ivan Gilbert was also a Primitive Baptist minister. However, Uncle Lemly had been "out of fellowship" (excommunicated) from the Hardshell Baptists, so he joined the Softshell Baptists until shortly before his death when the Hardshells welcomed him back into fellowship. I'm not sure what the difference was between the Hardshells and the Softshells, except that the Hardshells seemed to be much more conservative and *hard shell* than the Softshells. Rumor had it that Uncle Lemly had made a small contribution to a Methodist church to buy a church bell. As the Primitive Baptists considered anything like a bell to be an idol, Uncle Lemly had committed a sin, even though he had naively made the contribution out of the kindness of his heart

Incidentally, years later Andy Griffith wrote a song about two old hound dogs named Noel and Lemly, as the twin Primitive Baptist preachers were cousins of his.

There are seventeen Primitive Baptist churches in eastern Tennessee and southwest Virginia who are No-Hellers, which means that they believe that there is no hell after death; that the hell that does exist is in this lifetime. They still believe in predestination; the predestination is that we will all enter the gates of heaven. They base this belief on Jesus' words recorded in John 14:2, *In my Father's house are many mansions: if it were not so I would have told you. I go to prepare a place for you.* The No-Hellers believe that Jesus was including everyone—*a place for you*—to be included in the Kingdom of Heaven.

However, Grandpa's brand of Primitive Baptists believed in double predestination. I already knew about the Presbyterian belief in predestination, but I couldn't get my mind wrapped around the notion (doctrine) of double predestination, so I asked, "Grandpa what does double predestination mean?"

"What is to be will be (I already understood that) whether it ever happens or not." That second part really stumped me.

I must have had a quizzical look, as Grandpa went on to say, "But I'm not gonna go lay my head on the railroad track. That'd be tempting the Lord. It's not right to be tempting the Lord."

I didn't know why the Lord would be tempted to decapitate Grandpa, if the double predestination rule was in place, except maybe because he would be so foolish as to lay his head on the railroad track which would, itself, be predestined.

When Mamma was concerned about Uncle John's drinking, she said, "Mr. Gilbert, John has such respect for you, I feel that if you speak to him about his drinking, it will help him to stop."

"It's all in God's hand. When the Lord has prepared for John to stop drinking, he will." Sometime after that John did give up the bottle and started teaching Sunday School in a Methodist Church. Then Grandpa flew into action to dissuade John from devoting his religious attention to a heathenish church. In that instance, he didn't wait for the Lord to speak. I'm sure he would say that it was in God's plan for Grandpa to speak to John on behalf of Himself.

The Primitive Baptists don't believe in religious education, seminary training, salaried ministers, missionaries, religious icons or musical instruments in the church.

They believe that the Lord, God Almighty, would lead you to do what you needed to do and free will or choice had nothing to do with it. When a person is born he/she is already predestined for heaven or hell. A preacher will even say in his prayer, "I hope, O Lord, that I may be amongst the elect, but not my will but Thy will be done."

No amount of study, repentance or even waywardness would change that choice already destined for you at birth. When one asks about backsliding, that can't happen as you're already elected either for heaven or for hell.

My maternal grandfather was a Methodist and said of Presbyterians, who also believed in predestination were "Just Primitive Baptists, who've moved to town." It's been noted by other writers that seldom would you find a Primitive Baptist church in town, even a small town. It was, and continues to be a rural church.

When Daddy was small he loved to go with Grandpa to the church meetings, particularly the Association Meetings, which would last all weekend. By time they had forded the first creek in the buggy, Grandpa would be two verses into the "Romish Lady," a song warning of the dangers of popery.

Daddy experienced a terrible event at an Association Meeting at Aaron's Corner Primitive Baptist Church when he was only six years old. Grandpa was conducting the service inside the church, as he was the moderator. Daddy was just hanging out alone outside when he saw an old man with a long beard start to go into the church. The old fellow fell on the doorstep and died. Daddy started crying, and the folks trying to help the old man thought Daddy was some of his kin, but Daddy didn't even know him. This experience prompted Daddy to reject the Primitive Baptist faith because they provided nothing for children or teenagers.

A few years ago, my younger sister, Evelyn, and I decided to go to the Sunday service at Snow Creek Primitive Baptist Church where Grandma and Grandpa Gilbert are buried. Grandma died in 1948 and was buried in-style with the church full of flowers. It was the first time she had ever ridden in a Cadillac. I don't recall anyone ever giving her any flowers while she was alive even though she did so much for others. Aunt Bea with her husband and son always lived with Grandma in her boarding house, and her sons ate at the boarding house at least a couple of times each week. I must admit there wasn't a better restaurant in town. Any kinfolk who came from the mountains to look for work in Winston would always stay at Grandma's boarding house on North Liberty Street. When she died, they all sent flowers.

Grandpa died in 1962 and was given a funeral ceremony with as much pomp as would befit the Church Moderator but within the limits of the decorum of the Primitive Baptists who were as dour and doleful as Grandpa Noel himself.

Evelyn and I got to the church just as the service was starting. It wasn't Association Day, so there wasn't a large crowd. The church had been modernized with brick on the outside walls, modern plumbing and electric lights. However, the meeting room still contained no musical instrument or icon . . . except a surprise on the wall behind the pulpit; a large photograph of Grandpa Noel with the same dour and doleful look I had remembered while he was still among the living saints.

The next week, Evelyn called her daughter, Toni, in Texas, but reached Chris, Toni's husband, instead. She said, "Chris, you know I have repeatedly told you how fortunate you are to have me as a mother-in-law. Well, I have new information to substantiate that claim. In your Catholic church you have crosses, crucifixes and statues of saints.

"This past Sunday, Reid and I went to a Primitive Baptist Church in Virginia. Primitive Baptists don't believe in having any icons, even crosses, inside or outside the church. However, this church had a huge picture of my grandfather on the wall behind the pulpit, where in most churches there would be a crucifix or a cross or a picture of Jesus in Gethsemane. You probably weren't aware how closely kin I am to sainthood."

At least once each summer, when I was growing up, we would go to one of the Association Meetings. In addition to a lot of preaching, there would be "Dinner on the grounds," although the dinner was not on the ground but placed and shared on a long table under the canopy of white oak trees.

When I was 16 we went to the Association Meeting at Aaron's Corner Primitive Baptist Church. On the last day of the meeting, Sunday, the sacraments (pronounced with a long a as in "sacred") are celebrated. As there were no baptisms appointed, the only sacraments were the

Lord's Supper and foot washing, both of which were conducted with the church members sitting in chairs under a brush arbor behind the church building. Non-members stood outside the circle and observed.

The elements for the Lord's Supper were provided by church members; one of the men contributed his home-fermented blackberry wine, and the bread was baked by one of the women in the church. The elements were blessed by all the present elders before passing the bread and wine around the circle. Each communicant pinched off a bite of the bread, then handed the loaf on to the next person. The wine was then passed from person to person with each one taking a sip. One old fellow was enjoying it so much that one of the elders had to persuade him to pass it on so others could partake.

Of course, modern folks would take exception to everyone drinking after each other out of the same chalice. In those days, we all drank from the same dipper out of the water bucket. We never seemed to fare the worse for that.

The foot-washing was particularly interesting to me, as I had never witnessed the ritual before. Wash basins were filled with water for the members to use for washing the feet of other members. Men washed men's feet and women washed women's. It was important for people to wash the feet of others for whom there may have been some misunderstandings or contentions during the past year.

Foot washing was adopted by the Primitive Baptists as a sacrament based on the example of Jesus washing the feet of his disciples as recorded in the 13th Chapter of John. He said to them (John 13:15), "For I have given you an example, that ye should do as I have done to you."

After the sacraments and lunch, the preaching continued in the church with the men and boys sitting on one side of the church and women and girls on the other. There were even two gender- specific doors. In the songs, the women harmonized with the men's lead voices.

Several preachers sat on the dais, sharing the water dipper and informally talking with each other about who may be led by the Lord God to have "somethin' to say."

One preacher, Elder Sam White, related his feelings about a recent dream—a familiar topic with Primitive Baptist preachers. The dream was about the death of Brother Noel Gilbert (Grandpa) and worries about "What will we do when Elder Gilbert leaves to be with the Lord Almighty?" It turned into a virtual funeral eulogy with everyone—including Grandpa—sobbing and plumbing the depths of grief. Next, the official Annual Association Meeting was called to order. Elder Noel Gilbert, being the Moderator, presided.

"The Lower Mayo Association Meeting is now in session. Are we all in fellowship? . . . If any brother or sister has contentions with the association or with one another, now is the time to voice your issues."

A couple of concerns about the cemetery and the church roof were discussed before Grandpa dismissed the meeting with "If there be no more issues, then we are in fellowship and will proceed to the culmination of the Association Meeting of the Lower Mayo Association in the year of our Lord, 1947. Brother Jarrell, would you heist a tune before the benediction?"

Brother Jarrell tried a couple of notes before he settled on a baritone beginning for "On Jordan's Stormy Banks I Stand." Not only were there no icons in the meeting room there was also an absence of musical instruments, aside from the human voice. There were also few hymnbooks, so Brother Jarrell was prepared to "line the hymn." This meant that the song leader would speak or chant a line, then the congregation would sing that line. This interspersing of the spoken and sung words was a kind of antiphonal with an emotional catharsis.

I was familiar with the hymn and wondered if they would use the old words or would include some more modern words, i.e. the second line of the hymn was, *and cast a wistful eye*. Unfortunately in some more recent hymnals, someone has switched the word *wistful* to *wishful*, which I feel is a less interesting term. Another line from another hymn has been changed from *Dear Lord and Father of mankind, forgive our foolish ways*. It originally was *Dear Lord and Father of mankind, forgive our fev'rish ways. Fev'rish* is much more descriptive than *foolish*. Of course, the Primitive Baptists would use the more primitive wording. I was not disappointed . . . but I digress.

Knowing the hymn as I did, I wondered if Brother Jarrell was going to use all the verses. It soon became apparent that he was going to use them all, and the reason was soon apparent.

By time the second line was finished, the preachers had begun embracing each other, which signaled the congregants to do likewise, including all of the congregation—not just the church members. I could tell this was going to take a long time. I saw brothers embrace each other, even though they hadn't spoken in six months. As the people embraced each other, many were bidding each other *God be with you* for another year, and as they embraced, they released tears of personal baggage and animosities.

Years later, while studying Greek theatre, I wondered if the catharsis those audiences experienced was anything like the catharsis of a Primitive Baptist Association Meeting.

More recently I have fantasized about a dream to have a Primitive Baptist Association Meeting which would include political and religious leaders from the world stages and cathedrals and mosques and temples. We would sing *Amazing grace, how sweet the sound, That saved a wretch like me. I once was lost but now am found, Was blind but now I see.*

Do you suppose that if we could line *Amazing Grace* together while embracing each other, we could then compassionately sing *now I see?*

Maybe a good foot washing would also be efficacious.

UNCLE SAMMY JANE

Uncle Sammy Jane was Daddy's uncle and our great-uncle born in 1865 too late to fight in the War Between the States. He was Grandpa Noel's older brother.

Grandpa and his twin brother, Uncle Lemly, were the babies of the family and became Primitive Baptist preachers when they were still in their twenties. As preachers, I suppose they both were of the opinion that as such they had to be terribly serious . . . at least display a countenance of awesome spirituality. Uncle Sammy Jane said that they were "dour and doleful, and if thet's whut religion does fer yah, I ain't got time fer it."

Actually, Uncle Sam's real name was Samuel Green Gilbert, but in Patrick County, Virginia if there were a lot of boys with the same name, such as Sam Gilbert—on a whole mountainside of Gilberts—the boy was given his mother's name as his second name. . . . just to keep them identified, don't you know. His mamma was Martha Jane Cassell Gilbert. His grandmother, Mary "Polly" Gilbert, lived to be more than a hundred.

Some of the boys would carry the name with them for the rest of their lives. Uncle Sam has a granddaughter, Violet Pennick, living in Roanoke, and she still refers to her grandfather as Papa Sammy Jane. I'm sure she has no other Papa Sam, but he would seem somehow incomplete without his full name . . . the name he "goes by."

In order to keep the women's name distinct if there were too many sharing the same name, they would be given their husband's first name as well as his last name . . . Cousin Sallie Tobe, Cousin Bessy Bob. This informal naming should prove fascinating to a sociologist or anthropologist.

Uncle Sammy Jane didn't have time for religion, because life was too full of wonderful opportunities for tomfoolery, and seriously professed religion could put an awesome burden on his brand of fun.

He was as gregarious as Grandpa Noel, but in a different sort of way. On a Saturday he'd walk to Stuart—catch a ride if he could—and walk up one street and down another (there were only two parallel streets), stopping at every store in an attempt to swap his pocket watch or jackknife. "How much to boot would you give me?" he'd ask. He had no intention to part with either one of them, but this little ritual gave him an opportunity to talk with lots of folks.

He worked at many jobs from blacksmithing and farming to railroading. A bit of wisdom gleaned from his railroading days was, "If you can't enjoy the train ride, the ticket ain't hardly worth the price."

Uncle Sammy Jane also worked for a while in the tan bark yards. In the timbering process, the inner bark of the felled hardwood trees would be stripped to be used in tanning leather and preserving the hides of slaughtered or hunted animals. He had managed to get the job of cook, or "cookie." One cold, December morning before fixing the usual hominy grits, oatmeal, bacon, country ham, sausage, bread (both biscuits and pone) and gravy (white sop and red-eye) he started brewing up a couple of huge pots of coffee. In fact, it looked as though he had no notion of cooking anything but coffee.

Uncle Sammy Jane was the kind of trickster who could time his jokes when they were least expected—they actually were much better that way. All the boys could hardly wait that cold morning for their "wakin' up" coffee, but soon after their first big swigs of coffee they were all running out into the snow and vomiting. What he had done was to brew a big pot of Prince Albert Smoking Tobacco in the place of coffee. As it was told later, the boys had earlier played a trick on Uncle Sammy Jane by putting some ambeer (tobacco juice) in his white lightning to color it up a little. They didn't get much work done that day, but I'm sure the boys thought twice before they decided again to play a trick on Sammy Jane.

In March 1889, Uncle Sammy Jane married Lelia Shelor who bore four children, three girls and a boy. I never knew Aunt Lelia, as she had left Uncle Sammy Jane before I was born.

His second wife, whom he married in January, 1916, was Martha Fain. I always knew her as Aunt Mattie. They had one daughter, Nell. One day when I was only six we were visiting Uncle Sammy Jane and Aunt Mattie. I was fascinated by the way she talked, so I asked, "Aunt Mattie, why do you talk like a hillbilly?"

Aunt Mattie, not quite hearing this said, "Stella, what did thet young'un say?"

Mamma answered, "Uh . . . he didn't really say anything. Reid, keep your mouth shut."

The reason Uncle Sammy Jane's first wife divorced him was that he wouldn't give up his drinking. She gave him an ultimatum to choose her or moonshine. When it was obvious he couldn't turn away from his old pal, John Barleycorn, she left for Baltimore to work as a seamstress until shortly before her death in 1940. She was buried at Wayside Church, five miles out of Stuart, Virginia and about a half- mile up the road from where Uncle Sammy Jane lived. After her funeral he walked every day up to the cemetery and sat by her grave for twenty to thirty minutes. He continued this daily devotion until shortly before his death at the age of ninety in 1955. He is also buried at Wayside between his two wives.

One summer Sunday afternoon, Daddy and I were visiting Aunt Mattie and Uncle Sammy Jane only the year before he died. As we sat in their front yard in the shade of a Chinaberry tree, Uncle Sammy Jane whittled on a short wooden peg. He poked the whittled stick toward Daddy, asking him what it reminded him of. Daddy said it looked a lot like a corn shucking peg. Aunt Mattie ventured that it looked like a gambling stick. He simply turned it around and said, "Nope hit jest looks like the other end."

After a short while he said, "Pete, you know they're buildin' a addition onto High Point Baptist Church."

Daddy said, "Yeah, Uncle Sam, how's it goin'?"

"Aw, they jest got the underpinnin' finished." An underpinning of a building, is the foundation. Uncle Sammy Jane whittled some more in a spate of silence. "Pete, you know what some fool done last night?"

"What was that, Uncle Sam?"

"Some fool come by thar last night, an' put up beer bottles, an' whiskey bottles and wine bottles all 'round thet underpinnin' . . . When them nice church folks come to church this mornin', they seen thet filthy stuff lined up all 'round their new addition underpinnin' . . . Weren't thet terrible?"

"Uncle Sammy Jane, who in the world would do such a terrible thing as that?"

As Uncle Sammy Jane quickly commenced some vigorous whittlin' he answered, "Oh, I ain't got no notion in the world."

By his demeanor we knew that he had done it the night before while walking back from carousing in Stuart. Not only was Uncle Sammy Jane able to time his pranks, he didn't even have to be present when the event transpired.

Later in the afternoon, Daddy said, "Well, Uncle Sam, I guess we'd better be getting' on home."

Aunt Mattie said, "Pete, why don't you an' Reid stay fer supper? We ain't got much, but what we got, you're welcome to it."

She and Daddy carried on a little duel of words, finally with the result that we stayed.

All through the meal, she kept saying, "Pete, we ain't got a thing fitten to eat." She opened a home canned jar of peaches, which Uncle Sammy Jane loved. She again said, "Sorry I ain't got a thing what's fitten to eat."

Uncle Sam had already filled his bowl, but then pushed it to the middle of the table.

Daddy said, "What's wrong, Uncle Sam?"

"Ain't nothin' wrong with me."

"Now I can tell somethin's botherin' you."

"Mattie said there wadn't a thing fitten to eat, an' I make a habit of not eatin' what ain't fitten to eat."

Even after some cajoling from Daddy, he wouldn't eat another bite. Aunt Mattie was what he called "a querelsome woman".

In his enjoyment of the fullness of life, I always felt that Uncle Sammy Jane was as spiritual as his younger twin brothers, Grandpa Noel and Uncle Lemly, who in some respects had restricted life only to the "dour and doleful."

GREAT-GRANDMA CLARISSA JANE BRINKLEY

Although I had never met her in life, I discovered Great-Grandma quite serendipitously while digging around in my folks' basement. At first I had no notion who she was, as her picture was so covered with mold and dust, so I put her out into the open air where her features began gradually to clear. She seemed to be emerging from the depths of abandonment by her own stubborn willpower. I checked on her every day, and after about two weeks I became frightfully aware of her glowering eyes, and no matter where I would stand or move in the room, her determined stare would follow, if I could see her face from where I had hung her.

Behind a convex glass in an old-fashioned oval frame the tight lace collar of her blouse rose just beneath her clenched jaw, almost to her severe chin. The small lens of her wire spectacles seemed to intensify her gaze. Her hair was gathered into a sumo wrestler's bun.

Mamma had told me some things about Great-Grandma Brinkley, so I was not surprised at her demeanor as I began to know her better through observation of her antique portrait.

Great-Grandma and Great-Grandpa Brinkley lived at Pine Ridge on the outskirts of Mt. Airy, North Carolina. They had three children: a girl and two boys, and I was told that she apparently had no particular concern for the girl's well-being, whose name I never knew. The two boys, Winfrey and Roy, were guarded zealously from the wiles of young girls in the neighborhood, close by where the original Siamese, twins Eng and Cheng Bunker, had married sisters, daughters of a local tavern keeper. The twins settled down after years of traveling with the Barnum and Bailey Circus.

Of course, Eng and Cheng, being Siamese, had a Siamese name, unpronounceable for local Mt. Airy folks, so they chose the name *Bunker*, because they had been told Bunker Hill was an important site in American history.

The proximity to the twins and their large families may have had nothing to do with Great-grandma's worry about *her boys,* but it was an open secret that the Bunker wives had connived, with the encouragement of their mother, to marry the strange foreign boys. It was well known that they had been paid well by Barnum and Bailey, and could thus support families. After they married, they each, with their wives, had adjacent cabins where they reared large families. Such a marital setup, of course, caused a lot of gossip and a great deal of smirking about how the conjugal beds were arranged—the boys being joined permanently by a large ligament at the chest.

Great-Grandma was shocked by such neighbors, but even more scandalized by the rumors about things you weren't supposed to talk about. This may very well have prompted her to set up a determined guard for her boys. She understood the strength of girls but, worrying about the vulnerability of her boys, she had no notion of allowing any girl to entrap either one of them. There were no girls worthy of the Brinkley boys—no one she was aware of at any rate.

This worked for a while, until 1901 when Winfrey, my grandfather, at the age of thirty, met and married my grandmother, Van Della Mae Edwards, who was only eighteen at the time. Great-Grandma put two and two together—(1). outraged at the Bunker family arrangements and (2). knowing full well the ways of young girls (having been one herself, not so many years before), the sum of all this was that that strumpet Edwards girl had entrapped Winfrey into *wedlock.* She likely focused on the *lock* part of that word. She knew that Grandma Della Mae had gone to school with those two passels of Bunker kids.

Her protection of Roy worked permanently, as he was never ensnared, thus living a long life as a bachelor. She was so angry at the young couple that she refused to visit them until after their second child, Uncle Bob, was born in 1908. Great-Grandma may have compromised some of her earlier values of unacceptable goings-on, as she divorced Great-Grandpa Brinkley and married a Mr. Rose.

It wasn't difficult to read this old tale anew in the demeanor of that severe photograph gazing at me with those piercing eyes.

Grandma Brinkley had kept the picture in a secluded closet, probably not wanting to face her constantly. When Mamma inherited it, she must have stored it away in the basement, then forgetting it. Although she could remember her grandmother, she seemed to be spooked by the photograph. She told me that it would be quite all right for me to take it.

It moved with me and my young family several times without incident until in 1969 when we moved to an old farmhouse near Plain, Wisconsin.

As the old house was so large, each of my three daughters had a bedroom. My wife and I had a bedroom, and I had a study, where I was finishing the writing of my PhD dissertation. My study, overlooking the vegetable garden and a creek to the south contained my huge roll-top desk, my books and all my papers. It seemed to be the perfect setting for Great-Grandma to hang and observe—whether approvingly or disapprovingly, I didn't know—all of my academic efforts.

It was about this time that I noticed that my daughters had developed an interest in Great-Grandma (their great-great-grandma). They loved to bring their friends upstairs, open my study door slowly, as quietly as possible, and point to the staring picture, without daring to say anything, until they would slam the door shut and fly squealing down the hall, bounding down the steps, several at a time.

Great-grandma moved with me several times after that with nothing new happening of which I was aware until I was on the faculty of Ohio State University. She hung over the fireplace mantel in the master bedroom in my house on Frambes Avenue in Columbus. She continued to glare, seemingly content to do so.

When my wife, Robin, and I were in London in 1989, we received a phone call from her brother, Erin, who was rooming in the Columbus house. He seemed anxious to ask us how we were doing. I said, "Everything's fine here—how about in Columbus?"

He said, "Something like really strange happened here in the house."

"What was that?"

"I have this new girlfriend."

"Erin, there's nothing strange about that."

"Well, we were in my room, and she left to like go to the bathroom. When she returned, she said, 'Why didn't you tell me Maggie was an older woman?' [Maggie was a student also living in the house.]

"Maggie's not an older woman. She's a graduate student in the Art Department."

"She said, 'Well this older woman, dressed up in a strange antique costume, stuck her head in the bathroom door and looked around as though she was looking for someone'. When I asked her if I could help her, she didn't say anything. She just left.'

"She then told me she wanted to see Robin's picture, so I took her to your room, where I knew there was a picture of Robin. When she looked in there, she saw your grandmother's old picture and said, 'That's the old woman who stuck her head in the bathroom door.'

"That kinda freaked me out, but then like when I took her home and came back to the house, there was that old woman like sittin' in my big rockin' chair in the livin' room. So I couldn't spend the night in the house that night."

I asked, "Has anything happened with my grandma since then?"

"No, but I keep my door locked and my pistol loaded and cocked."

I joked, "Do you suppose a door or a bullet would deter her whenever she may be on a special mission?"

We talked about other things, and apparently Great-Grandma stayed in her resting place on the bedroom wall until we returned from England.

When I related this tale to my daughters, Karen, my youngest, said, "See, Daddy what I told you?"

"What do you mean, 'What I told you?'"

"I told you when we were living in the old Bindl farmhouse in Plain, that old woman would walk up and down the hallway every night. My bedroom was right across the hall from your study, and she scared me to death. That's why every night I would climb into bed with Tari or Adrienne to keep away from that old woman."

Years later, when Karen grew up, she consulted a medium to release the frightened little girl and the severe great-grandma to travel their own respective paths.

I moved Great-Grandma after that to West Virginia, where again she kept surveillance over my proceedings, but when I left that state, I packed her carefully in a new cardboard casement due to her fragile condition.

When I started dividing various family heirlooms with my daughters, neither one of them wanted to take Great-Grandma home, so she rested in a storage shed in Spring Green, Wisconsin, until I could send her to a niece, Mary Kay Gottenstrater, who had expressed a keen interest in welcoming her into her home, and, of course, into her life.

My niece is the daughter of my younger sister. Mary Kay was always the adventurous sort, so was interested in meeting her great-great-grandma.

Mary Kay extricated Great-Grandma from her glass encasement and discovered another picture behind her. It was the picture of a similarly old gentleman with a long beard and sad eyes. Mary Kay made smaller copies of the pictures and sent them to me. We assume that the old man was my great-grandfather. Knowing of Great-Grandmother's story, I was no longer mystified for the melancholy eyes of Great-Grandpa Brinkley.

I'm anxious to know what further adventures Mary Kay will experience with Clarissa Jane Brinkley when they finally meet.

Mary Kay's husband is Cuban and may very well be vulnerable to the charms of Great-Grandma as she will probably hover over their household just as she did over mine, and more particularly over her own, before becoming encased in a picture frame—just attempting to protect her boys from the trickery of predatory girls.

PART II
MY MENTORS

It is difficult to know where to start and certainly where to stop when one recalls one's mentors over the years of learning and living. I could begin officially, I suppose with Miss Pauline Jones my first grade teacher, whom I adored. But there is Mrs. Jewell Darnell my Sunday school teacher, who baked me my own sponge ring cake on my 7th birthday. Also Virginia Fulp, who was only a few years older than I. She was also a Sunday school teacher and gave us, out of her allowance, a Christmas gift of chocolate covered cherries every Christmas. I suppose that was when I began to understand that the teacher who can feed the body . . . even with goodies . . . is likely to be able to feed the mind and the soul. My high school and college teachers were also responsible for instilling in me an interest in continued learning.

However I will limit the number of my mentors to seven:
    Rev. Ralph Reed
    Richard Chase
    Professor Robert Seaver
    Charles Weidman
    Etienne Decroux
    Sidayo Kita
    Professor A. C. Scott

THE REVEREND RALPH REED

"Well, boys," Preacher Reed said. "It looks as though we've got ourselves an official troop of the Boy Scouts of America."

Gene Winebarger said, "Well what number are we?"

"We're Troop 100 of the Old Hickory Council of the Boy Scouts of America."

My brother Ott said, "That sounds pretty good. I don't often get a hundred on any tests at school. But now it means that I'm a 100 percenter."

No one questioned him what we were 100% of, but it was somewhere between 100% of scoutery or 100% of tomfoolery.

The Reverend Ralph Reed, who was usually referred to by us boys, as Preacher Reed, was the most influential person in my teen years . . . aside from family, that is. I was twelve when I became existentially aware of parishioners' attitudes toward pastoral leadership. That was when Preacher Reed was assigned as his first post-seminary appointment to Shiloh Church, our small Methodist church on a three-point charge also with Mount Pleasant and Mount Olivet churches in the Western North Carolina Conference of the Methodist Church.

That was several decades before Methodists added "United" to the beginning of their name, which happened when the Methodists merged with the E.U.B.s (Evangelical United Brethren). I suppose the Methodists (so named from the methodical ways of the followers of John Wesley, the founder of Methodism) were more comfortable with the word, "united," than with either "evangelical" or "brethren" . . . But I digress.

When Preacher Reed arrived in 1942 he was unmarried and seemed to have plenty of time to devote to the Shiloh Church members, particularly the young people. By establishing the MYF (Methodist Youth Fellowship) he was fulfilling his pastoral duty to that group of people in the neighborhood. He soon organized us boys into Troop 100. Although we were a rag-tag bunch of country kids, we were proud of being designated "Troop 100". That did make us feel kind of special.

We scouts were obviously visual misfits at all the Boy Scout parades, as none of us could afford a full officially-approved uniform. One of us would have the appropriate hat, another the shirt and still another the pants or shoes. Most of us did have the right red neckerchief. If we were to combine all of our sartorial luxuries, there might have been a complete uniform with a few extra neckerchiefs; that is except for the fellow who had almost all the right accoutrements. He was the only child of the owner of the cross-roads beer joint. He even had a merit badge sash, eventually filled with an impressive array of badges. He later became a professor (voted Most Popular several times) at Memphis State University. Another boy became a successful businessman owning several commercial truck lines. One drank himself to an early grave. A couple of the boys stayed on the farm and others moved to town to work in the mills. I traveled and matriculated, several times.

Even though we were disdained at parades, we were quite popular at camporees, because we country scouts already knew many of the things the city scouts had to be taught, like starting a fire and cooking bacon in a cast iron skillet over an open fire. They didn't even know how to use an axe or a hatchet.

But I digress again, as I had begun to describe Rev. Reed, whom we boys called "Mr. Reed," perhaps to de-sanctify his ecclesiastical title in order to narrow the distance between us, yet maintaining the respect for our age differences.

Even though he took us camping to Snake Mountain, hiking to Walnut Cove, swimming in Old Field Creek and mountain climbing at Hanging Rock State Park, he hovered over us like a mamma hen taking care of her biddies. While camping, he was the only one who drank coffee, and he always made sure that he boiled an egg in the coffee to add some calcium to the brew. At Hanging Rock he worried about us getting too close to the edge of the rock cliff, attempting to explain to us the danger of some kind of disorder, which was the opposite of *acrophobia* (perhaps acrophilia?) which certainly was not a problem for us, as we did indeed love high places. He was afraid that we might suffer from that sickness which impels you to jump off those elevations, whether on top of a barn or the crest of a mountain ridge. I'm afraid that there were times when we took some unnecessary risks, just to tease him.

One time, after a twenty-mile hike, he cautioned us about drinking too much cold spring water while we were so hot and sweaty. One of the boys, who later imbibed too heavily in another kind of liquid, assured Mr. Reed that he knew what he was doing and guzzled a half gallon of the welcome water. Shortly he doubled over with stomach cramps and bellowing like a foundling calf.

My brother and I walked the two miles to Shiloh Church for the scout meetings, and of course there was a two-mile hike back home. Occasionally, if it was raining or snowing, Mr. Reed would give us and a couple more boys a ride back home. He lived in the opposite direction. Every time he did this, he would say, "Now the reason I'm giving you boys a lift is because I expect you to do the same when you're grown up and can give some boy a lift, when it may be needed." Many times I've thought of this admonition when I had such occasion to help someone, even though they may not be a boy scout.

Rev. Reed was well liked by the church members in all his three churches, but particularly so in our church, Shiloh. Of course, we boys were great fans and weren't intimidated by our age differences or even frightened by his vigorous preaching. Actually, preaching was one of his long suits, as far as the adults were concerned.

It seemed that the womenfolk were more impressed with the young preacher than the menfolk and paid real special attention to his personal nourishment at the periodic food-on the-ground occasions. That's when they would make sure he would take a healthy portion of their lovingly-prepared provisions. It didn't take us boys long to notice that the mothers with marriageable-aged daughters were especially solicitous of Mr. Reed's attention, probably harboring all kinds of marital fantasies for those daughters. As mentioned above, he was single when he was assigned as shepherd of the flock at Shiloh.

However, it became generally known through the grapevine that our new pastor had a girlfriend down near Charlotte, and before long it was announced officially from the pulpit that he was engaged to be married to the girl friend who had been studying music at Queen's College. After the wedding, Mr. Reed introduced Mrs. Billie Pennington Reed to the church members at an obligatory church gathering where everyone greeted her politely. They were obviously withholding judgment until she proved herself worthy on one hand or more likely on the other hand committed some social *faux pas* (or at least would be considered unladylike in our Baux Mountain society). The most apparent arbiters of acceptance—or not—were the mothers, noted above. Oh, they were polite enough, and smiled when necessary, although when their lips smiled their eyes did not.

Having studied voice at college, Mrs. Reed had a lovely operatic singing voice. Even though music was an important feature of the church activities, her manner of singing was just too much with her soprano high notes and her predilection to hold her hands together out in front of her ample bosom. The boys on the back pews snickered whenever she was in full voice, and the mothers looked stonily toward Mr. Reed seated behind the pulpit. It is true that forgiveness was a major tenet of our religious creed, but the disappointed mothers had not yet forgiven him for bypassing their own lovely offspring.

This attitude prevailed even after the first child, Mary Elizabeth, was born and joined her parents in the Methodist parsonage. In fact, the knowledge that something unmentionable was happening in the Methodist parsonage bedroom, simply added to their pique. It is generally expected in Methodist congregations that the pastor will have several well-behaved offspring, but that their conception is not similar to that in the congregants' bedrooms.

When anyone recognizes this paradox, it should be pointed out that there was only one virgin birth, a couple of millennia ago.

Of course, potential grandmothers would warm up a bit over any new infants no matter to "cottage or manor born." Potential pastoral heritage was held in even higher esteem. This jurying manner continued apace until Mrs. Reed brought the baby to a church service one Sunday morning when Mary Elizabeth was less than two months old. Everyone oohed and aahed over the baby before the service began, and she was well behaved through the early part of the service . . . the prelude, hymn, scripture, Apostle's Creed and prayer. However when Mr. Reed started sermonizing, Mary Elizabeth began demonstrating that she had inherited her mother's powerful lungs. Mrs. Reed tried quite unsuccessfully to shush the baby, who would diminish her tone and volume only sporadically.

Rev. Reed was growing evermore frustrated while Mrs. Reed was becoming increasingly embarrassed. Some church attendees were sympathizing with the sermonizer, others with the young mother, while the boys were enjoying the distraction from the preaching and wondering what the conclusion of the standoff might be.

Suddenly Rev. Reed transferred his attention from the pew sitters in general to the specific attention of his wife, saying with a bit of irritation in his voice, "Dear, would you please take the baby out to the car." His wife wrapped the baby more closely in the blanket, holding her close to her breast, hastening to the end of the pew and down the middle of the church aisle. Tears were flowing visibly down her cheeks as she tried unsuccessfully to muffle her sobs.

After she disappeared completely from view out the church door, Mr. Reed might as well have finished the worship proceedings . . . no one was paying attention any longer to his admonitions for piety and the Christian life.

Immediately following the benediction, the congregation dispersed to survey the situation of the young mother and baby ensconced in the ministerial automobile outside. All the mothers, particularly those mothers of eligible daughters, had dropped their hostility toward the minister's wife, commiserating loudly with her and her public humiliation.

When their favorite pastor emerged from his ecclesiastical robing and out the door and down the stairs to secular and marital reality, their glares dressed him down effectively demonstrating their diminished view of him and his attitude toward womenfolk and their own maternal responsibilities.

Mrs. Reed had been duly affirmed by the previously backbiting church ladies.

As I recall, the text for the next Sunday's sermon was Mark 10:14, "Suffer the little children."

When James Starbuck saw that in the worship bulletin, he said, "Well, Preacher Reed suffered from his baby child, last Sunday."

Of course that set all the boys on the back pew to tittering.

At the age of eighteen, I left Baux Mountain for Brevard College, where Rev Reed had also begun his college education. That was 1949, the year that the bishop appointed him to a city church in Greensboro.

Emerging from a conjoined epoch of scouting and growth, both the Rev. Ralph Reed and E. Reid Gilbert entered cautiously, but optimistically, into the post-war era with the potential of perilous waters as well as newly enhanced mountain top experiences.

THE LEGACY OF RICHARD CHASE

"No, don't slide your feet across the floor. Pick 'em up like ploughin' in a field." Thus my introduction into the authenticity of folkways or at least folk dancing by Richard Chase.

Back in the '50s when I was in college at Brevard then Duke, I came across a fellow who introduced me to my own heritage and has inspired me in my activities since then in the ministry, education, theatre and my own writing. I don't recall where or when my first meeting with Richard Chase occurred, but after that first meeting I was sure to attend whatever workshop or class he may have been conducting anywhere within my geographical vicinity.

Of course, he'd always have his books along with him and almost apologetically introduce them, as he wholeheartedly agreed with Tom Hunt who was reputedly to have said, "No, it'll not do just to read the old tales out of a book. You've got to tell 'em to make 'em go right." As a matter of fact, in his preface to *The Grandfather Tales*, he wrote, "So, you try it. After you have learned the tales in silent print, shut the book and 'tell 'em.'"

He was always insisting on authenticity. Whenever he would teach the group some of the country dances, he would get quite upset with me because I liked to do the "buck an' wing" or the "Carolina shuffle," where the feet would slide across the floor and stomp the hardwood planking. "No!", he'd say, "Pick up your brogans like stepping over furrows in a ploughed field. Remember, they were ploughboys."

I'd done my own share of plowing with a mule and a bull-tongued plow, but I'd never tried dancing, even the country dances, in the ploughed field. Whenever he was looking, I'd try to do it his way.

One of his icons was a small St. Christopher statuette, the protector of all travelers. He would tell of the time he was driving across one of the mountains and wrecked his station wagon. It was in the days when the body of the station wagon was built of wood. He said, "I always carried St. Christopher with me, because those were some terribly rough roads in North Carolina and Virginia. And when that station wagon slid off the side of the mountain there wasn't enough of that wood left bigger than a piece of kindlin'. But I was okay and St. Christopher survived as well. He's been traveling with me ever since."

Knowing that I was studying to enter the Methodist ministry, he wrote me a brief note, "There's an abandoned Methodist Church on Beech Mountain. Now when you finish your seminary studies you must come to Beech Mountain and fill that pulpit." I folded the note and put it in my wallet along with my other important cards and a little money. The note survived several wallets, but somewhere along the way it disappeared, just as my resolve to honor Richard's request had.

There was something inspirational about Richard's personality and work, at a time when I was used to inspiration coming from preachers. His inspiration went beyond churchiness and into the very soul of life, the mountains and our heritage. Quite often since then, when I have worked with high school and college students in Kentucky and West Virginia, I've attempted to instill in them the same pride in their Appalachian heritage as Richard had inspired in me.

In addition to including the Mummers Plays in *The Grandfather Tales*, he also taught them to a bunch of us. This led me to attend a couple of Christmas folk workshops at Berea College, where I learned more about the Mummers Plays, including the theatrical sword dance.

I was so intrigued by these folk plays and dances that I considered focusing on them for my graduate work in theatre. Even though that didn't happen, later in 1989, while teaching at Ohio State University, I received a grant to research the plays in the small towns and hamlets in England during one Christmas season—the time when most of them would be performed.

There I met Doc Rowe who introduced me to the Cecil Sharpe Dance Society. He had been so intrigued with the ancient rituals performed in the villages each year that he had been filming them for thirty years.

At Heddington Quarry I observed a fascinating performance of the local Mummer's Play on the village green. The actors were pleased with my interest, but when asked about any connection with later developments in English Theatre, they walked away. I abandoned that research approach and simply used whatever I could learn from that performance and others I had observed.

As esoteric as they were, it's surprising how often I've used elements of them in teaching Movement for Actors and in some theatre performances. The sword dance was just the ticket for beheading John the Baptist, when I directed *The Play of Daniel* at Josephenum College and Seminary.

Even outside the mountains, I found that Richard's stories, particularly the Jack Tales, were a delight to audiences, young and old, and introduced them to a bit of the celebration of being from the mountains.

A specific time this happened was when I was on a Fulbright assignment in Thailand working with Professor Wayuppa Tossa in her Folklore Program at Mahasarakam University. When I was introduced to the Thai trickster character, Sri Thananchai, of course I saw parallels immediately with our Appalachian trickster, Jack, whom Richard had introduced to so many of us. In fact, while I was there I wrote most of the stories of *Trickster Jack*, which was later published by Wheatmark Press.

No matter "where I may have roamed oe'r land or sea or foam", there would always be something that would remind me of my own mountain heritage. It was certainly permanently ensconced in my psyche by Richard Chase and his absolute devotion to the people and culture of the Southern Appalachians.

He was quite right that there's much more in those stories and tales than first meets the eye on the printed page. You've got to tell them from your own heart and your own sense of wonder and playfulness.

PROFESSOR ROBERT SEAVER

I was fortunate in 1957 to receive a fellowship for the new Religious Drama Program, offered at Union Seminary (NYC). The department was funded by a special grant from the Rockefeller Foundation. It was under the leadership of Bob Seaver.

Although Bob did not have theology degrees, his graduate study of Speech and Communication from Northwestern University was substantial for the instruction of theology students, specifically in Homiletics (preaching). It seemed that most of the students in the program were not interested in the profession of theatre, but merely to enhance their Sunday School dramatic programs.

My involvement in the program consisted of acting in several productions as well as directing a production at the Riverside Church. Bob cast me in a production, which we rehearsed in Boston, before taking it in 1959 to the Uniting Synod of the United Church of Christ. The other actors were professional.

Teachers and mentors influence a person in a diversity of means. Bob's influence on me, aside from the constant support, were his challenges.

One day before his class, I was chatting with Dick Phillips, who was an aspiring NY actor. He had been cast in an Off-Broadway production. I asked him about the message of the script. "What's your visceral response to the existential nature of the role?"

"I don't know."

I had just finished Perkins School of Theology two years earlier, where we students, as well as faculty, were constantly challenging each other's credo and accepted beliefs. At Union, I and several other Texas ex-patriates, were dismayed to discover that no one was questioning their earlier religious beliefs. So my confrontation with Dick was in that context.

"You mean you've committed yourself to a public production and have not explored those issues?"

"Reid, it's a role, and I haven't been cast for quite a long time."

Professor Seaver had come in and had heard the last part of our chat. "Reid could you spare a few minutes after class?"

"Of course. I'd be glad to."

Seavers' charge to me after class was quite succinct, but forthright. "Twenty years from now, the Dick Phillips's of the world will be doing theatre. The Reid Gilberts will be talking about it." Nothing further needed to be said, but when I find myself becoming too academic in assessing my participation in theatre, I recall Bob Seaver's admonition.

Professor Seaver was successful in having several notable literary and theatre personnel meet our class. Henzie Raeburn and E. Martin Browne were in residence for quite a while. They had organized the Religious Drama Society of Great Britain. Henzie was a wonderful actress and Martin had successfully directed in West End, particularly *Murder in the Cathedral*. W. H. Auden also was a guest lecturer.

On another class occasion, Bob was directing me in a scene. Apparently he was unimpressed with my movement ability. Standing close to me, he put his hand on my shoulder and pushed slightly. I must have been off balance, as I stepped backward. He said, "It's obvious you don't know how to move on stage. Your balance needs work. Can you stay for a moment after class?"

"Oh, yes."

After class, he said, "I've arranged for you to study movement at the New Dance Group Studio on W. 56th Street. The modern dance lessons should help your stage movement."

Never did I feel threatened or upset with his challenges. I accepted them because of my assurance he cared for the professional welfare of his students.

Actually his pushing me into Modern Dance led to two more mentors, Charles Weidman and Etienne Decroux.

It was a few years later the Professor Seaver saw me in a performance, IKKAKU SENNIN, a Japanese Noh drama, directed by Sidayo Kita.

I played the role of a koken, who sits quietly, immobile, upstage until it is necessary to retrieve a prop or straighten a kimono for one of the other actors.

After the performance, Professor Seaver said, "I still don't know how well you can move, but I could see that you really know how to remain immobile."

CHARLES WEIDMAN

Charles Weidman was a pioneer in the early days of modern dance, having been a dancer with the Denishawn Dance Theatre which toured Asia in 1925. Later he collaborated with Doris Humphrey in establishing a dance pedagogy, The Humphrey-Weidman Technique.

In 1958 while enrolled in a master's program of Religious Drama at Union Seminary, I had the opportunity to meet and study with Charles. Robert Seaver my acting teacher there told me that I needed movement training, so he arranged, personally, for me to take modern dance lessons at the New Dance Group Studio. I didn't need another item on my plate. In addition to fulltime study at the seminary, I was pastor at the Vreeland Avenue Methodist Church in Paterson, NJ, and my wife and I were expecting our first child.

My initial classes were not with Charles, but for the subsequent term I enrolled in his repertory class. I was immediately struck by his commitment to his work and his encouragement for his students. Toward the end of the term there was some opposition from the New Dance board of directors for leasing a performance space. Charles maintained that teaching his repertory made no sense, if there was not an opportunity for us to perform.

After class one day, I went to the men's dressing room to change and saw Charles there sitting all alone, almost as though in meditation. His hair was slicked down and he was wearing a tie—both things being unusual I thought. The scene reminded me of a naughty school boy who had been summoned to the principal's office. He told me that he had been asked to present to the board his rationale for a need for a performance space.

Subsequently the space was approved and we had two sold-out performances at the Henry Street Playhouse.

After that, while still in New York, I studied Mime with Etienne Decroux before landing a theatre teaching position at a small college in Kentucky, where I taught mime as a part of the acting course.

Some years later I was planning a Mime festival and contacted Charles to see if he would present a workshop and perform there, and as I was planning a trip to New York I would like to drop by and discuss the matter with him.

When I got to the city, he greeted me at his studio and introduced me to a young friend, who was a sculptor and painter. The two of them had been collaborating on The Theatre of Two Arts. He asked me if they could demonstrate their work. Of course I agreed and was treated to a performance of this intriguing work. In a dance sequence Charles would don a large piece of brown paper, somewhat like a kimono, and his partner, while they both were dancing, would paint the paper, using it as a canvas. Another dance involved a thick, but malleable, wire, which was twisted into various shapes as the dance proceeded. When the dance ended, the newly twisted wire would be a finished sculpture.

I felt like royalty, indeed, for a command performance by these two innovative artists.

Unfortunately, the plans for that festival didn't materialize, but in 1974, Charles, at the age of 74, did perform with his young company at the International Mime Festival at Viterbo College in Wisconsin. I had insisted to the planning committee that Weidman must be invited as he had usually included Pantomime of Style in his Modern Dance performances.

After his performance at Viterbo, I went backstage to congratulate him and found him in the dressing room, sitting all alone with his hands folded in his lap, almost as though in mediation (again).

In greeting him I said, "It was so good to see your work, Charles, after all these years."

With an almost astonished look, he said, "Did you like it, Reid?"

"I thought it was wonderful. Your young dancers have certainly learned your technique. I particularly enjoyed your solo dance of the Gettysburg Address."

His childlike response was, "I'm so glad you liked it."

We then discussed his ongoing work and dance vision and my study and performing of Japanese Noh Theatre with Sidayo Kita.

The next time I heard from Charles was the following Christmas. He sent me a triptych, composed of three panels of cardboard. On the first panel was a picture of a Japanese man in a dark kimono. Written on the photo was "Mr. Charles Weidman, with Best Complement, Koshiro Matsumoto, Tokyo Oct, 1925." On the third panel was a picture of a dancer in full Kabuki costume and make-up. Under the picture was written "CW in The God of the Mountain."

On the panel between the two pictures was a handwritten explanation of the two panels.

> In 1925 a most memorable time in my life as a dancer was the achieving of the role of God of the Mountain in Momiji Gari from Japan's great actor-dancer Koshiro Matsumoto. He said that I "was good."
> (The rest of the panel contained Charles's description of that great Japanese epic.)

That was the last contact I had with Charles. He died a few months later.

I framed the treasured triptych and hung it in my computer room where I could see it daily.

Charles was the consummate artist, always creating new work with the demeanor of childhood wonder.

ETIENNE DECROUX

Marcel Marceau—better known simply as *Marceau*—was unquestionably the best-known mime in the world. He enjoyed audiences on every continent, except perhaps Antarctica. He didn't seem to speak penguin language even in mime.

In 1957, prompted by a poster showing lips and two eyes with eyebrows, I was intrigued enough to purchase tickets to see this famous mime at the New York City Center Auditorium. My curiosity was well rewarded, as this small man with two assistants, Gilles Segal and Pierre Verry, told stories evoking a wide range of emotions and sentiments. He accomplished this with minute but definitive movements of the hands, the eyebrows, the mouth; indeed the whole body without uttering a sound. With him we swam under ocean currents and soared above the clouds.

I was mesmerized, never dreaming that I would ever meet this fantastic artist or pursue his art form.

However, in 1959 I had the opportunity to study mime with Etienne Decroux, a master mime teacher from Paris. When I enrolled in his classes in a walkup studio on Eighth Avenue in New York, I was unaware that he had been Marceau's teacher. I studied with him for eight months, until I moved to Kentucky to take a faculty position at Union College.

For the next several years I used the mime exercises in teaching the importance of body language and character signature in actor training. These mime principles were useful for the classes I taught at Union College, the University of Wisconsin, the National School of Drama in India, and Lambuth College.

I was given the opportunity in 1970 by a physician friend of mine to use his wonderful vacation retreat as a studio to teach mime to his daughter and his houseboy. I accepted this invitation and founded there the Valley Studio and the Wisconsin Mime Theatre and School. As I was fortunate to be able to employ some of the best international mime, clown and dance artists, the *New York Times* called Valley Studio "the center of mime training in the U.S."

In 1975 I accepted the position of Administrator of the International Mimes and Pantomimists (IMP). In this role I was in touch with a wide array of worldwide mimes. Pierre Verry, Marceau's partner, was the French representative of IMP. Although I had not met Marceau face to face—or should I say, "white face to white face?"—I did get to meet him on a snowy day and evening in Milwaukee, while he was on tour.

From 2:00 pm to 2:00 am we visited in between TV interviews, his performance and a late dinner. In his hotel room, he confronted me about the critical reviews of mime performers who used whiteface, as he did. I was the editor of the *International Mime News,* and many of the reviewers would criticize the white face mimes, implicitly denigrating Marceau's work. I assured him that I was concerned with the shallowness of this point of view. I also told him that I wouldn't censor any of the writing, and that I was planning to write an editorial—not to defend his work—but to warn against the insipid dangers of any orthodoxy. He told me that Decroux, his teacher as well as mine, would no longer speak to him. Decroux claimed that Marceau had bastardized the art form.

Some people thought that Decoux's irritation was his use of the white face. Marceau quite correctly said, "I didn't invent white face. Even the Greeks used white face to emphasize facial expressions." He went on to say, "Everything I do, I learned from Decroux."

One evening in his weekly lecture, Decroux said (in French of course) "It is all right to whittle an 18 inch wooden figurine. However you have not made your dramatic statement until you've attacked a 20-ton boulder of granite with a mallet and chisel."

I remember the metaphor quite well, as I had just finished whittling a small wooden figurine of Adam. Band-aids covered my war wounds.

It was only years later that I saw someone come close to attaining Decroux's standard for mime performance. Steve Wasson and Corinne Soum, his wife, were using Decroux's Coporeal Mime principles to perform major epics and Greek myths, thus attacking "the 20-ton boulder of granite."

The short pieces of Marceau and many others, Decroux would call pantomime, with a great deal of use of face and hands. Whereas corporeal mime is focused on the movement language of the entire body.

I felt that some of Decroux's irritation was only jealousy, as Marceau was well known worldwide, and only those people in the theatre world knew of Decroux.

Marceau was particularly concerned with the younger mimes who seemed to have rejected Marceau's style of mime. He said, "After all, the mime students in this country were introduced to the art of mime through my work." He was quite correct about that and he went on to say, "All of the styles and techniques I use were taught to me by Decroux. Why would he be unhappy with me, and why would the new mimes turn their backs on me?"

Even though mimes may be silent onstage, they are more loquacious than almost any other group of people except, perhaps politicians. Marceau once warned a news reporter, "Don't get a mime to talking."

In his hotel room at 2:00 am this small man was sitting, twisting his fore finger in his curly hair and commiserating on the lack of respect from Decroux (the father figure in the family of mime) and the younger mimes (the siblings in this odd family). Here was Marcel Marceau, beloved of millions of fans, distressed in his aloneness from his artistic family.

One of the summer instructors at Valley Studio, was Carlo Mazzoni-Clementi, who had founded the Del' Arte School of Physical Theatre in Blue Lake, California and was probably the world's greatest authority on Commedia Del Arte of Italy. Carlo had studied with Decroux and had toured with Marceau. He knew both men well.

He told me that when Decroux was in New York in December 1958, he had been invited to Carnegie Music Hall to deliver a lecture-demonstration of mime. Carlo said that both he and Marceau were in the audience. As he and Marceau were reminiscing after the presentation, Marceau said, "Carlo, would you go backstage and ask the master if I could come back and extend season's greetings?"

Carlo assured him in his most grandiloquent, effusive style that he would do that.

Backstage, Carlo congratulated our teacher on the eloquence of the presentation and the grandeur of the evening. He then said, "Monsieur Decroux, in the audience this evening was Marceau. He would like to come back and extend to you season's greetings."

Decroux paused for emphasis and said, "Ah . . . Marceau! He lives in the cathedral, and he is the pope. But I, Decroux, live in the catacombs (his studio was in his basement), but I am Jesus Christ."

That night the pope did not get to speak with Jesus Christ.

Carlo also related this event to several others in the mime field.

PROFESSOR A.C. SCOTT

When in 1962, I started my ministry at Grace Methodist Church in Belleville, WI, I also matriculated at the University of Wisconsin Graduate Theatre Program. My first graduate TA (teaching assistant) was as a stage hand at the Memorial Union Theatre under the tutelage of Fred Buerki. Papa Buerki, a name which he encouraged with all his students, loved the title and often used it himself. Almost every summer he arranged for European theatre tours with his students. I never opted for those excursions, but it's been told that Fred would often announce to the hotel personnel, when he checked in, "I'm a bachelor. These are all my children."

He was an old agnostic reprobate, who had not darkened a church door since the funeral of his beloved mother many years earlier. Knowing that of him I was surprised by a rumor from one of the other graduate students that Professor Buerki was going to surprise me one Sunday morning and attend my church service at the Grace Methodist Church. The student felt it would be unfair to me for such a surprise. I thanked her and thus was not alarmed a few weeks later when Papa Buerki showed up early in his yellow Lincoln convertible for church. Students filled his car and two more cars were filled with students.

As the morning worship started, I announced to the congregation that the new attendees were friends of mine from the university and urged them to treat them kindly.

As usual when the service was over, I would stand on the stoop outside the front door, wishing the congregants blessings for the coming week. After nearly everyone had left I was standing in that usual spot and talking with Papa Buerki, standing on a lower step. He said, "I need to know how you knew we were coming to your church service?"

Adjusting my ecclesiastical robe, clasping my hands together, glancing toward the heavens, I replied, "I have connections you know."

It wasn't often that anyone could upstage our dear professor, but on that occasion he blurted out, "Everything in the service was okay until now, but that pronouncement is just too much."

Shortly after that first summer, I needed to focus on a specific area of theatre study. At first it was somewhat difficult to choose, as I had enjoyed all aspects of theatre literature and performance while teaching at Union College, 1959-1962.

However, coinciding with that moment of decision, a new professor joined the UW Theatre Department. Professor A. C. Scott, a Brit, had served in the British Foreign Service for many years in China. During that tenure he had developed a great interest and expertise in the Chinese theatre.

I was hooked right away, perhaps as a final opportunity to follow the gypsies of which Mama had warned me so many decades ago. She had said, "They'd take you way off yonder." I had also been intrigued with any Asian speakers or leaders in church youth assemblies. I suppose one doesn't need any more impetus to commit intensive study and travel.

Professor Scott welcomed me into the small group testing the waters of Asian Theatre. Although his lectures utilized theatre scripts, film clips as well as Asian Theatre history and critiques, he felt that the only way to begin to understand that exotic art form, was to get involved with the actual theatre practice.

With that in mind, he obtained for me a Rockefeller grant to study and participate in a special project at IASTA (Institute of Advanced Study of Theatre Arts). The timing for my potential involvement was a bit awkward, as I had ongoing responsibilities with classes, family and my pastorate. Professor Scott had obtained places for two graduate students in the IASTA project. The other candidate told me that his involvement was precluded by his family and graduate obligations.

I had similar duties, but I also had the Grace Methodist Church Commitment. However, I was able to get another pastor in a nearby town to conduct Sunday services at Grace Methodist during the three months I would be gone. My involvement in Japanese Noh Theatre with Sidayo Kita is detailed in another chapter.

The next year, 1965, Professor Scott had run interference for me in obtaining a Fulbright Award to research and teach theatre in India. That year was significant in so many ways: family, career, cultural understanding.

That was the beginning of an exciting adventure for the family. Of course, preparations for the journey kept everyone occupied for weeks: medical shots, purchase of appropriate clothing and packing in as few bags as possible. My wife, Luan, had been quite frugal in packing everything in one suitcase and a standard size college footlocker. We could buy more clothes in India.

The Fulbright Foundation had supplied information and travel vouchers for the trip, which was to be via an ocean liner. Ms. Olive Reddick, the Fulbright director in India, was a former missionary and was convinced that the only way to travel was by ship. She no doubt, never had the opportunity to travel such a distance with three little girls.

Saying Goodbye to Belleville and Grandma down in Monroe was bittersweet. The drive to New York for boarding was rather uneventful, except for stopping in Delaware to visit my sister and the other grandmother.

Going through customs and additional boarding necessities was fairly routine and uneventful. The girls were having a marvelous adventure, though somewhat more daunting than a trip to Grandma's.

When we were safely ensconced in our tiny stateroom on a lower deck, we climbed to the upper deck to view our own departure. Luan and the girls went to the aft railing, while I stood back to take a picture of the beginning of this family adventure.

Before I'd even raised the camera, an overwhelming panic hit me. I saw three wonderful little girls, my daughters: red head, brunette and blonde, waving, "Goodbye, Lady with the torch".

I wondered, "What the devil am I doing . . . taking these children to India for a year?" I then began remembering exotic tales of danger and sickness told by previous travelers.

I also recalled years earlier when my mother one day yelled at me and my siblings, "You kids run into the house and close all the window shades. Be real quiet."

"Why Mamma?"

"The gypsies are coming."

"I know they steal chickens, but why are we supposed to be scared of them?"

"They steal little children."

"If they stole me, what would they do with me?"

"Oh, they'd take you way off yonder."

"Really!!!?" That sounded like a wonderful opportunity to celebrate with the gypsies whom I'd often seen camping in a grove of white oak trees behind Colvard's General Store.

Coming to my senses, returning to the beginning of the year-long sojourn, I wondered, "Has the spirit of the gypsies kidnapped me, after Mama's warning so many years ago?"

That was a risk, worthy of my adventuresome nature, but "What right do I have to take these innocent children halfway around the world to an exotic country with questionable health issues…If something happens to them, I'll kill myself."

I had to put my fears at rest, as we were now on our way to *way off yonder*, on a month-long ocean voyage to the fantasy land of swamis, bearded Sikhs, camels and rickshaws.

Sailing into the Bombay harbor we could already hear the commingling sounds of street hawkers, traffic and drum music. We could also smell the pungent spicy odors from the street vendors. Our train trip to New Delhi was fairly uneventful.

The Fulbright staff had arranged for a nice little apartment in Nizzamudin East. To have us feel at home, our landlords served us ice cold

Coca Cola. We visited in their lovely living room, displaying Indian art and fabrics.

In addition to my research I taught Mime at the National School of Drama. My students later became leaders in the theatre and film of India. One of my students, Om Shivpuri, played Nehru in the film Ghandi.

After several months, I was asked to perform at the National Indian Theatre Conference. Kamaladevi said, "We'll have you perform at the end of the Conference."

"That's fine."

"No, we can't do that."

"Why did you change your mind?"

"Because you're so good, no one will remember what anyone else performs."

"Why are you saying that. I don't believe you've ever seen me perform."

"You're an American . . . I have a feeling about Americans. If you decide to do something, you'll do it well. If you perform last, no one will remember anything anyone else performs."

Just try to live up to that billing. I don't recall whether I was last or not. I was the only foreigner to perform, but I was the only one everyone could understand. There are 14 major languages in India, and all of them were used in the scripts performed. Not everyone could know all the languages, but everyone could understand Mime. I also had the opportunity to perform Mime with an Indian mime, Irshad Panjatan.

The whole family had fallen in love with India and its people. Impressed by the trip, Tari, years later, would return to adopt a small girl in Mumbai and an infant girl in Nepal.

Not only did we survive *way off yonder*, it was a significant part of my Asian Theatre Studies, and it proved to be a happy incentive to an extended family.

SIDAYO KITA

Is the Noh Theatre, drama or opera or dance or mime?
Thus Sidayo Kita introduced us to the ancient Japanese theatre.

In 1964 I received a Rockefeller Grant to serve for three months as Sidayo Kita's American assistant at the Institute of Advanced Studies in Theatre Arts (IASTA) in New York. This was the first time a Noh director had ever taught or directed performers outside Japan, and had never directed non-Japanese, even *in* Japan. This was a marvelous opportunity for me, as well as for the professional New York actors invited into the project.

We would be studying the vocal and movement techniques of the Noh, while simultaneously rehearsing *Ikkaku Sennin* (Holy Hermit Unicorn) for a public performance at the end of the three months. Jerome Robbins came almost every morning to observe our rehearsals.

A stage was built against a wall in an upstairs space of IASTA on 42nd Street. (You see, I have played Broadway!) It was built of sanded, but unfinished, Japanese cypress boards, elevated three feet off the rehearsal room floor. In Japan the Noh stage was an eighteen-foot square. Ours was a twenty-foot square to accommodate the larger American actors.

On each corner of the stage was a post, holding up a canopy. The upstage right post was called the *shite pillar* (pronounced "shtay"), as this was the general area for the position and movement of the shite, the protagonist of the drama.

Downstage right was the *eye-fixing pillar*, which was a visual indication for any of the actors that it was at the corner of the stage. This was necessary because while wearing the heavy wooden masks the actors could not readily see the floor. If they were to look down to see the edge of the stage, the mask would be too dark, thus interrupting the flow of the drama, but would allow the actor to see the post at the edge of the stage.

The pillar downstage left was the *waki pillar* which was the home territory of the *waki*, the antagonist or secondary character.

The musicians sat along the upstage left edge of the stage. They were situated next to the *flute-player's pillar*. Directly upstage left of the *flute-player's pillar* a small sliding door leading to the backstage was the *hurry door* for the entrances and exits of the musicians. The door was only four feet high, thus the musicians had to crouch both to enter and to exit. This of course prompts the Japanese bow of respect to the audience and to the stage, itself.

A stylized painting of a contorted pine tree covered the upstage back wall.

Connected to the upstage right corner of the stage was the *hashigakari*, a ramp or pathway leading from the mirror room to the main stage area. In front of the *hashigakari* were three small pine trees placed in a white gravel pathway or eave drip line; this reminded both performer and audience of the roots of the Noh as being out of doors.

The unfinished floor was to be finished, to our surprise, by the student actors each morning, as we cleaned the floor on our hands and knees with bean curd encased in a damp cotton cloth. Not only did this keep the floor surface pristine, but a bit of oil oozing from the bean curd created a beautiful finish over a period of several weeks. Street shoes were not permitted on the stage floor, as they would leave a black mark, particularly from the sidewalks of New York.

Many more details of the Noh come to mind, especially the movement, the vocalization, the masks and the costumes. The movement is slow, but contained like holding a strong team of horses with tight reins. The feet have a kind of cotton sock called a *tabi*, which caresses the polished floor.

The costumes are gorgeous brocaded kimonos with large *obi* tied in huge bows in the back. The main characters wear wooden masks with elaborate headpieces. Every character carries a fan, which may be used as a tray, a pitcher of sake, a sword or any other intended prop.

The most important lessons were those of time and space. It has been said of Noh Theatre that, "One watches an actor bound across the stage, 12 inches every twenty minutes." And yet even with that pace, years of time are encapsulated into a fifty-minute performance.

Another lesson of time is the time—several weeks—for a finish to be put on that unfinished pine floor, by the actors on their hands and knees cleaning the floor with bean curd. An American stage would have been finished with an overnight drying paint.

In the space of a twenty-foot-square stage, we see beautiful damsels, evil wizards, grieving mothers and devout monks crossing rivers and traversing mountains.

A term Kita-san introduced, *yugen*, could not be translated into English. One might attempt to approximate the meaning by calling it beauty, effervescence, aura, electricity. It is that quality which one finds from time to time in a marvelous work of visual or performance art. Kita-san translated it by saying it was "a lotus blossom on the end of a dead branch of a tree."

"Impossible!" one might say, and yet we find it there at unexpected times and places, whether in the arts or in life. The pity is that we can't force it to happen. We hope to experience and accept it when it is there.

An occasion of *yugen* was in a performance Kita and I shared at the University of Wisconsin. He was playing the role of *Hagaromo*, a heavenly princess. She had lost her cape of feathers, which had been found by a local fisherman. It was so lovely that he wanted to keep it to give to his wife. When *Hagaromo* explained to him that she cannot return to heaven if she is not wearing the cape, he relents and gives it to her.

The character, as a gesture of thanks, waves the fan toward the earth (stage), but Kita dropped his fan that evening. When I later asked why he had dropped it, knowing that the movement has kept the same choreography for centuries, he said, "Because I felt like it."

Of course, that was a moment of *yugen* for him, and as the master actor he had a right to transcend the tradition and technique. If, as an apprentice, I had taken such liberties, it would have been a grave mistake.

As I reflect on it, perhaps the experience of studying and performing with Kita-san, was somewhat like sliding down a rabbit hole with Alice.

The Noh theatre experience was certainly a wonderland beyond any childhood dreams or fantasies I might have conjured up earlier or dreamt of years later.

The greatest lesson in my Noh experience was the absolute sense of respect, if one can understand that the basic meaning of *re-spect*, is to *look again*.

The floor is polished every day with a great deal of respect. The actors caress the floor with their tabi-clad feet. When the actor dons the mask, it is first placed in the actor's lap so that he can regard its exterior visage. After several minutes of regarding the exterior, the mask is then turned over for further meditation on the interior. Then the actor moves his face to the mask—never the mask to the face.

Kita-san helped me understand that the Noh Theatre is a disciplined performance of respect; stage preparation, masking, costuming, and for tradition, itself.

PART III
OTHER FOLKS ALONG THE WAY

Besides those folks closest to us, such as family and teachers, we encounter many wonderful people along the way. I have been especially fortunate to have encountered marvelous folks in high positions, such as politicians and entertainers, as well as everyday people from the Appalachian Mountains to train depots of India. Many of the other amazing folks (extended family, students, and colleagues) I'll simply keep in my memory bank and leave them publicly unsung.

IT'S A SMALL WORLD

My cousin, Eddie Burchman, after reading some of the incidents in my life journey, emailed me that he was impressed with the many places I had traveled and the adventures I had experienced. He went on to say he sensed I had enjoyed that, and he had stayed close to home in Winston Salem and hadn't done a lot of different things and he had enjoyed his life.

I was pleased that he was able to respect my style and vicissitudes of life and that he had likewise appreciated his own journey and circumstances without envy or condemnation either for me or for himself. What a refreshing way to accept one's own life while admiring that of someone else!

When I emailed him that I was going to Peru, he replied by saying that he wouldn't know the first thing about going to Peru, except to go out to Highway #52 and head south toward Winston, but that he wouldn't know after he got through town where to turn.

As a *bon voyage*, he wrote, "Hope things continue to go well for you, and your journey takes you where you really want to go." I can't imagine a more positive blessing from one's kinfolk.

Musing a bit on the myriad miles one might travel or the divergent paths one might take, I recalled incidents which brought to mind the old song, "It's a Small World After All,", such as running into an old high school classmate, Jack Walsh, in the Chicago airport twenty years after graduation.

In 1966, while living in India, for some reason I had occasion to go to the Indian Parliament House, which was not my usual haunt. I had previously met Prime Minister Indira Gandhi briefly at a social event, but I don't believe I had arranged a tryst with the Prime Minister for that morning.

As I was ascending the expansive stone steps, I saw an American descending toward me from about thirty steps above. I sensed a familiar face, confirming the recognition as the gap between us narrowed. Incredulously, I blurted out, "R. Harold Hipps, what are you doing in India?"

He replied, "Reid Gilbert, I could ask the same of you."

R. Harold, a Methodist minister from the North Carolina Conference, had been a great inspiration to me in my teen years when I attended youth assemblies at the Lake Junaluska Assembly in the summers. He had demonstrated through song and folk dancing that the religious life was not just dour and doleful, as I had recalled from Grandpa's Primitive Baptist demeanor. How ironic that the last time I saw the Rev. R. Harold Hipps was on the Parliament Building steps in New Delhi, India. We had a wonderful chat for a few moments, reminiscing of earlier years and catching up on the ensuing time frame.

In 1976, when I was Director of the Wisconsin Mime Theatre, I was booked to perform at the McFarland Elementary School a few miles out of Madison, Wisconsin. The principal asked, "Would you mind if one of the mothers of some of the children attends the performance?"

"Not at all! You're paying for the performance and have every right to invite whomever you please."

After the performance a red-haired woman, balancing a toddler on one hip, came to the stage and told me, "I have been planning to teach mime at church camp this summer, but I can't do those things you were doing—and I even majored in physical education."

Detecting a southern accent up there in Yankee Wisconsin, I asked, "Where are you from?"

"I grew up in Winston Salem, North Carolina."

"You're Emily Butner?"

This clearly confused her. "Well, yes, I was Emily Butner, but I'm Emily Butner Wallace now."

I quickly solved the mystery while stunning her further. "You may not remember that we dated a couple of times back in 1953."

"You mean you're *that* Reid Gilbert?"

I suppose I hadn't impressed her very much on our dates, but I did look a little different now with the white mime make-up.

Later, I found out that she told her three school-age daughters that she used to date the mime, who was at school that day. Of course they found that hard to believe.

When I related this incident to my friend, Barbara Banks, she asked me what year that happened. I said I was sure it was 1974. She then told me that in 1972 when her son, Paul, was born in Madison she shared the hospital room with Emily Butner Wallace who gave birth to her fourth daughter.

In 1998, Phil Faini, the dean of the College of Creative Arts at the West Virginia University, was asked to send a representative to a conference on aging to lecture on aging and the arts. He must have thought I was qualified—particularly the aging part—so he asked me to address the conference. I gladly accepted.

In the hallway outside the conference room I noticed a man handing out political pamphlets, and at the conclusion of my remarks he approached me with a broad smile, almost as though I should know him, which I assured myself I didn't.

After introducing himself, he asked me, "How long were you in Wisconsin?"

I realized I had mentioned Wisconsin a few times. "I lived there for years. My PhD is from the university and two of my daughters still live in Madison."

He inquired further, "Do you recognize the name, Jon Patrick Hunter?"

"Absolutely! He's one of the best journalists in the state. In fact, I was the associate minister in his church, the First Unitarian Society of Madison. How do you know Jon Patrick Hunter?"

It was my turn to be stunned. "He's my daddy."

Jon Blair Hunter became my state senator. It was later I thought to myself, *It's a good thing I didn't say anything bad about his daddy.*

In 2009, after moving to Tucson, one day I was filing some of my personal papers, including some from years before. I came across a letter written to me in 1981 from Sande Zeig, a former mime student at Valley Studio. She was writing at that time to inquire of the possibility of performing at a Mime Festival I was organizing in Milwaukee. She started the letter with, "A long silent voice from your past emerges." She had been an excellent student and had continued to progress in the performance world.

When I unearthed the letter, I thought it would nice to attempt to Google her, as I had done several times with students and friends from many years before. I found an email address, which I thought was in New York, so I emailed her informing her of my annual trek to New York, and that it would be nice to make connections again after all those years. I signed off with "A long silent voice from your past."

Fifteen minutes later I opened an email; *Reid, I am amazed and happy to hear from you. But . . . the most amazing thing is that we live ten minutes from each other. I live in Tucson now by Sabino Canyon. Sande Zeig.*

It is indeed a small world after all when one considers those chance meetings of old familiar faces in strange out-of-the-way places. I sometimes wonder whom I might have missed in an airport on the way to somewhere.

On the other hand I am just as mystified in this small world to meet someone whom I have not known before and will probably never ever see again, one such incident being at the San Jose airport in Costa Rica on March 14.

As we were waiting to board the plane for Atlanta I noticed a young girl, in her early twenties, who had a mask hanging on the outside of her backpack. I admired the mask and told her, "I collect masks from various countries. Did you make this one?"

"Yes, in a craft class."

On the plane we were assigned seats next to each other. As we talked, she told me that she was from Germany and had come with a group of young people to volunteer for six months in a school. They had chosen Costa Rica because it was reputed to be the safest country in Central America. However, she had been robbed there three times. On one occasion someone had broken into the cabin where she and others were staying and stole everything. At another time, policemen stole her things. The third time she and a friend were robbed at gunpoint. She looked at the book she was reading and said, "Although I'm enjoying reading this book, it is just a material thing and is really insignificant to my life."

I thought what a wonderful lesson she had learned about letting go of material possessions without anger or remorse of the loss of her *things*. We talked a little about her educational and career plans. I asked her if she would be flying on to Germany from Atlanta and if someone would be waiting for her.

She said, "Yes, my *Vater* will be meeting me at the airport."

I thought how fortunate she was to have someone waiting for her and how fortunate he was to have such a perceptive daughter. Of course, I reminisced about my own daughters and a granddaughter who was about her age.

As we began deplaning in Atlanta, she said, "You collect masks don't you?"

"Yes, I do."

"Would you accept this one as a gift from me?"

Overwhelmed by this gesture, I said, "I would be most grateful and honored . . . Would you be so gracious as to sign it?"

She took my pen and signed *Jill Koehn* in the inside of the mask.

Her mask is as highly valued in my collection as the Italian masks by Stanley Allen Sherman and Balinese masks by I. B. Anom.

Speaking of I. B. Anom, I experienced another strange coincidence. I was introduced to Barbara Banks by Robert and Derry Graves. We had not met in person, when I called her in Tucson from Wisconsin, where I was spending the winter in 2006.

She, knowing of my interest in Asian Theatre, recounted a recent tour she had made to Indonesia.

She said, "I met a marvelous master mask maker there."

"Would it have been Ida Bigosh Anom?"

There was a brief silence. "How would you have known?"

"Of course, I wouldn't have known that he was the artist you might have met. But he is a friend of mine, and I have a couple of his masterpieces."

I. B. Anom was the mask maker to whom she was referring.

More recently (Feb. 2015), I wrote a story about an incident that occurred in 1968 at Lambuth College, where I was teaching. I rewrote it into a one-act script and submitted it to the Old Pueblo Playwrights annual New Play Festival. It was accepted, and I was editing it with further rewrites. I was anxious to get in touch with Bob Dickerson, the student who had been picked up by the FBI for burning a flag. A week before the staged event I got an email from Bob, even though I had not been in touch with him since 1969. He said that he had been discussing drama with a former fellow Lambuth student and felt he ought to get in touch with me whenever he thought of theatre. What a surprise to hear from him. I asked if he had been in touch with his best friend, Ron Baker, with whom I had only recently reconnected. He had not, and I was able to put those old friends back in touch with each other.

On the weekend of the reading, my friend, Barbara Banks, had scheduled a clay workshop. Friday, after the first day of the workshop, she said that the workshop instructor's husband was from Tennessee. So on Saturday we shared dinner with the instructor and her husband.

He confirmed that he was from Tennessee and had grown up in Jackson. I said, "I taught at Lambuth College in Jackson."

He said, "I attended Lambuth."

I told him about the script and the flag-burning incident. He was enrolled at the time I was teaching and had remembered that a student had got in trouble for something in a cemetery. The next day he attended the staged reading of the incident which happened when he was a college student so long before.

On that same weekend I was autographing copies of my book, *What Matters*, as gifts for the actors presenting my script. The previous summer I bought 100 copies and enjoyed selling and giving them away. When I started to sign one of the books, I noticed just inside the front cover, "Christian Courageous". I wasn't adverse to Christian heroes, but I had not written that in my book. Examining the contents further I realized that an entirely different book was printed inside the cover of my book.

I thought that I might as well read at the least the first chapter of a Christian martyr at the time that Diocletian was executing Christians. The subject/victim in the first chapter was Ardalion. The irony was almost unbelievable, as Ardalion was a mime. *Had someone deliberately put this story in one of my book covers for a message to me and my career as a mime?*

And I wonder what the message is: *Have I not been courageous enough? Have I not been Christian enough? As a mime should I be preparing for my own execution for my beliefs?*

It's indeed a small world whether bumping into old friends *in* faraway places or meeting new ones *from* faraway places and long ago times or messages about my own life choices.

SISTER WILLIE MAE TYGER

In the 1960s, an interesting organization with a fascinating title emerged in Jackson, Tennessee. As I was a recently appointed faculty member at Lambuth College, I had the opportunity to encounter this organization through the colorful personality of Sister Willie Mae Tyger . . . an equally fascinating name and person.

I met both the organization and the person a couple of years before Dr. Martin Luther King was assassinated in Memphis, only eighty miles away. I had heard of Sister Willie Mae when I attended a community organization dedicated to improvement of race relations in Jackson. It seems that any time there was something amiss down in Fite's Bottom, Sister Willie Mae would go marching . . . and I do mean marching . . . to City Hall to confront either the mayor or chief of police, or both if she could find them both.

Fite's Bottom was a neighborhood of substandard houses located in a lowland area adjacent to Fite's Creek. The houses were owned by white absentee landlords and rented to low-income African Americans. All of the houses had been officially condemned; therefore the owners could not get permits to repair or even to paint them. However, they could be rented with an adequate excuse for neglecting the upkeep.

Sister Willie Mae had helped organize the neighborhood improvement association, and as its president, felt empowered both officially and morally to confront City Hall whenever the occasion demanded it. After all, she didn't really have anything to lose; she had no earthly goods to lose, and she did have all the respect she needed or wanted from her Fite's Bottom community.

Such a community, obviously, needs a defender, and the Fite's Bottom Improvement Association, and the Fite's Bottom champion came in the form of an elderly, childless matriarch, who feared neither City Hall nor the Jackson Police Force. If the community's streets required repairs or garbage pick-up attention was needed, Sister Willie Mae would head downtown to City Hall.

I was told by Mayor Conger that whenever she was seen climbing the City Hall front steps, the alarm would go out by someone, "Oh, Lord! Here comes Sister Willie Mae." Early on they had attempted to exit the back stairs, but even if they escaped undetected, they knew she'd sit there until they had to return. She had all the time she needed whenever she was on a mission. And if Sister Willie Mae's mission wasn't completed on the first day, they knew she'd return early the next morning. She'd say, "I got all day, Honey."

The Fite's Bottom folks were generally employed, if at all, in menial, low-paying jobs. However, in true entrepreneurial spirit—I really mean spirits—they would seek other opportunities to bolster their financial status. As Madison County was legally a "dry" county, those with a thirst for alcoholic beverages were reduced to obtain their poison in back alleys or other unusual locales, such as a black community like Fite's Bottom.

This arrangement provided opportunity for Fite's Bottom folks to pick up a little cash and for the imbibers to avoid having to go out of state for their refreshments. However, it did involve the risk of a clash with the "Man". The upstanding white citizens could meander down to Fite's to collect their rent; often in a liquid state.

Sister Willie Mae confided in me that most of her neighbors in Fite's Bottom, including herself, at one time or another had fit the title of bootleggah. The illicit use and/or sale of liquid spirits didn't detract from the religious spiritual fervor of Sister Willie Mae or her fellow church members. It became onerous only when it was imbibed in too heavily or incited domestic violence; that would then begin to slide into the "sinnin'" category.

"Moderation in everything," was practiced, though seldom if ever spoken in the black community One preacher was overheard saying, "I believe I can preach a little betta, if I have a little toddy just afore I step up behind the pulpit."

Sister Willie Mae told me, "The Poh-lice would come to my house, even when I won't to home an' step up on my nice clean bed with their muddy boots."

"Why would they do that, Sister Willie Mae?"

"They's lookin' fer likker a'course, an' they could look up into my attic by standin' on mah bed."

"Did they find anything?"

"No, the po-lice nevah found nothin' untoward in mah house . . . not that time anyways."

Of course, in Sister Willie Mae's church it was the custom every Sunday for a church member to invite the preacher home for Sunday dinner after the meeting. It soon became time for Sister Willie Mae's young neighbor, who was only recently married. "Oh she fussed an' she fumed about what to feed the preacha. I said, 'Why Honey, you just feed the preacha what you feed youh own man.'"

"Oh Sister Willie Mae, thet won't do atall. I feed mah own man beans, an' it don't seem fitten to feed the preacha beans."

"Chile, you just let me feed Brother Tolliver. I'll handle this for ya."

The day the new preacher was going to dine with Sister Willie Mae, he brought with him two young preachers from Nashville. Sister Willie Mae served fried chicken, mashed taters, green beans cooked with fatback, sweetened iced tea and had even baked a sweet tater pie, accompanied by all the aromas of a Southern-home-cooked Sunday dinner.

Just before she served the pie, she said, "Brothah Tolliver. I unnerstan' you ain't gonna have nothin' to do with no bootleggahs."

"Thets' right, Sistah Willie Mae."

"An', I unnerstan' you ain't gonna eat in no bootlaggahs' house."

Still unaware of where Sister Willie Mae was heading, he again responded, "Thet's right, Sister Willie Mae."

Standing there next to Brother Tolliver, while holding the sweet tater pie like a golden chalice, she simply announced, "You's heah ain't ya?"

The preacher gulped loudly, as his knife and fork clatterd onto the Blue Willow china plate.

The young preachers were incredulous that he or any other Black preacher would have made a declaration like that. "You mean that you said that in a colored church in Tennessee?"

He couldn't answer them, seemingly having lost his voice and all appetite for any more of Sister Willie Mae's Sunday "fixin's."

After some hearty laughter, the two young preachers didn't feel obliged to share with Brother Tolliver the "Sweet tater pie."

At one of our city-wide community action meetings she told the assemblage that the police would come down to Fite's Bottom at odd, unannounced times, day or night, to raid some black man's home for illegal alcohol. As Madison County was officially dry even a bottle of wine would be contraband.

This sounded incredulous to me, so I sought out Sister Willie Mae after the meeting. "Sister Willie Mae, whenever another police raid happens like this, would you give me a call?"

"Hit might be in the middle of the night."

"That makes no never mind. I just want to witness this my own self."

"Perfessor Reid, Ah'll shorely do it."

Within a couple of weeks, as I recall, I got a call from Sister Willie Mae on an early, cold Saturday morning. "Perfessor, they's heah."

"Who's there, Sister Willie Mae?"

"The po-lice is heah goin' all over my neighbah's house an' woodshed and even a ol' beat-up car out behin' the house. An Perfessor, I'se tellin' ya the gospel truth. This neighbah, he ain't doin' no bootleggin' an' moover, he ain't nevah done no bootleggin. An' him not even to home. He already gone off to work, an' jus' his little woman an' baby theah, an' them fat-assed po-lice is trompin' all over the place."

Sensing Sr. Willie Mae's rising vituperation as well as my own earlier announced interest, I answered, "I'll be right down, Sister Willie Mae, with my camera."

When I arrived with my unloaded camera, I greeted Sister Willie

Mae, who was standing with about twenty other neighbors across the street from the raiding party. Everyone but Sister. Willie Mae, was quiet; standing with folded arms and staring intently, without visible expression, at the enforcers of the lawmen conducting their "duty."

I began snapping the camera lens, as though I was getting a lot of interesting photographs of this quasi-military operation. They had already torn the hood and trunk off the disabled car and had ripped some of the weatherboards off the side of the house.

Seeing a white face attached to a body, seemingly taking incriminating photos, the leader of the raiding party walked toward me, greeting me with, "It's a pretty cold morning, isn't it?"

"Yes, it is. Could you tell me what's going on here?"

"Well, we're just investigating a complaint."

"What kind of complaint?"

"You know, about liquor—bootleggin' an' all. These colored boys get involved with liquor an' beat up on their wives or girlfriends, who then call in an' make a complaint."

"It's my understanding that this fellow is at work."

"Yeah, we got a warrant to go pick him up at the plant."

"It's also my understanding that he's never done any bootlegging or had any complaints about any involvement with illegal alcohol."

"Well, there is now, 'cause we found it."

"Found what?"

"A half bottle of wine . . . out in the woodshed."

"That doesn't seem like bootlegging."

"No, but it's just as illegal—as this is a dry county, you know."

"Just how dry is it?" I asked.

"Whaddaya mean?"

"Is champagne also illegal?"

"Oh, yeah."

"Did you raid the Madison County School Superintendents house last Saturday morning?"

"Why would I do that?"

"There was an article in the *Jackson Sun*, last Monday describing a champagne breakfast which the superintendent hosted for our congressman. Did you raid that drunken bash?"

"There was no complaint made about that. We simply respond to complaints. We don't just go and harass law abiding citizens."

"If I made a complaint about that party, would you have raided it, or do you leave the politicians alone and just come down to Fite's Bottom for fun?"

"I've already told you too much. I've got work to do."

As he turned away, I said, "Well, have a good morning. I'll see if the *Jackson Sun* would like to have these pictures." trying to bluff him into thinking I had actually taken some incriminating documentation of him and his men at work.

Sister Willie Mae told me later, "Ya know, Perfessur, they didn't charge that boy with nothin'. They jus' let him go. Maybe you an' yo' Kodak made a diffurnce thet mornin'."

"Let's hope, Sr. Willie Mae, that somethin' will help you and your neighbors in your efforts to make a permanent diffurnce in Fite's Bottom."

EDNA and AUGIE

Edna Meudt and August Derleth—often regarded in the same league as Zona Gale—were titans on the Wisconsin literary landscape during the last half of the twentieth century. They were good friends, living in adjoining rural counties. Although I barely knew Derleth ("Augie" to his friends) Edna was a close friend, almost a surrogate mother to me. An Irish poet, James Liddy, called her a "literary witch because of her intuition for personal sorcery."

Valley Studio (my mime theatre and school) was right across the creek from Edna's home place and adjacent to her grandparents Kritz's homestead. The one-room Kritz School, where Edna received her early education, was less than a mile up the Upper Wyoming road from us. Actually, we bought the schoolhouse, moved it to our campus, painted it brown and used it for a ballet studio, fully utilizing its hardwood maple floor.

First meeting Edna at the Uplands Arts Council art gallery barn, I was mesmerized by her poetry readings. She was accompanied by her fourteen-year-old grandson, Chris, who was also her ward. Her poem, "The Summer Day That Changed the World," introduced me not only to her and her life, but also the creative energy of the *Valley of the God Almighty Joneses* (Frank Lloyd Wright's family) as well as the tragedy of the 1914 murders at Taliesin.

In her poem about Taliesin she recorded the events of that fateful day through her eight-year-old eyes. It seems that she had been invited to a birthday party for Margaret Cheney who was visiting her mother, Mamah Borthwick (Frank Lloyd Wright's mistress) for the summer. A psychotic servant, Julian, heeding the voice in his head, had locked all but one of the doors of the dining room, then set the place on fire while everyone was having lunch. Whoever was able to escape the fire was met with a hatchet outside the one unlocked door. Five adults and three children lost their lives that day. Edna was lucky to have arrived late.

When Edna was already a published poet, she and a Wisconsin historian were inspecting the graveyard at Unity Chapel, the family church of the Lloyd Joneses and the Lloyd Wrights. As they approached Mamah's gravestone, the historian said, "I wonder if anyone knows who is buried here."

Edna replied, "I certainly should. I was there the day she died . . . I've been thinking about writing a story about that."

"Oh, no! You can't write a story about such a horrific event."

No one could ever tell Edna what she couldn't do. She wrote the story but discovered that prose didn't capture the drama or the emotion of the tragedy. Her poetry did. Her reflections of the events were captured at the end of her poem in these lines:

O generations!—Whatever it is we are—never the same after some ruined hill is climbed and we meet face to face the Thing that makes it Was.

The apprentices at Valley Studio were always pleased whenever I invited Edna to share some of her poetry with us in front of the fireplace in the common room. They, being a part of the '70s generation, were intrigued with the poems of her farm life, but more particularly of her love life.

Her meetings and readings with us were coffee and saffron-bread occasions with rumoring and apparitions—but no dogmas (never dogmas). She claimed she was the world's only Roman Catholic atheist.

Edna had left Wyoming Valley before the Wisconsin Mime Theatre and School found it.

As a teenager, she was deemed ready—by her parents—for matrimony, so they arranged for her to marry Peter Meudt, a successful farmer near Dodgeville, fifteen miles away and several years older. She seemed to sum up this portion of her life with one phrase from her poem, The *Round River Canticle*: Auctioned to an unfriendly world . . .

Although she was in a loveless marriage, she was not devoid of love.

Many of her poems chronicled this love, much to the embarrassment of her children and grandchildren. Her response to them was, "A poet is honest if nothing else."

The object of her love was a Roman Catholic priest who reflected her love in his own emotional life. However, they both had vows—she, her marriage vows and he, his priestly vows—vows which they never violated. Even in their reciprocal love letters, they remained circumspect.

Father Dan spent the last five years of his life—while in declining health with cancer—in the home of Edna and Peter. Then, after the deaths of Peter, Edna and Father Dan, whenever I visit the house—currently the home of her grandson, Chris—the room where the Right Reverend Daniel Coyne died is referred to as "Father Dan's room."

Of all Edna's poems dedicated to Father Dan or celebrating their love, the most poignant is "I Most Regret":

I most regret never having danced with you
To ever-pervading music in a ballroom never seen . . . When I slip through
O dance me toward the Sun!

One Saturday August morning, at the end of the first week of a new studio session of fresh new faces and energies, I called Edna to invite her for afternoon tea later that day. She readily agreed, and then we chatted about sundry things. Before hanging up she said, "Reid, you know my acceptance to your invitation is contingent."

I replied, "Contingent upon what?"

"Oh . . . an act of God or a natural disaster!"

"Edna, why do you always say things like that? Of course I would understand if something drastic were to happen before then."

After the phone call, the school cook served a scrumptious lunch, as usual, in the dining hall. At about two o'clock I saw an ominous cloud south of us in the Dodgeville direction. In about thirty minutes the phone rang. I knew it was Edna.

When I picked up the phone and greeted the caller, Edna calmly said, "This is Edna."

"Yes, I know! What happened?"

She answered, "I'll have to cancel the invitation. A tornado just hit here, taking down several trees, breaking tree branches and pushing the barn off its foundation. I'm particularly distressed that the larch tree at the side of the yard was uprooted. It was at least 100 years old, and I've always been so fond of it."

After a few more exchanges, I said, "We'll be there tomorrow morning to help you clean up."

"That would be wonderful."

The next morning the mime actors and students trekked to Edna's to clear up the debris from the storm. We couldn't do anything about the barn, and she had already arranged for a construction company to send a crane the next day to upright her beloved larch.

One of our new apprentices, Cleatious Goldman, was Jewish and Blackfeet Indian. He looked at the upended root ball of the larch and asked, "Edna do you have any clean white sheets which you would allow to be torn up?"

"Yes, I do."

She then yelled at Chris, "Chris, get that old sheet I washed on Monday."

Chris brought the sheet, and Cleatious ripped the sheet into two-inch wide strips, which he then tied around the larch root ends now exposed to the air.

Edna watched studiously and asked, "Cleatious, why did you do that?"

"So that the tree spirit would know we haven't abandoned it."

Although Edna is no longer among the living, the larch has made it into the new century.

Shortly after the tornado incident, August Derleth was visiting Edna and inspecting the damage to her yard and barn. Another mutual photographer friend, Dale O'Brien, was also visiting and took a picture of Augie with an ancient, though bedraggled, maple as background. When the film was developed a distinct death mask of Derleth was outlined in the tracery of the tree branches. Augie died two weeks later.

Edna then inspected the maple from the point of view of the camera, but could not detect the death mask, which had been revealed in the photograph.

In his younger days, Derleth had built himself a home, which he called *A Place of Hawks*. When his friend, Frank Lloyd Wright saw the house, he proclaimed, "Derleth, you've built yourself a barn,"

To which Augie replied, "Why not, Frank? A bull will be living in it."

Recalling his bullishness reminds me of the one time Augie and I had a confrontation. Edna had arranged a conference at the Madison Unitarian Meeting House for the International Poetry Society, of which she was president.

She asked if I would choreograph and perform a mime-dance based on a Derleth poem, "Childhood." I agreed to do so, utilizing the various levels of the meeting room which Frank Lloyd Wright had designed. At that time I was also assistant pastor there.

The audience responded appreciatively to the performance, but Derleth informed me in no uncertain terms, "That may have been your childhood, but it certainly wasn't mine."

To this day I do not know what inspired my temerity to answer this Wisconsin giant of letters:

"It was not necessarily my childhood either, but there's something you writers need to understand; once you've written and published a piece it is no longer yours. It's like a child and has a life of its own. If you want to keep this literary child for yourself, you must simply put it in a dresser drawer and take it out occasionally to enjoy it."

Both Augie and Edna seemed to be stunned by my brashness.

It was only later that Edna thanked me. "That was exactly what

Augie needed to hear—and from someone who understood, and from another field of the arts."

Both Edna and Augie are gone, but I remain grateful to have been a part of their creative family.

> We choreographed her Round River Canticle
> To discover that she had not left the valley;
> She keeps flowing back.
> The round river epitomizes her poetry
> Which spurts into politics and historical figures and
> Images to reflow or
> Reflower through herself.

VERNA MAE SLONE

Many people are confused about the pronunciation of *Ap-pa-la-chi-a*. Even Webster has it wrong; but what can you expect; he was a Yankee from Massachusetts. Linguists tell us that Shakesperean language—word usage, phraseology and dialect—is more prevalent in the North American Southern Appalachian Mountains than anywhere else in the world including the British Isles. When the English and Scotch-Irish settled in the Appalachian hills and hollows they brought and retained the Elizabethan language.

Shakespeare ended his Sonnet *cxvi* with "If this be error and upon me proved, I never writ nor no man ever loved." Now only a Shakespeare or a hillbilly could have writ that. I have enjoyed reminding school children in the mountains that *hillbilly* is a praise word, as the word *billy* is an old Scottish word, meaning "friend." Therefore, if someone were to call you a "hillbilly," simply thank them and agree that you could be a pretty good mountain friend.

Studs Terkel interviewed the famous and not-so-famous in his decades of radio interviews on his Chicago radio show. I attended lectures and appearances of several of his famous guests, particularly Eleanor Roosevelt speaking on social issues, and Dylan Thomas reading his marvelous Welsh poetry. Actually I met two of the less famous, who were from Kentucky.

I met Jean Richie, from Viper, Kentucky, who had performed and helped preserve many of the traditional folk songs of Appalachia.

A much closer acquaintance from Pippa Passes, Kentucky, was Verna Mae Slone. It must seem rather ironic to some folks to hear of an Appalachian town, Pippa Passes, named after a Tennyson poem. When Verna Mae was interviewed by Terkel, I was especially intrigued by her account of honoring her father by collecting stories about him and printing them in a mimeographed booklet for her children and grandchildren.

On a trip to the south with my daughter, Karen, we stopped by Verna Mae's home for a visit. While teaching at Union College in Kentucky, I had lived a few miles across several ridges from Verna Mae. Her neighborhood was in one of the most isolated communities I had ever seen in Virginia, North Carolina, Tennessee, West Virginia or Kentucky.

We found Verna Mae to be hospitable, charming and quite erudite. I had already bought her booklet, *In Remembrance* which I found exceptionally well written and insightful, not only about her father, known as "Kitteneye," but also about life in general.

In the foreword of her memory book she exhibited a great deal of love for her family and some anger at those who had written about mountain folk.

"So many lies and half-truths have been written about us, the mountain-people, that the folks from other states have formed an image of a gun totin', baccer spitin', whiskey drinkin', barefooted, foolish hillbilly, who never existed, but was conceived and born in the minds of the people who have written such things as *Stay on Stranger* and the *Beverly Hillbillies*.

She told Karen and me about life in that part of the Kentucky hills and related some of the stories in the book about her father. After a couple of hours and a mountain repast of cornbread, soup beans and buttermilk with fresh salad greens, we proceeded on to North Carolina to visit my dad.

A few months after that visit I agreed to perform on a PBS television show with David Crosby, entitled "Appalachia and Other Folk; Songs and Tales." I wanted to tell one of Verna Mae's stories about her father, so I called and asked if she would give me permission to tell about "Kitteneye and the Gourd Dipper."

She replied by saying, "Why, law me, yes! If you tell that story on television that'll be just that many more folks knowin' about my daddy, won't it."

It seems that Kitteneye and some other local men had been summoned to a murder trial over in the county seat of Cattlesburg in the steamy dog days of August. On their way home, awalkin' down the dusty country road, they was all awishin' fer some cool spring water in the worst kinda way. The road was so dry thet ever' time one uv 'em would take a step there'd be little puffs uv dust come up from all 'round their brogans [work shoes] jest like steppin' on a dried puffball mushroom.

They, theirselves, was so dry, they couldn't even spit. The 'baccer, they was tryin' to chew—why they just had to dry-mouth it. They'd all seen a water spring on the way to the court proceedin's an' figgered they'd stop by there for some water, an' sure 'nuff just as they rounded a curve, there it was ahead on the upper side of the road.

But standin' beside the spring was an ol' woman, the filthiest-lookin' woman, Kitteneye had ever seen. They figgered it was her spring, and it was; they asked if they could have some water outta her spring. She said, "O my, yeah! An' I'll dip it out fer yah."

She then reached fer the gourd dipper which was ahangin' on a tree saplin' there an' started adippin' it in the water an' handin' it to first one feller an' then 'nuther.

Now, a gourd dipper is made out uv a gourd with about a 18-inch stem (fer a handle) an' about a quart-size body (fer the dippin' part). In order to prepare the dried gourd, a body would cut a circle in the bowl to clean out all the seeds, then cut the stem end to clean out the handle of any dried stringy stuff. I used to dip the whole gourd in the spring and drink water right outta the handle like "sippin' cider through a straw."

As Kitteneye watched the hospitable proceedin's of this dirty woman sharin' her portion of life's water with his friends, he even noticed that she had 'baccer juice adribblin' outta the corners of her mouth.

He shorely didn't want to put his mouth on that gourd dipper where thet ol' woman's nasty lips had been. But just as the other fellers had finished havin' water, Kitteneye figgered out how to have some water—it was terrible hot an' dry—so he taken the gourd with "Thank ye, Ma'am!" turned it aroun' an' drunk the water right out through the stem handle.

That ol' woman said, "Why, I declare, young feller! I ain't never seed a body drink water out of a gourd dipper . . . the way I do."

I've told that story on many an occasion since.

Verna Mae finished the foreword to her Remembrance book as she wrote "With God's help I hope my brain can tell my hands what my heart wants to say."

Can anyone ask for more?

After that, Verna Mae wrote several books on the Appalachian language.

RED CREEK FRIENDS: STONELEDGE

For a few years my post office address was Red Creek, West Virginia.

Actually, the creek itself was some distance away. Before the town had a post office, the most prestigious citizen was an Irishman named Flanagan, prompting the accepted name of the community as "Flanagan Hill." The reason it didn't retain that nomenclature for the new post office, was that the then political leader of the burg was a republican and Flanagan was a democrat, and the new leadership could not abide by the fact that the town would be named for a democrat. (Or the whole situation was the other way around, but at any rate for political purposes it had to be called something other than "Flanagan Hill".)

In the summer of 1990, it occurred to me that it was time for me to acquire a few acres of mountain land. I asked my friend, Joan Davis, who lived on a small island, Gladwin Island, at the confluence of the Glady and Dry Fork rivers in Tucker County, West Virginia, if there might be available land in the area.

"There's a fellow up the ridge off the Jenningston Road, who has some land for sale. I hear that he's quite anxious to sell. His name is Roy Mallow, and I'll look up his phone number for you."

I called Roy and arranged to meet him that afternoon. It was a Sunday, so he wouldn't be working that day. I was amazed at the beauty of the place, which included 150 acres and an older house. Close by were four other modern houses owned by family members.

As my wife, Robin, and I were conducting a workshop on Gladwin Island, we had opportunity to go often up to Roy's place, where we would sit on the porch and visit about weather, land, politics and other significant topics. On the fourth or fifth visit I said to Roy, "Roy, I need to apologize to you."

He said, "Fer what?"

"Although I love your place here, I don't know what I was thinking about, because I can't even make an offer on it."

"Well," he said, "That don't differ none atall. Come whenever you please, whether you ever buy it or not."

We talked a bit longer, and I commented, "I don't think I've ever seen the Dry Fork River so dry as it is this year."

Kevin, Roy's seven-year-old grandson, quite stoically said, "Maybe that's why it's named the Dry Fork."

These were folks I definitely wanted as neighbors.

When we got back to Columbus, where I was teaching at OSU, Robin obtained a position at Ohio Wesleyan University, which prompted us to think we might be able to make an offer on the Mallow farm.

Unfortunately (or fortunately for us) in October, Roy and Sylvia, Roy's wife, declared bankruptcy. I discussed that with my banker in Thomas, WV, who was also the Mallows' banker. I asked him if it would be agreeable to him if we paid off the mortgage and returned the deed to the house and a few acres to Roy and Sylvia. He said that he had no objection, but we couldn't make any official agreement, because of the ongoing bankruptcy procedure.

It took several months for the bankruptcy hearing to convene. Robin and I drove from Columbus to Clarksburg, WV, making sure we'd be there in plenty of time. When we arrived, a couple of land developers were already there. They looked as though they were from the Southwest with cowboy hats and boots and turquoise rings. As they paraded up and down the hallway of the courthouse, I heard one say, "We're gonna make a heap of money offa this place."

Robin said, "We can't outbid those fellows."

I said, "Well, the fat lady hasn't sung yet."

When we were seated in the courtroom, the judge started the proceedings and immediately said, "We have an offer here from Mr. and Mrs. Gilbert, and I think we'll go with that."

One of the developers, who could have been cited for "contempt of court," promptly announced to the judge, "When I go to an auction, I expect it to go to the highest bidder."

The judge calmly said, "This isn't an auction. It's a bankruptcy hearing, and it's not our intention to take anyone's home away from them. With this arrangement the bank is happy—their loan is satisfied; Mr. and Mrs. Gilbert are happy—they have a place they can enjoy; Mr. and Mrs. Mallow are happy—they will still have their homeplace. Everybody's happy, 'cept you two fellows, and I'm sorry about that."

I don't think I had ever before seen steam rising from the crown of a man's head.

Roy and I became good friends—almost like brothers, and when I got ready to build a house on the place, I asked Roy if he'd be interested in building it. He agreed, and as I wasn't an architect, I'd make rough drawings and measurements of what I wanted and discuss the feasibility of the plan with Roy. Whenever I'd ask him if a certain thing could be done, I'd wait for his answer, "Well, it *could* be done." The longer it took him to answer would give me an indication of how difficult it was going to be. As Roy was a carpenter, mason, plumber and electrician I trusted his judgment implicitly.

Roy had a friend, Pete Ellender, whom he introduced to me. Pete lived between our place and Red Creek in a house he'd inherited from his grandmother. He didn't have a car, but would ride his lawnmower to the Red Creek Post Office Community Center, which was about a quarter of a mile of a dangerously twisty road from his house.

He was noted for his ability to fix lawnmowers. I stopped by one day to ask if he'd fix my chainsaw. In his stuttering answer he said, "N-n-no R-r-eid, I d-d-don't fix chainsaws. I j-j-ust fix l-l-l-awnmowers."

Pete attended the Flanagan Hill Methodist Church regularly, and one Sunday morning, when I attended, Pete stood up in the testimony time of the service and said, "E-e-every S-S-Sunday morning I get to c-c-come to the church an' r-r-ring the church b-b-bell, an' I p-p-p-praise the Lord for that." It was probably the most honest and heartfelt testimony I'd ever heard.

Roy, on his way to town, would always stop by to see if Pete needed anything or wanted to go with him. When Roy died suddenly one afternoon of a heart attack, Pete said to me, "R-r-r-eid, we've l-l-l-ost a g-g-ood friend." I agreed that we had indeed lost a wonderful friend.

Not too long after Roy's death and before I left the mountain, Pete died—also of a heart attack. At his funeral the undertaker attempted to ring the church bell—Pete's church bell—as the casket was being taken to the gravesite the bell broke, and so far as I know hasn't been rung since.

Roy had lost the family farm to bankruptcy. Some newcomer now owns the house Pete inherited from his grandmother. The house I designed and Roy built (Stoneledge) had to be sold as a divorce settlement. But that's the way it goes; no one can ever really possess the land.

On one occasion when Roy and I were on one ridge of the farm, looking across the creek at another ridge, he'd say, "Now that rock bluff is yours, an' it goes all the way to that hickory yonder." It was almost as though Roy was telling me that he was shifting his stewardship of the hills and woods to me.

I must now acknowledge that someone else, besides myself, must be the caretaker of that portion of Mother Earth.

Now, years later, Roy's grandchildren still refer to Stoneledge, as "Reid's House".

One of his grandchildren, Logan White, lived right beside my lane where I would have to pass when I'd drive off the ridge to Jenningston Road. One day when I was driving to Thomas, as I came off the hill, Logan and his friend, Collin Waybright, came running out to the road to stop me. So I stopped and we talked; about hound dogs I believe. It was a typical mountain scene with a guy in a car, stopping to talk with a couple of other mountain guys. The age difference was inconsequential, even though I was 70 and the boys were 10.

In West Virginia a person would know the neighbors, even several miles away. In modern cities it would be unusual for a person to know people in the next apartment or two houses away.

Although I have met many famous people—politicians, performers, writers, theologians (from Washington to New Delhi, from New York to Las Vegas)—I have never met any person more genuine, honest and compassionate than my two Red Creek friends, Roy and Pete.

To My Red Creek Friends

Friends who've met in the arms of fate,
Close-by neighbors who had to part,
And though our paths must separate
I recall with a saddened, though grateful heart.

Having lived the life of a gypsy, roaming the world geographically and career-wise, I always felt the need to stabilize with a home in the Southern Appalachian Mountains, having grown up in the hills of North Carolina; a home that I would design with roots in Mother Earth, yet reaching for the clouds of Father Sky.

When we met Roy and rambled the farm, I felt we were at home with the place and with Roy and his family. I began formulating house ideas, while finishing my last years on the faculty of OSU. Joan Davis, when seeing the spot we had chosen for the house, said "This site needs a castle."

Although never having met or studied with Frank Lloyd Wright, I had been greatly impressed with his work from the Mossberg House in South Bend to the Guggenheim Museum in NY. His principle that a house should never be situated on the top of a hill (as the integrity of the landscape would be compromised) influenced my decision to place the house on the edge of the ridge above a stone ledge, (thus the name of *Stoneledge*) leaving the top of the hill to be landscaped for drumming purposes, picnics and memorials with its own name of Angel Circle. Planned for the Angel Circle (not completed) were a croquet court and a glass sculpture, *GABRIEL GREETING THE NEW DAWN*. As the house faced directly east, the sculpture would refract the sun rising twice during the year (the equinoxes) as the sun moves gradually from a southerly dawn to a northerly one, and vice-versa. The prismatic sun-rays would then beam directly down the lane to the front of the house. By the way, the lane is lined with 38 Norway pines, and expands at the top of the lane with Red Spruce, guarded by Pyramidal Arborvitae.

It was important to have the house belong to the land; thus several decisive choices:

1. As the farm had belonged in the Mallow family since 1929, I had hoped Roy would agree to build the house. He agreed to do so, so we shook hands on it, never drawing up any kind of written contract. It was also a reasonable choice, as Roy was a stone mason, carpenter, plumber, electrician, etc.
2. Since a child, I had landscaped with stone and worked with wood. I had whittled small pieces of wood and even soapstone from near my childhood home. While a teenager I had also worked for a small neighborhood sawmill. The decision for wood and stone (no drywall) seemed reasonable to me.
3. It was important, also, to have the house built of indigenous materials; thus, the stone from the farm as well as the lumber. After the portable sawmill would finish sawing a pile of logs, Robin and I would load the new lumber on the farm truck and load the heavy green boards into the barn loft, where we would *stick* them for air drying. One of the white oaks in the "dark woods" was not supposed to have been cut, but, as a red oak had fallen in the fork of the white oak, it was cut, leaving the massive crotch, which could not be milled. Robin felt terrible about the mistake. She felt something special should be done with the fork. She and I worked for several days with a crosscut saw to cut a piece out of the middle of the fork. Not being able to finish that,

we had the workers use a large chain saw to complete the cut for a piece to be inlaid in the foyer of the house. Roy laid the crotch so that the two trunks pointed to the two wings of the house. It had not completely dried, and it continued to shrink, displaying a wondrous array of veins, as well as colors. It now greets any visitor entering the front door.

John McBee, Roy's son-in-law, bulldozed the road and the spring, water lines and septic tank. As John began digging the basement, Roy insisted that we dig all the way to solid rock because, "That tower is going to be mighty heavy with all those rocks."

Thus the house has an extra lower level, not planned earlier.

I realized that there were going to be spectacular views from the top of the tower, so I planned a flat rubber roof for the fifth level roof garden. All of the other roofing is metal, as it reminded me of the old house where I grew up and where I loved to hear the music of the rain. To the west, one sees the Dry Fork River and the Otter Creek Wilderness area, which will never be developed. To the north, one can see Mozark Mountain and Bright's Chapel, as well as some neighbor houses. One sees up the lane to the east, the Angel Circle and beyond that, Canaan Mountain. To the south are the crescent meadow and Rich Mountain and Middle Mountain.

I wanted a strong center (heart) of the house, so I designed an octagonal tower to be built of stone.

Above the unexpected basement would be the kitchen on the second level, octagonal of course, as the kitchen would be at the heart of the house. We wanted a Scandinavian style masonry stove which would have a baking oven and could provide heat for 24 hours with one good strong fire.

Norbert Senf from Canada built the core of the stove and delivered and installed it. Roy and his crew finished its exterior masonry. The stove also has a loop of water line to heat the water in one of the two water heaters. The wall to the left of the stove is also stone, as it will be behind the old wood range. On the wall opposite to the masonry stove is a corner cupboard, which I built with a rescued antique corner-cupboard front and our walnut boards. Beside it is a breakfast nook, which I built with two-inch-thick walnut boards. At the west side of the kitchen is a covered balcony To the north is the laundry room, at the corner of which, is the planned spiral staircase to the basement. To the east is the mudroom and a half bath and storage space behind the living-room fireplace.

To the south is the dining area, then the living room with a Heatalator fireplace. The beams and mantelpiece are built of poplar hand-hewn beams from Robin's grandfather's barn in Indiana. At one side of the living room is an open deck. Also there is a multi-sided solarium with a stone floor to catch the water from watered plants as well as the warmth of the southern sun.

The heart of the third floor is the dance studio with full-length mirrors rescued from my sister's Texas house, which had been destroyed by a flood of the San Jacinto River. Built into the north wall is an antique post office desk from northern Wisconsin.

The front foyer entrance door is made from a solid Columbus YWCA door, into which Roy built one of the four leaded, beveled glass panels from an old home in Columbus. The panels have been sandwiched between two pieces of glass, thus becoming panels of three thicknesses. The wall sconces were rescued from a Gothic-style Madison, Wisconsin church which was updating its style, so that university students would feel more comfortable. All of the foyer walls are of cherry. I made sure we would have boards long enough for the foyer, sixteen feet long, so that there would be no piecing. The guest bedroom and bath have several "rescued" features.

The master bedroom has walls of walnut and cherry. The southeast partial wall is ideal as a bed headboard or background for a filigreed headboard. That wall is composed of slabbed walnut planks sawn from a dead walnut tree that was still standing. We put the boards on the floor to see how they might come closest to complementing each other, like a jigsaw puzzle, before we had them fastened to the wall. Behind the partial wall is another solarium with a fieldstone floor. On each end of the wall is a wrought iron curtain rod, which can be swung to conceal the solarium or toward the bed to simulate a canopy bed. The wonderful old glass wardrobe case was in Mr. Jim Cooper's haberdashery store in Thomas. The medicine cabinet in the bathroom is an old cupboard found in a garage in Columbus. The mirror is from my sister's house. Off the bedroom is a covered balcony, which is great for watching storms brewing in the summer or for meditating on the purposes of life.

    The fourth level is the library, which has a wainscoting of walnut containing both the dark and light grains of the tree. The bench and railing are built of two-inch-thick walnut boards. On one side of the library is a spiral staircase to the roof garden area on the fifth level. Planned for the roof garden is a storage area which is to be cut next to the chimney wall.

    The front porch has a high roof with two columns and a crossbeam. This gives a kind of Japanese feeling to the front entrance. The wall sconces there are from my sister's house. Directly in front of the porch is a stone veranda with the three edges echoing the sides and angles of the tower. All castles need a moat and a drawbridge, but the best I could do was simply to design a bridge to the two stone columns guarding the entry. These columns are topped with wrought-iron light fixtures from my sister's house. Immediately in front of the columns is another stone octagonal veranda. Two stone seats there are placed on the north and south edges.

    It is a wonderful house to come home to and a difficult house to leave.

On a West Virginia ridge
A house made of wood and stone.
Known simply as STONELEDGE,
An equal there is none.

Containing labors and streams
And history of the past,
It waits for fresh dreams
Of new hopes that will last.

BUT FOR THE GRACE

There, but for the grace of God, go I, thus John Bradford, the martyr, supposedly mused while still a young man, when he saw a group of criminals being led off to their execution.

Although this remark was supposedly to reassure me that I was in the protective hands of the Almighty, I always wondered what the poor prisoners might be saying.

This event was often cited in my seminary studies, as a pertinent example of the theology of Divine Grace. However, it seemed extremely odd to me that no theologian, or even impertinent theology student, had wondered or surmised what the poor criminals were saying as they looked into the gawking crowd and saw the holy John Bradford ogling them.

Many years after seminary, I was awarded a Fulbright Grant to research theatre training in India. Travel there was problematic, but at least fascinating. I had already visited Kalakshetra Theatre School in Madras and Darpana Academy in Ahmedabad. I then headed to south India aboard a train to Cheruthuruthy to study the Kathakali dance theatre. It seemed that we were making all the local stops across the midlands of India.

As I had been cautioned to eat only fully cooked or peeled food, I had been subsisting for days on oranges, bananas and peanuts. I had promised myself that I would bite the bullet, pardon the pun, and order a full course of South Indian fare at the next station. My palette was complaining of the monochromatic offerings of the past few days.

Shortly after boarding at Poona—wheels clanging, steam hissing and brakes screeching—the train belched into a small equatorial depot. Station peons were scurrying in circles with occasional tangents into vending shops and then into train cubicles to take orders for all kinds of local merchandise, especially food. I thought, *This is now my chance to be daring and sample the local cuisine.* Upon hearing the menu list I ordered tea, chapattis, rice and chicken *ala* something or other.

The belching engine continued to rumble and shake as though alive, while its thirst was being quenched by the water tank overhead. It certainly seemed ironic in such an arid region that the water would be allowed to overflow the train's appetite, spilling over the engine and across the tracks.

While waiting for my order, I was entertained by the people milling around on the depot platform, while scores of monkeys scurried across the station overhang as well as on the train, itself.

The marauders were reaching through the barred windows, searching for anything that may have been of gustatory interest to them. My cell mate teasingly grasped the probing arm of a little old man of a monkey, who squealed with fright until he was released to scamper back over the top of the car.

As my lunch was delivered, other uninvited guests continued to reach through the bars to grasp something for themselves from this strange invading foreigner. The odoriferous curry blended somewhat uncomfortably with the other usual fragrances of a bustling Indian train station. I began to break off a piece of the chapatti to sop into my soupy mixture of chicken and lentils and Indian herbs. Of course this must be done with only one hand—the right hand—as the left one is reserved for other purposes.

I then observed a small bedraggled girl walking toward me across the opposite parallel tracks. She had obviously spied me, the only light-skinned train traveler, whom she rightly assumed would share some of his bounty of food with her.

She was about five, it seemed—the age of my middle daughter securely ensconced at home with her mother and sisters in a comfortable New Delhi apartment. Approaching my open window, she lifted a brass begging bowl. Dividing my "loaves and fishes" with her, I returned her bowl with our shared lunch and an English spoken greeting.

Without saying a word, she reached her tiny hand repeatedly into her bowl while her dark haunting eyes withered me small in her gaze.

Seemingly unconcerned about the ingredients of the food—whether forbidden meat or not—she seemed to ponder this stranger with a gold-banded watch on his wrist. She continued to stand immobile between the opposite tracks, still visually focused on her target of the stranger, as the train groaned out of the station.

I imagined her saying, as we pulled away, *Vahan lekin liye Ishwar charna main hai.* which translated into English is, "There but for the grace of Vishnu ride I."

John Bradford, take note!

HARRY NOHR

Harry Nohr was a retired postmaster from Mineral Point, Wisconsin, when I first met him. He was a small rather quiet man, who, years earlier, had developed a keen interest in woodworking. I should really say that he was more interested in the wood than in the working. However, what he did with a knot or burl of hardwood, was nothing short of spectacular.

On his lathe he could transform a gnarly bit of wood into a beautiful bowl, almost paper thin. I believe three of his bowls are in the Smithsonian collection of American Wood Craftsmen.

I once asked him how long it took him to finish the piece once he had found the wood. Without hesitation, he said, "Four years!"

"Why so long?"

"If the wood is dried too fast it will check (crack) when I grind it to a thin veneer."

"That must be how you can get the bowl so thin."

"Yup!"

"I suppose it gets a little complicated from beginning to end."

"Ya betcha! I sometimes wet it down a bit to keep it from dryin' out too quick."

"But what's the most difficult part of the whole process?"

"Findin' the wood."

Incredulously, I countered, "Harry that doesn't make much sense. The ridges and valleys of Southwestern Wisconsin are covered with trees . . . even good hardwoods."

"Ya don't get it?"

"Apparently not."

"Ya need to understand. I look for burls, knots twisted roots an' such. It's the swirled troubled grain that I want. Wood that has known no adversity is not very interesting."

It was then I reflected on the striations, variegated colors and whorls in his finished bowls, and realized that his implication of straight-grained wood may be fine for flooring. Only those burls and knots, that had withstood fierce wintry storms and scorching summer sun were worthy of the craftsman's efforts. Then one might rightfully celebrate the internal design for display in an art gallery or on the family dinner table.

At certain times I have felt the need to remind myself . . .

"Persons who have known no adversity aren't very interesting?"

> Traveling through wintry storms and
> Enduring sweltering summers
> On life's journeys and vicissitudes
> I hope the metaphor of gnarly wood
> Might help me avoid
> Any personal dull attitudes.

HERBERT FRITZ

In 1968, Dr. Dean Connors, a pathologist at St. Mary's Hospital in Madison, bought the old Newton Farm on Upper Wyoming Road, approximately three miles from Frank Lloyd Wright's Taliesin. He contacted Herbert Fritz, a former apprentice of Wright's, to upgrade the barn and house for a pleasant country home. Herb had followed Wright's suggestion that the Taliesin architecture students should buy farms in the area. Thus Herb bought the old Jordan farm, dubbed it Hilltop, across the road from Taliesin and less than a mile along the ridge from the back acreage of Dr. Connors's new place.

Herb moved the old house a few yards up the hillside at an obtuse angle to the barn. He added a front porch to the house, a two room basement and a kitchen addition toward the barn. The roof of the new kitchen extended toward the barn to form an elegant breezeway, connecting the house to the barn.

After a couple of years, Dr. Connors discovered that this new residence was too far for a daily commute to his work in Madison, so I used the barn for mime instruction for his daughter and houseboy. While I was finishing my doctoral dissertation at the University of Wisconsin, I continued to use the space for instruction and then for living quarters for some of the students, as I had expanded the program into Valley Studio, the home of the Wisconsin Mime Theatre and School.

Dr. Connors became chairman of the Board of Directors of the Valley Studio, and in 1972 he and I conferred with Herb to build a dormitory on the hill behind the house and barn. The new building was rather plain with a large kitchen, dining room and laundry room. The upstairs floor was divided into two large bunk rooms, each with a restroom and shower. The building looked rather stark, sitting about twenty yards behind and approximately thirty feet higher than the original complex.

All the structures, including the old and new, were roofed with cedar shake shingles.

In another year Fritz designed another dormitory at an angle to the earlier one. The roof line again connecting the two dormitories at an obtuse angle, forming another breezeway

In 1976, the Valley Studio purchased an abandoned one-room schoolhouse, the Kritz School, from a mile farther up the Upper Wyoming Valley Road. Herbert had this old schoolhouse placed near the public road beside a huge white oak tree. This building received few changes, but it was painted brown to coordinate with the exteriors of the other buildings.

Every time that Dean and I discussed the angle of a new structure, Herb always knew the exact placement and the correct connecting angle.

Herb was not only our architect, but I was quite close to his family, having performed weddings and memorial services for members of the Fritz family.

Years later I held a mythic workshop for two weeks at Herb's place, utilizing his combination there, of old barns and a modern home built into the hillside.

Herb came often to chat with the staff and students about the relationship of architecture to residential as well as educational and arts spaces. When asked about the rather elaborate studio space of the lower dorm, which of course was at the end of the building, he explained that a structure should have an interesting beginning and a celebrative termination; the intervening spaces would take care of themselves. This principle was easily applied to the theatre and mimetic arts.

Herb's use of natural wood, reclaimed barns and old one-room school houses at Valley Studio were similar to his designs for his own buildings at Hilltop. This prompted one commentator to observe that Herb Fritz's style of architecture as primitive elegance.

GOVERNOR LEE DREYFUS

My political life . . . at least the early planning . . . began at the age of eleven in the fifth grade-if one considers a political career beginning with a definite conscious decision to enter the political arena. If, however, one considers politics as constant promise/com-promise, then politics enshrouds all of life.

Miss Blessing, with whom I had some issues, was my fifth-grade teacher. She and I had had a couple of arguments about correct answers on tests. The second time this happened she said, "I beg your most honorable pardon, but can you prove your answer?"

I replied, "Yes, Ma'am, the correct answer is in the geography book under a picture of the Himalaya Mountains." We looked, and there was the answer. Although I won that battle, I did not want another confrontation. I maintained an eagle eye on teachers henceforth...not necessarily a wise strategy.

Shortly after that skirmish we had a long questionnaire in the Weekly Reader. One of the questions was, "What do you want to be when you become an adult?" My answer was. "I plan to be president of the United States." I had no real idea what that meant, but it sounded like something worth achieving . . . I've become disabused of that notion.

Miss Blessing must have been impressed by my answer, as she asked me on the playground at recess, "When you become president, will you put me on your cabinet?"

I knew what a cabinet was; Mamma had one in the kitchen with some shelves for dishes, a tin-lined drawer for potatoes, a flour bin with a sifter and even an enameled countertop which could be extended for a larger working space.

I had no idea why Miss Blessing would want to be put on my cabinet, as I thought that would be rather uncomfortable, but I answered, "Of course I'd be happy to put you on my cabinet." Nothing more was said about this ambition of mine. However, my subsequent neglect of running for the presidency may have been the implied horror of Miss Blessing perched on the top of my cabinet.

For years after that my political involvement was limited to running for class president, student council president and similar offices, some of which were won and some lost. I did write a few politically motivated letters to editors.

Occasionally, I became somewhat involved politically with organizations to which I belonged. Having developed a keen sense of justice in the fifth grade, I hadn't learned to keep mum whenever issues came up, which were obviously headed toward wrong-headed solutions. In such instances, when the chairman of the meeting didn't want to deal with my proposed solution, s/he would name a committee, appoint me as chair and select committee members who were not likely to agree on anything.

During the Carter Administration, I did have the opportunity to confront or attempt to entertain several political types in Washington at a Wolf Trap congressional wives' luncheon, at Vice-President Mondale's home and at a Senate Finance Committee dinner party. On each occasion, after performing silently as a mime, for an encore, I would remind my audience that mimes can speak and would then urge the conclave of powerful politicians to support the arts, particularly the creative activities of children.

When Mrs. Mondale came to Milwaukee to represent the Carter Administration at a Festival of American Mime, her advance person was Marilyn Haft, an attractive young New York attorney. She and I were assigned, prior to Mrs. Mondale's arrival, to plan the itinerary around Milwaukee where the official entourage would stop for a few moments to observe performers on the streets and in the parks.

That morning when I got into the car I sat in the back seat next to Miss Haft. I must admit I was feeling rather important, being the Co-Director of the Festival, being chauffeured around by secret service men and sharing responsibility with such an auspicious person as an assistant to the Vice-President.

As I settled into the seat, Miss Haft looked at me and said, "What's your story?" Her tone was such that I thought she perceived me as coming on to her.

Perplexed, I said, "I beg your pardon."

She said, "Well everyone has a story, and I'd like to know what yours is."

Sighing a sigh of relief I realized that this was such a refreshing way to ask about a person, and have related that little confab in subsequent storytelling events to point out an interesting way to elicit a person's story whether in a political setting or not.

We did share our stories, as different as they were from each other.

Years later in West Virginia, I tried to twist some political arms, including Senator Robert Byrd's, to put a funded four-lane highway north of the town of Thomas instead of the earlier plans to put it between Thomas and Davis, across the Blackwater River gorge. I explained, as though they didn't know, "It will cost so much more to build the three-quarter-mile bridge across the canyon than to go north of Thomas with a much smaller bridge."

The engineer responded, "Oh, it's much cheaper to build bridges than it is to move dirt."

"Well, there's your answer to the budget of the whole road from Buckhannon to the Virginia state-line. Just build a bridge across West Virginia with a few off-on ramps." The guy looked at me as though I was crazy. "Well it was your technological assessment, not mine."

Some engineers and politicians seem to lack both logic and humor.

My most active involvement in politics was in 1979 when I volunteered to serve on the gubernatorial campaign of Lee Sherman Dreyfus in Wisconsin. I had known Lee socially and at the University of Wisconsin in Madison. What most impressed me was what he had accomplished for the arts at the University of Wisconsin, Stevens Point when he became president there.

I had also heard him speak at arts meetings. He would usually challenge artists and patrons by asking them to raise their hands if they had been in touch with specific politicians in the past week or month. There would seldom be more than a few hands raised. He would follow this by saying, "I called (Senator) Bill Proxmire, yesterday, and told him that he must support the proposed budget for the National Endowment for the Arts."

While he was president at UW-Stevens Point, there had been several student demonstrations. His response was to assure everyone that every day he would wear a red vest for anyone to identify him on campus to engage him in discussion of any burning issues.

There was also a faculty demonstration in the form of a petition, which a committee delivered to Dreyfus's office. After he reviewed with them the 19 demands, he said, "I agree."

The befuddled faculty asked, "What do we do now?" He was not being a smartaleck; he was simply letting the faculty know if they were ready to assume these responsibilities they should do so. He recognized that quite often academic administrators assume certain tasks, which were really in the province of the faculty, but which they had neglected to address.

When I saw him at a small social event after he had announced his candidacy for the governorship, I told him I wanted to be on his campaign to represent the arts. He said, "That's a good idea. Bankers, teachers, unions, businesses get involved in election campaigns. The artists never get involved until after the elections when they come to the politicians and hold out their hands asking for funds. The newly elected officials ask, 'Who are you?'"

Dreyfus was running on the Republican ticket, but the Republican leadership didn't trust him, as they were afraid he was really a "Republicrat." Subsequently he lost the endorsement of the statewide republican convention.

The campaign committee met at Stevens Point after the convention to decide on the next course of action. There was a strong sentiment to withdraw, as Lee had not only failed to get the republican endorsement but we had nearly depleted the campaign funds. It was then I came through with the winning proposal; "What Lee needs is a whistle-stop train. He is such a terrific orator and literally needs a physical platform from which to announce his political platform."

Lowell Jackson, who later became Secretary of Transportation, said, "Reid, you're just like all other artists with fanciful dreams where your brains ought to be. Why do you always make such far-out, weird ideas? Get realistic. We have almost no money and certainly not enough for a whistle-stop train. We can't even afford a school bus."

"My point exactly! I have an old-school bus which the Wisconsin Mime Theatre has been using for touring. It has a wonderful platform at the back with a steel railing. On the top of the bus is a deck we use for props and costumes. We could paint the bus like a train caboose, put a small oom-pah band on the upper platform, roll the bus up to the town square and release Lee through the back door to deliver his campaign message."

That's what we did, and it worked. There were times when we had to push the bus into the town square. I had warned them that the bus was a lemon, but that helped Lee successfully play the underdog candidate.

After Lee Sherman Dreyfus was elected governor, Time published a picture of the old bus in an article about the strange gubernatorial campaign in Wisconsin. I needed the publicity—the bus didn't need it anymore. It had served its political purpose and was retired to a Boy Scout ranch in New Mexico.

I was awarded a seat on the Wisconsin Arts Board, which gave me an opportunity to make some important political decisions about arts projects in the state.

Several years later when I was directing a professional theatre in West Virginia, Dreyfus, who was no longer governor of Wisconsin, called me and thanked me for keeping him and Joyce, his wife, on my mailing list. I had never heard of anyone being grateful for being kept on a mailing list of a non-profit theatre. That was an indication of his attention to detail and thoughtfulness. He then admitted that my "far-out, weird idea of a whistle-stop train" was the key to his successful gubernatorial campaign in 1979.

I thanked him for his thoughtful call.

A perfect example of reincarnation! The aged bus's first incarnation was as a school bus for hauling kids to school. In its next life, it was a touring bus for the Wisconsin Mime Theatre and School; then its life was as a symbol and conveyance for a political candidate. Its last life span, so far as I know, serves the transportation needs for a bunch of Boy Scouts.

Thanking Governor Dreyfus for his thoughtful call, I had already shelved my fifth-grade announcement to run for United States President.

CONNECTEDNESS
not connections, but connectedness
not things, but a state of being

We have probably come to the defining or divining point of history—either soaring to the heights of the human potential or falling into the chasm of human despair and degradation. The defining point would be the cross roads of consequential choices—the road taken or the road not taken. The divining point would be the prophetic look in to our very nature.

Both of these points were considered by Soren Kierkegaard, who has called them the *Either* Or, when the human being—indeed all humankind—must make a momentous decision, amidst swirling energies, pressures, desires and expectations of which many current events and writers are reminding us.

On my annual trip to the National Theatre Conference in NYC in October 2011, I took along the spring 2006 issue of *Parabola*, a quarterly periodical to which I've been subscribing since its inception in 1976. It was for leisurely reading in the air terminals and planes. Each issue has a shared theme for the articles, poetry and art work—that issue's theme having been "Shaking our Senses Free."

The article which captured my attention was "Common Sense," with an interview with Peter Kingsley. I was entranced with Kingsley's concern, stating that we have completely misunderstood Parmenides and Empedocles in order to focus on personal and cultural emphases on individuality. It may not be necessary for us today to remember the names of those Greek philosophers, but their message is important—the message that our senses have led us astray by depending too much on our individual sense awareness rather than embracing the totality of sharing the senses with the connectedness of the universe and, by this means, the whole cosmos.

To quote Kingsley: "The usual idea we have is that meditation, is to enlighten us, give us peace, or whatever. But for these people, meditation is not for oneself. It is an act of service for the sake of the cosmos. The purpose wasn't to get something out of it. It was to attune oneself to the cosmos for the sake of the cosmos."

Kingsley feels that in misreading or misunderstanding Parmenides and Empedocles we have been going down the wrong road for two-and-a-half millennia by ignoring the fact that the human race was not fully human and still today is suffering from the same misconception: that Aristotle introduced us to our total humanity by making us aware of our own self-awareness. What was, and is, missing is the connectedness.

Of course we have been reminded from time to time of the necessity to incorporate understanding and effort in our connectedness, as Aldo Leopold reminded us, "Everything is connected to everything else." However, we seem to continue to be impelled outward by individual greed and withdrawn inwardly by personal fear.

Too often we performers think that we pursue our art for self-expression. However, that is an insufficient reason to foist our self-expression onto the public, if there is no need of celebration or understanding of the aesthetic appreciation by that public to be shared in that art.

I have scolded buskers, street mimes and clowns about thrusting themselves too assertively to people, particularly children, who are often frightened by these well-intentioned performers. However, it became clear to me that those aggressive street performers needed the audience more than the unsuspecting audience needed them.

Someone had sent me a fascinating animated email, showing a chalkboard lecture by Jeremy Rifkin. The basis of the presentation was to introduce the theory of "mirror neurons," which attempts to explain the empathic experience toward other peoples' misfortunes and pains. I have noticed that when I see someone stumble, I have a similar feeling of alarm and physical recoil as that of the stumbler.

A researcher, in attempting to ascertain the brain activity during a specific difficult task, attached electrodes to the head of a chimpanzee and then recorded the brain waves when the hungry chimp attempted a difficult task of cracking nuts. While the subject was still hooked up, a human being—not a part of the experiment—came into the lab and upon seeing the nuts, attempted to crack them. The chimp's brain waves behaved in the same manner as when he, himself, was attempting the task of cracking the nuts.

Rifkin reminded the class that we experience the emotion of another person as we sense a character's emotion in a stage production. According to him, we are soft-wired for this sharing of emotion. The classic Greek theatre understood this phenomenon, utilizing the shared empathy by its concern for *catharsis* at the end of the performance. In the Japanese Noh theatre, the same phenomenon is known as yugen. In both of these theatre forms the dramatists strive to share the connectedness in mutual emotion of empathy—perhaps in Rifkin's term *mirror neurons.*

He goes on to explain that in the human journey we have evolved this connectedness. Prehistoric man shared empathy with those within his family or clan—anyone who would be within shouting distance. According to the researcher, this evolution expanded later within faith communities and still later within city-states and now into a global phenomenon. He does not account for the fact that many people continue to restrict their empathy to those within their family or religion or nation-state. Unfortunately, we're still far from embracing a global shared empathy.

To empathize is to civilize and inversely one might affirm that to civilize is to empathize. Giovanni Boccaccio, in his writing *Di Cameron*, started that classic opus with the statement, "It is important that we all take pity of people in distress." Politicians take note.

Both Boccaccio and Shakespeare, although literary titans in their respective cultures, took themes, stories and language from the folk—the peasants, probably much to the chagrin of academics who would assume that that connectedness comes from more heightened sources. Shakespeare wrote and printed many words heard first from his connectedness to the baser citizens of the populace with its "folk vocabulary".

Back to Rifkin, who cites the global response to such natural disasters as the earthquake in Haiti and other global suffering. He also maintains that this empathy is extended to all sentient beings and indeed the whole global community of living and inanimate beings.

Certainly anyone with a devoted pet would agree that emotions are shared between people and their pets, each being quite capable of empathizing with the other. When I was enduring a trauma in my life, one of my wife's cats, while I was dressing, stood on the back of a chair and lifted his velvet paws to stroke my face while looking sadly into my eyes.

Rifkin would, no doubt, agree with me when I suggest that this connectedness of empathy is at work when an adult of one animal species will care for the foundlings of another species, i.e. a mature pigeon keeping baby rabbits warm, a mother dog breast-feeding infant kittens; a barn owl and cat becoming playful friends (a nursery rhyme perhaps). More recently an experiment at the University of Chicago demonstrated the empathy between "lowly" rats, who would rescue a fellow rat from an entrapment even before taking proffered food.

A tragic example of this connectedness was a report of moving young elephant calves from one part of Africa to another part where the elephant population had been depleted due to illegal poaching. When the calves matured there was a grave problem as the young bull elephants had become rogues and were needlessly killing other animals such as hippos. The reason for this was that the young males were not raised in a community of older males, such as uncles, who would have taught them proper behavior.

One of the young bulls could not be retrained and had to be euthanized. The event of his demise was truly touching, as his sister stood by watching him slowly fall . . . even attempting to help him stand.

She stood there awhile and started to walk away but turned again one more time before she joined the herd . . . the rest of her family.

A mother tree makes room for new seedlings, provides nutrient and even shortens some of her own roots to make room for the seedlings.

On a lighter note, it has been reported that a study has been conducted in which dogs empathize with their owners by yawning when their owners yawn . . . even by merely hearing the sound of the owners' yawn.

Surely it is no stretch of the imagination to accept in this context that human beings may indeed be blessed with the soft-wiring of *mirror neurons*. Just consider the behavior of nesting birds, caring for their young or the colony of honeybees following their queen.

It may surprise us to realize that even that gloomy writer Edgar Allen Poe wrote that, "This opinion, in its general form, was that of the sentience of all vegetable things." Can someone account for the growth of a tomato vine from one small seed? A few years ago a study was conducted of plants reacting to persons, who had earlier harmed the plants.

Of course Rifkin's statement is a reiteration of Leopold's statement of the connectedness of all things, except here he has pursued it in a more scientific manner. In the light of that thesis, I have become aware that the recent political movement in the Mideast (Arab Spring) is really a major example of this connectedness and mirror neurons. It will be tragic if we do not recognize it as such.

On January 18, 2011, I attended a lecture by Dr. Claude Swanson, the author of *LIFE FORCE, The Scientific Basis*, which is Volume II of *The Synchronized Universe Series*. In the lecture he discussed *remote viewing, precognition, telekinesis, psychokinesis and kirlian photography*, all of which were specific instances of connectedness, which he maintains holds everything together in the universe.

His lecture reminded me that when I was in both India and Thailand, I felt strongly connected to my home farm and the whole Appalachian Mountain culture where I grew up. In fact, when I was in

India (1965-66) I wrote a three-act play, *Twixt Heaven and Hell*, which was set in the mountains after World War II. While in Thailand (1997-98) I wrote *Trickster Jack*, a collection of stories about the Appalachian trickster, Jack.

I was particularly interested in Swanson's statement about the vacuum: *In many ways it seemed to me that the vacuum was precisely where the connection between the distant stars and the small particles of quantum physics come together. All those particles out there are constantly radiating energy . . . Might this not be one of the missing ideas of the long sought unified theory?*

To be perfectly honest, much of the discussion of quantum physics —though fascinating—is beyond my understanding. However, the importance of the vacuum relates directly to my own work in the theatre, particularly the art of the actor. Too often the actor, as well as the director, seems to be concerned with positive space: the space the body occupies and with little concern for the negative space—that space between him and other actors as well as between himself and stage props and furnishings. A great deal is going on in the negative, unoccupied space and should be better understood and utilized by the actor.

When two actors on stage, or even two everyday individuals, move closer or farther away from each other the drama changes. In a workshop situation I will have two actors stand as statues five feet from each other. I then pick up one of them—the lightest of course—and move him/her to only inches from the immobile other one. It becomes apparent that the drama has changed even though the positive (occupied) spaces are the same.

Negative space is also of concern to the sculptor as well as to the architect and Japanese potter. The architect, who concerns himself primarily with the outward appearance of the structure and with little regard to the empty (negative) space within, is hardly worth the title of architect. Everyone is aware that an electric arc travels through negative space.

In the Japanese Noh Theatre the actor regards seriously the negative interior space, so that the outward appearance can more effectively connect with the audience. In fact in the Noh theatre, the word for negative or empty space is "potential".

The theatrical pause can be regarded in a similar way to that of negative space. Harold Pinter developed a whole playwriting career based on the strength of what has come to be called "the Pinterian pause." Even Beethoven acknowledged the importance of the negative time period when he claimed that his most important task was arranging the pauses between the notes.

The point of discussing the negative of space and time is to recognize the importance of the negative in the context of connectedness, just as Swanson has stated that it is in the vacuum where the basic connection is made.

It is rather ironic that quantum physics is now pursuing what various religions have been attempting to say for millennia. However it was the well-known Catholic theologian, Thomas Merton who urged us to take "flight from disunity and separation, to unity and peace in the love of all men." He also suggests that our suffering allows us to be more than who we believe we are and greater than ourselves by our connectedness to ourselves and to others. This connectedness is what we understand as *com-passion*, the sharing ourselves with the sensibilities of all others.

In Thailand, one may hear in the jungle the wailing song of the gibbons. It is a mournful, keening sound and, according to legend, is the song of the gibbon widows, whose husbands have been taken away. The song is meant to re-establish the meaningful family connections of the gibbons.

The Dalai Lama stated: "We must recognize that the suffering of one person or one nation is the suffering of humanity. That the happiness of one person is the happiness of humanity."

The Buddhism of the Dalai Lama, as well as the other world religions focus much of their attention on the need for and practice of making and maintaining the connectedness with the divine being(s). From Brother Lawrence's *Practicing the Presence of God* in medieval times and the current Christian celebration of the Holy Communion to the *glossalalia* (speaking in tongues) of some Christian evangelical communities, the connectedness is apparent.

In northern India male Hindu devotees dress as women—no, they are not transvestites—in order to assume the role of the *gopis* (the heavenly milkmaids, who wait on the needs of Krishna). By this practice, *Raganuga Bakti Sadhana*, they are making the connections to the divinity, as the gopis have the closest relationship to Krishna.

In Asian theatre there are three audiences: the obvious audience out in front of the performers, the performers on stage who comprise an audience for each other, but the most important audience being the ancestors and the gods. All performers everywhere hope to make connections with some audience.

This divine connectedness of the performer, as well as of the Hindu devotees, is then returned to humanity to make the circle of connectedness complete: from mortal to divine and return; from material to spiritual and return; from animate to inanimate and return. As a matter of fact, the reverse is also true, i.e. from divine to mortal, from inanimate to animate. Who can account for the influence of the mountain on the human being?

It must also be woefully admitted that too often these circles are quite often broken or segmented and the potential two-way trust in everyday individual, as well as national, life becomes truncated and lifeless.

It seems to me that the awareness of this state of connectedness is more crucial than ever before, not simply because in Jeremy Rifkin's assessment we have evolved to this global inter-connectedness of empathy. But also because it seems that many people and even religions and nations are pulling back into themselves for fear that to empathize in a mutual connectedness will somehow swallow them up, destroying the human being. Some fear that they are losing their individuality, while simultaneously the reaching out is more for the greed of obtaining additional perks, funds or adherents.

Parabola: myth and the quest for meaning, to which I have earlier alluded, devotes each of its issues to a theme. It is a quarterly periodical and in its forty-year history it has never devoted a single one of its 140 issues to the theme of CONNECTIONS or CONNECTEDNESS.

However when I look closely at its past issues, I am aware that all of them relate to connectedness either directly or indirectly: the first issue, No. 1, *The Hero* is succeeded by *Magic, Initiation, and Rites of Passage*. Each of these deals with connections: hero with his rescued persons, magic with its illusions, initiation with its initiates, rites of passage with their connections between the recruits and the establishment. In the first 2011 issue, Vol. 36, No, 1, which is now subtitled "Where Spiritual Traditions Meet," the theme is "Suffering," while exploring the connectedness of suffering between person and pain or empathy from one person to another.

This brings us back to Leopold's statement. "Everything is connected to everything else."

Could we be at that point where the prophet, Isaiah, foresaw, "And the wolf shall dwell with the lamb, and the leopard shall lie down with the kid."? (Isaiah 11:6)

On the other hand we might regard the warning of the great battle of Armageddon, as described in Revelations: the final warfare of mankind when meaningful connectedness is no longer honored.

Perhaps this is the ultimate and only true choice of humanity—to embrace the evolution of this illuminating connectedness or retreat into the more usual acceptance of the darkness of fear or egocentrism of greed.

TRACY ARM GLACIER

    the immensity of the particularities
        and the cohesiveness therein
comprise the vastness of the glacier
        the depth of the fjord
                and the profile of the granite

        the raindrop doth not a torrent make
            and acting alone makes little impression
however when conjoined with similar chemical molecules
        reacting to forces of gravity
                they fill the crevices between the mountains

        the single snowflake acting independently
            may inspire with its unique geometric lacework
but when clasping hands with sister snowflakes
        they amass the grinding glaciers who in their turn
                etch the features on the face of the boulder

    the individual may impress with soaring accomplishment
        of earthly human achievement
but when collaborating with galactic forces of the universe
    we contribute to the preservation of our natural inheritance
    and assist in the highest attainment of human potential

PART IV
EDUCATION

Education has been a major part of my life's trek; from the disappointing late start of public school to degrees from five institutions of higher learning. Of course, I recognize that education is not confined to bureaucratic academia. Therefore I've included people and events outside the classroom. Also, the reader should find my experience with important lessons from the children, fascinating.

FUDGING THE FUDGE
OR
THE BEGINNING OF MY EDUCATIONAL JOURNEY

In April 1936, we moved down to Powhatan County in eastern Virginia to live with Uncle Bob in the Brinkley family home where Mamma had grown up. Daddy and Mamma wouldn't have chosen to leave the Little White House, but the choice was not theirs to make, as Daddy had lost his job at the mill and we *all* lost our new home.

Uncle Bob lived in a big, old eight-room-plantation home (not on a par with Tara) with 200 acres, many of them tillable for enough vegetables for summer sustenance and the potential for canning for the winter. It was on the edge of a large swamp bordering the James River.

Even though I didn't want to leave our new house, I was looking forward to starting school in the fall, as I would be six in November.

This was the first time I had been involved directly in farming, although I was always intrigued with what I had observed indirectly. We had had a cow and chickens at the Little White House, and we often visited Uncle Sammy Jane in Patrick County, Virginia where he lived, raised big gardens and ran a blacksmith shop, which included shoeing horses. Once when we visited Uncle Sam, I asked him about a small pen-like affair made of sturdy, newly debarked timbers. It measured about six feet high, eight feet long and three feet wide.

Uncle Sam said, "I had to build that for a high-spirited young stallion which I shod."

I was horrified to think that Uncle Sam would have shot a young horse—or any horse, for that matter. "What did you have to shoot him for?"

Uncle Sam, realizing that I had heard "shot" instead of "shod," teased me a bit by saying, "Well he was just too much for me."

"Well, you didn't have to go and shoot him."

Neither Uncle Sam nor Daddy had ever seen me so upset.

My education was beginning even with misinformation and misunderstanding. My values were also beginning to develop with an appropriate balance of political gusto.

"Learning the ropes" . . . or rather the education of dirt farming at Uncle Bob's—was the first time I had ridden a mule bareback. It was the last time also, for a while, as my mule—the stubborn mule-headed critter—decided to walk under a clothesline, which was high enough for him but not for his baggage . . . me. Fortunately, I had already obtained enough commonsense to grab a hold of the clothesline, simply sliding off the rear end of 'ol Dan.

We (Uncle Bob, Daddy and I) made a pretty good crop of vegetables, but it was already becoming apparent that the other two sides of this triangle weren't exactly compatible. Uncle Bob was too quiet, almost sullen, and Daddy talked too much. Uncle Bob observed, "A clattering tongue is a knob on the end of a branch of ignorance." Many years later he queried me to see if I still remembered that tidbit of wisdom.

Even though the planting, hoeing and cultivating was hot, dirty work, the gathering of the harvest was not only exciting but also educational. Who could have guessed that one 'mater (tomato) seed had produced that whole bush with all those red 'maters? I was particularly fond of the small, cherry 'maters, which we called "tommy-toes." The pulling of the roasen-years (roasting ears), snapping off the beans, cucumbers and squash and the grubbing for the Arsh taters (Irish potatoes) were simply preludes for some mighty fine eatin'.

Pullin' the cornstalk blades for winter fodder for the cows and mules was particularly onerous as the drying leaves were sharp enough to cut a body's hand. Cutting of the cornstalks was fun, especially when we bunched them together like little teepees all over the corn field. We used the corn shocks to pretend to be red Indians.

When Daddy and Uncle Bob cut the wheat with the handheld grain cradle, tying the sheaves and stacking them against each other to dry, I began to understand what the church song meant: *Bringing in the Sheaves*.

The farm had a bit of history with a couple of rundown slave quarters behind the big house as well as some ditches, which had been used as trenches by the Confederate Forces in the Civil War, which was locally called the War of the Northern Invasion.

All this had happened a long time before my grandparents bought the place in 1918. I had made up a good ghost story which I told Susie, about seeing wispy rebel soldiers on silent horses—I then began to see them, myself, for real and even to hear them at night when the wind would blow through the ancient maples and rattle the louvers on the window shutters.

I knew that at the end of summer, in September, school would be starting, and I could hardly wait. Every Sunday, starting in the middle of August, I would ask Mamma, "Is school starting tomorrow."

"No!" she'd answer, "It'll still be a couple of weeks." I was anxious to get my formal education started, being particularly interested to get to know what was in all those big old books.

I had begun to mark off the days on the calendar until September 8 stood unmarked, all alone.

Tomorrow is it!

I was up and ready before anyone else, which was unusual for me. Daddy was going to take us in the old Dodge, as the school bus didn't come all the way through the swamp to our place. Susie was going to be in the second grade, having already started to school in North Carolina the year before. Uncle Jack, who was living with us, was entering the fifth grade and I . . . I was going to be in the first grade, starting on a grand adventure, even without the gypsies.

Mamma had packed lunches for all of us *scholars*, as we expected to spend the whole day there. We had all had our vaccinations. Jack was wearing his new overalls; Susie had on a fluffy pinafore with a huge ribbon in her hair; and I had on new knickers, which whispered when I walked as the corduroy pant legs brushed against each other. I felt mighty big and grown up.

At the two-room school, Daddy enrolled Susie and Jack before it was my time. The teacher in charge asked Daddy about my birth date. He answered, "November 15, 1930."

She immediately said, "He's not old enough to start school. He has to be six."

I couldn't believe my ears, as I jumped to my own defense, "I'll be six years old on November 15, 1936."

"But you're not six years old *now*, are you?"

"No, but, but, but…" I sputtered; attempting to further argue my case.

Looking at Daddy and completely ignoring me as though I weren't even there, she sternly stated, "Sorry, but those are the rules. No child is to begin school before the age of six."

How was I going to wait another full year to start my education?

This was my first bitter lesson of the recalcitrance of institutional bureaucracy. I was utterly devastated, even humiliated, crying all the way back home as the old Dodge bumped the five miles back over the rutted road. When Daddy parked under one of the old maples he told me to come on into the house. I refused. Mamma came out to get me. I refused. *Why would I need any grown-ups who set up these silly arbitrary regulations?*

I spent the rest of the day in the back seat of that car. Opening my lunch bag, I peered into the contents before slowly lifting out and munching on the tasteless sandwich. I wanted to get even with that teacher, but didn't know how.

That was also when I began the suspicion that there was a silent mysterious tension, or even warfare, between those people attempting to learn and those pretending to teach. Many years later in graduate theological seminary this was finally articulated in a student newspaper:

> A student wrote "Definition of a theology professor: A person who, finding a young theology student with a candle, takes him by the hand, leads him down a dark alley and blows out the flame."
>
> A theology professor answered "Definition of a theology professor: A person who, finding a young firebrand, douses the fire to prevent the church from being burnt to the ground."

Adding flame to my early matriculation woes and piling insult onto my delayed education injury, at Halloween the school was going to have a fund-raising party, and the whole family was expected to go. I knew that teacher was going to be there.

Mamma was planning to take fudge with black walnuts. She asked me to crack the walnuts, which was a tough job as the shells were so hard. Of course, I had to take off the outer hull, which always left a dark stain on my hands, and my clothes too if I wasn't careful. I knew I wasn't to eat any of the walnut kernels while I was still working on them. It was like not eatin' blackberries when you'd be pickin' them for jam.

However, I did expect a little earned reward when the walnut-filled fudge came out of the oven. The aroma was overwhelming. I had smelled it all the way down at the barn.

I went runnin' into the kitchen. "Can I have a piece of fudge now, Mamma?"

"No, we have to take them to the school where we'll sell them."

I continued to protest. "Do you mean I'll have to buy this fudge after all the work I did? Can't you just fudge the fudge a little for me to test it?"

"Yes, Honey, you'll have to buy it, and no, Honey, I can't fudge the fudge for you to try. It's for the school."

For the school that won't let me attend!

I was beginning to develop a keen sense of justice or perhaps of injustice. What kind of a world is this, filled with institutions forbidding me their services, yet expecting me to develop a product to sell for the benefit of said institution?

How will I ever get revenge?

The answer to my revenge question didn't occur to me until many years later. Although they prevented me from starting my education in a timely manner, when I knew I was ready, I got even with the whole bunch of those Philistines.

I stayed in school the rest of my life—twelve years of college, culminating in a PhD in Asian Theatre—and they couldn't do a darn thing about it.

SENATOR CLYDE R. HOOEY

In 1942 our high school was mysteriously burned. As it was across the railroad track from the Smith Reynolds Airport north of Winston Salem, we school kids were convinced that Ol' Hitler had done it. It didn't occur to us that there were many more likely targets for the Nazis to hit than a small rural school in North Carolina.

J. Hugh White, the principal, and all the other school personnel moved into the gymnasium what they could salvage, augmented with whatever else could be obtained during the war time.

The next year, the gymnasium burned, thoroughly convincing us of foul play. As no new buildings could be built during the war, the school authorities arranged for old barracks to be reconstructed for classrooms. A cafeteria was rigged in the shell of the gymnasium. Each classroom was heated with an old potbellied coal-burning stove, forcing us into an educational situation similar to my father's school when he was a boy in the mountains of Virginia.

After the war ended we were promised a new high school, which was finished just as I entered my senior year in the fall of 1948. It was a magnificent million-dollar structure with huge expanses of glass.

For the dedication of the new building Senator Clyde R. Hooey was invited to address the student body and all the county-wide educators. As the newly elected president of the student council, I had the opportunity—the frightful task—of sharing the dais with all the dignitaries and delivering a short speech, accepting the gift of this marvelous facility. I don't remember what I said, but I do remember Senator Hooey and his address.

A tall man with long silvery hair, Senator Hooey wore a swallowtail Carolina-blue coat with a fresh red carnation in the lapel. For an hour he spoke of federal aid to education without looking at a single note. His major point was that, "The chilrun of Nawth Kerlina are as deservin' as the chilrun of New Yoik City, to benefit from the rewards of international commerce in the New York harbors." I was impressed with his southern gentleman appearance, his senatorial demeanor and his stentorian oratory.

I was also impressed with his audacity to talk about federal aid to education when all other southern politicians were usually too timid to speak of anything that might be contrary to states' rights and responsibilities.

Moving ahead by several years—forty to be exact—I was preparing to perform in Washington for the Senate Finance Committee Dinner Party hosted by Senator Russell Long and his wife, Carolyn.

Mrs. Long, who insisted on calling me in her southern drawl, "Doctah Gilbert," was duly impressed that I had remembered Senator Long and his speech so long ago. She told me that she grew up in Shelby, NC (the hometown of Senator Hooey) and had gone to Washington as the senator's secretary.

Mrs. Long continued, "Ever' day that the senate was in session Senatah Hooey wore a swallowtail coat with a fresh boutonniere to the senate chambers. An' he nevah drove or took the limousine . . . thet would be a waste of the taxpayers' money. No, he took the F Street streetcah.

"One mawnin' on the streetcah, while holdin' onto one of the ovahhead hand straps, a young fellow comes up to him an' says. 'Pahdon me, but who are you?' He had apparently been observin' Senator Hooey for severul mawnins, an Ah suppose he was somewhat mystified by his formal attiah.

"Senator Hooey straightened himself up to his full 6'2" stature an declahed, 'Ah'm Senator Clyde R. Hooey from the sovrun state of Nawth Kerlina.'

"The young fellow. backed up and looked the senator ovah from his silver hair to his polished shoes, and said, 'Well I knew you were somebody'"

As I reflect on that autumn morning of 1948, I'm sure Senator Clyde R. Hooey was telling us Mineral Spring High School kids,

"Ah want you to know thet you are somebody."

WARMING UP MY COLLEGE DORM ROOM

After attending a small junior college (Brevard College) near the Smokey Mountains for two years, in 1951 I transferred to Duke University, where I was assigned a room in Dormitory G. Bernie Welch, a high school and Brevard classmate, and Paul Weeks, a pre-med student from somewhere in eastern NC were assigned as my roommates in a dormitory, otherwise occupied by Yankee boys, mostly from New York and New Jersey.

We didn't have very much in common with the northern boys, except we were all enrolled at Dook. They did a whole heap of drinkin' —strictly forbidden then—on weekends. By Monday morning the restrooms reeked with the stinky sweet smelly residue of spirits in otherwise empty likker bottles, which were deposited in the trash cans in the head, so as not to be left in their rooms to identify the boys who were the imbibers. The maids who cleaned our rooms and made our beds every day would surely have reported them.

The Yankees found us North Carolina boys rather amusin'. If the door was left open, one of 'em from Brooklyn would often step into our room and stand by the door just to hear us talk. We would invite him in, "Come on in an' grab a seat."

"I don't want to sit down. I just want to listen to you talk." He would continue to stand while listening to our strange speech patterns. In fact, I think he was surprised that English could at times be detected in the utterances of our southern conversation.

It became obvious to us rather soon upon matriculating at that prestigious southern university—which was attempting to join the academic fraternity of the IvyLeague schools—that the Yankee boys considered the local IQs to lower the farther south they would travel on their academic trek to the Tar Heel state.

I think they had figured by the time they crossed the NC-VA state line, it was problematic whether we NC boys were studyin' at Dook or Dook was studyin' us. Dook did have a rather respectable Primate Department.

One evenin', while I was still at my desk astudyin' (my roommates were gone), Bill, a fellow from New Jersey, wandered into the room. He had a rather quizzical look on his face as he exclaimed, "Boy, it's cold in here." I had opened not only the door to the hallway but also the windows, as I couldn't sleep in a hot room. It was beginning to cool down a bit, it being in January.

Ah don't know why Ah done hit without forethought, sorta unthoughtedly, so to speak, but Ah assumed my back-home, up-mountain Baux Mountain dialect an' said, "Ah know hit, Bill, an' Ah'm tryin' to git hit wahmed up in hyar. Thar ain't nary stove in hyar, whut could be fired up fer warmin' the place."

By his reaction, Ah knowed Ah'd caught one, jest as any experienced fisherman knows when a good one's hit his line.

"But, Reid, you have the door and the windows open."

"Yeah, Bill. Hit's hot out in the hallway, so's Ah'm gonna git me a draft acomin' thru hyar to git this blamed room wahmed up."

"Reid, you can't warm up the room that way."

"Bill, now don't be a joshin' me an' pullin' mah laig, 'cause Ah've studded fisics too, an' Ah'll jest pull thet high-pressure hot air out twarge the cold low pressure air outta them winders, then Ah'll shet them winders an' hev me some wahm in hyar."

Bill was getting quite solicitous now, as he'd realized that the ra-diator was turned off. He explained. "Now I'm tellin' you, you have to get your heat from the radiator."

"Bill, you're a-pullin' mah laig agin. There ain't no ra-diator in hyar. (Ah was now tryin' to educate Bill.) A ra-diator's fer a auto-mo-bile."

He reached acrost mah bed and turned on the ra-diator, which started a sizzlin'.

"Oh, Bill turn thet dad-blasted thang off. Hit's gonna blow up. Hit starts a sizzlin' thet a way, ever' time Ah twist thet liddle handle knob to see whut hit might be fer." Ah quickly reversed the handle.

"But that's where you get your heat."

"Bill, quit a funnin' with me now. Thur ain't no way a body could git enny heat outta thet thang. There tain't no door to put the firewood in nur the ashes out, nur nuther a chimbley. Hit ain't even got a stovepipe."

Bill didn't say anything. He just shook his head sadly, as he walked out into the hallway toward his room.

Ah know Ah hadna oughter a done thet to pore Bill, but when you've caught a big one, you've gotta play the line as far as you kin.

The next morning when I went to the head to shave an' brush mah teeth, the Yankee boys wuz all in thur conducting thur own mornin' ablutions. The word musta been out about this hillbilly, whut didn't know how to turn on the heat in his room. Hit's so obvious when a fellow tries to avoid lookin' at you in a shared mirror, while deliberately lookin' in the opposite direction, speshully when thur's nothing in thet direction to look at.

So I just figgered, I'd finish the story, as I shared mah appreciation of this indoor outhouse. "Ya know, this shore is a con-ven-ient room."

One of the fellers ventured to reply, "Whatta you mean?"

"Waal, ya see them water sprangs over thar on thet wall? When ya pull down thet liddle handel, ya kin stick yer foot in thur an' wrench yer foot real good. But Ah'm atellin' ya now, thet sprang water ain't nearly as good to drink as the sprang water on Baux Mountain whur Ah come from."

By this time they knew I had turned the table on them and was pulling *their* legs.

A couple of years after that when I was visiting Duke and saw New Jersey Bill, he told me that he would be receiving his BA at the end of the semester. I congratulated him, but I still hadn't the heart or gumption to tell him thet I'd been afunnin' with him thet cold winter night.

His hair had turned completely white . . . I take no credit atall fer that.

BROTHER JOE AND SISTER LUCY

After graduating from Duke University in 1953, I traveled all the way, *via* train, from North Carolina to Dallas, Texas to attend Perkins Seminary at SMU. I felt that changing the geographical and cultural contexts of my academic pursuits would be an important element in my overall education.

The instructors at Perkins were impressive and quite eclectic. Professor Martin was a retired Methodist District Superintendent and taught Methodist Policy. In a class discussion of *The Methodist Discipline*—in an effort to impress on us the breadth of the instructions in the *Discipline*—informed us that, "*The Methodist Discipline* covers everything that a Methodist pastor may need to know, except how to baptize a fat woman in a shallow creek."

Ed Hobbs, the youngest faculty member, taught Theology. The basic tenet of which was "To love God and do as you please." One day in class, he was confronted by Robert Short.

"You mean I can do as I please?"

"Mr. Short, what do you please to do?"

Bob only sputtered, but years later wrote *The Gospel According to Peanuts*, which was probably his answer to Professor Hobbs.

Dr. Fred Gealy, an outstanding Greek scholar, who taught New Testament, was also a church organist and one of the contributing editors of *The Methodist Hymnal*. One day in a small seminar, a somewhat contentious Wisconsin student, whose name I can't recall, asked Dr. Gealy a rather confrontational question. It was apparent that the student was more interested in challenging the professor than in searching for an answer.

Quietly, with tears in his eyes, Dr. Gealy looked at the student and said, "To be perfectly honest, we don't know what we're talking about, but the point is, we must keep talking." One of my most enduring academic lessons!

Two quite different professors were Dr. Albert Outler and Professor Joe Matthews. Outler was a fantastic lecturer in Theology and could have competed with the comedy of Bob Hope if the audience could understand Latin, Greek and the classics.

Joe Matthews, an existentialist, was, without a doubt, the most theatrical member of the distinguished faculty. His philosophical hero was Soren Kierkegaard. Matthews taught Christian Ethics, delighting in badgering the students to respond to his dramatic statements. One day in class, a tall, quiet student, Bob Wilson from Minnesota, answered his challenge and began to debunk the entire outline of his philosophy, which Professor Matthews had chalked on the blackboard. Shortly after Bob started his deconstruction efforts, Joe, hopping first on one foot and then other, tried to counter, or at least, blunt, the attack.

The student, uncharacteristically, said, "Just be quiet until I finish."

The next day in class, Professor Joe said, "Yesterday, one of your classmates knocked me down and walked all over my guts. But I heard some of you murmuring, 'O goody!' You were all wishing it had been you, attacking your professor." Of course, he was delighted to get this kind of response—particularly from such an outstanding seminarian.

One day, while talking with a group of other students in the hallway, I was confronted by Professor Matthews: "What's the *word*? What's the *word*? The world is waiting out there for the *word*. Don't you have the *word*?"

My friends said I had an apt rejoinder, but I was so shocked that I don't remember how I had responded.

Sometime later, in his office, Professor Matthews asked me, "Why are you fighting me?"

"I don't know why you think I'm fighting you, except last week when Bob Short asked you a question, you said, 'You can't ask that.' and I simply said, 'But he did ask it and you oughta answer it.' I don't have a fight with you, but I do find your disciples incorrigible."

"What do you mean, 'my disciples'?"

"You may not be aware of it, but there are some students who are so enamored with you that they won't listen to any other professor unless he agrees with you. They are so enthralled with you and your style that they even walk down the hall like you, leaning forward with their hands clasped behind their backs."

Priding himself on his existentialist proclivity for battling tradition, he asked, "How can anyone make a system of what I say?"

"Well, everyone speaks out of some framework or context. Otherwise there's no possibility of any communication."

Thus endeth our conversation, and afterward I never received better than an average grade from him. I continued to enroll in his classes, as I found them exciting and stimulating.

It was true that several of the students, so captivated by the style and manner of Professor Matthews, were his unacknowledged disciples.

A second batch of students, who came to seminary with all their personal and religious answers—sans questions—intact, were summarily frightened by him. Even though they were required to take some of his classes, they figuratively put their fingers in their ears to keep his *apostasy* from getting into their brains. After all, they had observed irreverence in some of their fellow classmates. Having arrived with their religious beliefs already packaged by their earlier youthful religious creeds, they needed only a ribbon to celebrate the package.

A third group of students, of which I fancied myself, listened to Matthews, Outler, Gealy Hobbs, *et al.* and took whatever seemed to be pertinent and efficacious from each and all in our own spiritual quests and potential pastoral futures.

One of the comic theatrical events with Professor Matthews involved an older female student, Lucy Thibault, whom we all affectionately called, "Sister Lucy." Most of the seminarians were younger men, mostly in their early to mid-twenties. There were also a couple of young women studying to be directors of religious education and with barely hidden agendas of capturing a young "preacher man." There was even a club on the SMU campus of girls who were focused on eventually becoming preachers' wives…but without having identified their specific quarry.

A few older middle-aged men had switched from an earlier career and with various stories of their own version of being "called" when struck by a shaft of light from heaven on their own personal "road to Damascus". But their calling was more likely on an oil rig in East Texas or in a pick-up truck on Highway 81 to Enid, Oklahoma.

Probably the most unusual student was Sister Lucy, in her 50s. She was a retired school teacher from the bayou country of Louisiana and planning, we thought, to become a Methodist pastor to the Cajuns of her home state.

One day in a rather large lecture class, Professor Matthews was attempting to divide the budding theologues into small seminar groups. In the process of putting Sister Lucy's complete name on the board, he continuously had trouble correctly spelling her last name (Thibault). In disgust he said, "Sister Lucy, why don't you change your name?"

She immediately engaged the challenger in his frustration: "Brother Joe, if I could find an old, retired, widowed, Methodist minister, I would change my name."

Of course that terminated the class for the day, as everyone had to struggle to pick themselves up off the floor.

A few years after that, Brother Joe left SMU to establish the Ecumenical Institute in Chicago, but he probably never completely recovered from Sister Lucy's *repartee.*

As far as Sister Lucy was concerned, I never learned if she ever found her superannuated octogenarian.

LESSONS FROM SHAPECHANGERS

In the summer of 1987 I had collaborated with several other university instructors to conduct a mythic workshop at a Southern Methodist University extended campus near Taos, NM. This was one of several summer workshops dedicated to exploring the performance potential of a given Greek mythic theme. That summer was the myth of Oedipus. As the participants were from several ethnic and academic backgrounds, we also encouraged then to explore similar myths in other cultures.

We were fortunate to engage a couple of Native American artists in the Taos area to work with us. One of them, Bernal Carpio was a dancer and storyteller and had performed in a number of major films. He was also an authority on native rituals.

One evening he captured the attention of us all, by relating local lore, particularly the occasions of the return of departed souls, quite often as shape changers. We were all familiar with the stories of creatures who would change from human form into other forms, particularly that of animals. At times the reverse might also be true.

At eleven o'clock, it was time to go to our sleeping quarters. We were all pretty well spooked out about the potential of such occurrences in that area.

The traditional burying grounds were right across the road from where we were meeting. Picnickers had littered that sacred space with trash, including lots of plastic bags and even smashed styrofoam coolers. We couldn't understand such disrespect and irreverence.

My wife, Robin, and I went across the road to our sleeping quarters, a chalet type of building in a corner of the Native American grave yard. We climbed up the exterior stairs to the porch and then into our place.

After turning out the lights, we heard strange percussive sounds out on the porch just under a window. I had forgotten to lock the door, so hurried to do so; it refused to be fastened.

There was a curtain over the window, so whoever was causing the pattern of dance-like rhythms couldn't readily be seen from the inside.

Being the brave husband, I ventured to the window, at least to know what or who was producing the metallic sounds.

Parting the curtain ever so slightly, I saw what I had fearfully expected . . . the specter of a departed warrior with a black mask around his eyes and dancing an angry war dance.

Frozen in time and space, I witnessed the bellicose spirit transform into a raccoon bouncing on an inverted metal garbage can lid.

That was the only such experience I had until I moved to Tucson, several years later and had not even thought further about shape changers.

At 2:30 one morning I was awakened by a horrendous noise. Having been sound asleep and dreaming, I heard in the dream the sound of a cougar or mountain lion attacking from a boulder as I was hiking in the Sonoran desert. While crouching closer above me, the cougar uncharacteristically loosened an avalanche of rocks and dried, dead cacti. Fortunately, I heard the debris beginning to fall all around me before the cougar had a chance to pounce.

All of this happened in my dream in only a split second of actual time.

Then, waking up in a frightened sweat, I realized the noise was not only in my dream but was also real and coming from the direction of the walk-in closet.

I sat bolt upright in bed and began instinctively to ponder . . . no . . . to decide . . . to investigate the source of the clamor.

The trek to the closet was only about eight steps, but that gave me enough time to select the most logical, though fantastic, scenario of the event.

In the ceiling of the closet was a trapdoor from the attic—a trap door which could be an actual entrance into the closet if someone or some thing could have been in the attic. I quickly assured myself that there was no exterior entrance to the attic unless . . .

Then I realized that there was a swamp cooler installed in a window space in a wall of the attic—but there was no other opening . . . even a window.

However . . . if the swamp cooler were to fall out or be removed, the resultant opening would allow even a large creature, like a bear, to crawl in.

Several weeks before, I had seen a bobcat peering at me through the glass patio door. Actually, we were standing only about four feet from each other. He stared at me for a few minutes, then picked up his prey, a fluttering bird, and walked regally across the backyard and calmly climbed over the fence, grasping the wrought-iron bars like a simian.

If the bobcat could climb the fence like that, he could climb to the top of the roof and remove the swamp cooler.

On the other hand, the noise I heard from the closet was much more than a mere bobcat could make, even if he were to jump all the way to the floor, which was carpeted.

No! It must be something heavier than a bobcat.

Of course it couldn't be a bear, as there haven't been any bear sightings recently in the Tucson area. The picture of a cougar in our neighborhood was featured only a few days earlier in the *Tucson Star*.

It must be a cougar that knocked down the trap door. After all, it was a cougar in the dream, so this must be reality copying fantasy, rather than the other way around.

As I approached the closet in the semi-dark room, I could see that the closet door was closed, even though I had remembered it was open before I'd gone to bed.

There was no more noise—in fact no noise at all—since the big bang only a few moments earlier.

Not really expecting an answer, I called out, "Is there anyone in there?" To be truthful, I was praying that there wouldn't be an answer.

What would I do if I were to hear the roar of a mountain lion or a bear?

No answer . . . just an eerie silence.

I knew that the explosion had come from the closet, and I knew further that I had to continue the investigation.

The first move would have to be, open the door, which I started v . . . e . . . r . . . y c . . . a . . . r . . . e . . . f . . . u . . . l . . . l . . . y. The door barely budged. A huge weight was leaning or lying against the door.

Even after I pushed the door and bulky weight a few inches, I couldn't see anything in the dark closet without a light.

When the door was cracked just opened enough for me to reach in to the light switch, I hesitantly crawled my fingers over toward the switch, fearing that at any moment a paw or a claw would snatch it off.

Nothing happened until I was able to turn on the light.

What I saw of this heavy bulk was fur...plus a lot of other clothing.

My heavens! A burglar or homeless person has crawled up to the roof, taken out the swamp cooler and fallen through the trapdoor. He must have broken his neck, for there's no movement or sound.

With great effort, I pushed the door open wider until I could get my head in to discover the invader, whoever or whatever it might be.

There on the closet floor lay a whole wall storage unit, depositing all racks, clothing and shelving, which must have weighed a couple of hundred pounds. For some reason or other the whole unit collapsed in the middle of the night, pushing the door closed and holding it in place until my brute strength pushed it all aside.

The whole event reminded me of James Thurber.

Walter Mitty, step aside.

I AM A TEACHER

I Do Not Teach

To claim to be a teacher in one breath, then immediately to register a disclaimer of not teaching, is not a simple play on words. My point is that the teaching event is a shared experience with no one able to lay claim to the conventional notion of imparting wisdom from the teacher (all-knowing) to the learner (completely-ignorant).

I am in good company in this argument, as Socrates, one of the world's greatest teachers did not teach; he permitted the students to learn. He probably received his inspiration from the vocation of his mother, Phaenarete, who was a midwife. The word *educate* is derived from the word *educere*, which means to lead or bring out. It is the responsibility of the midwife to deliver or bring forth. The teacher has the same responsibility.

This is basically what the Socratic Method means—to bring forth from the innate understanding of the learner. Socrates demonstrated this by asking leading questions of an illiterate boy. In the process the boy proved the conclusion of a geometry theorem.

When I was conducting a theatre class in a West Virginia high school, one of the students confessed to me, "I'm not involved in the class 100 per cent, because I'm bored."

My response was, "It's not my responsibility to entertain you."

The next day I wrote on the chalkboard for the whole class:

It is not the teacher's responsibility to entertain, impress or judge.

It is the teacher's responsibility to open, inspire and challenge,

Unfortunately, too often the teacher is expected to entertain with all kinds of superficial fripperies. The teacher must avoid the temptation to impress his impressionable students, simply because his experience is usually more expansive than theirs. Even though the teacher may need to evaluate the level of the student's work, this should not be interpreted as a right to *judge*.

In the past there was a much greater need than now to impart data and information. However, in this information age it is much less necessary for the teacher to fulfill this role. This does not preclude the necessity of training. Any field of study needs a certain amount of basic knowledge and understanding. In math, language, history, the arts, etc., it is important for the instructor to share that underpinning—and there are various effective ways of doing this.

Teachers are often hamstrung with lesson plans, paper work and test scores. With this kind of pressure, it is difficult to find the time for students to explore, discover, observe and experiment.

For several summers in the late '60s I had the opportunity to introduce arts activities to junior high children in the beautiful driftless (non-glaciated) area of Wisconsin. On the first day of each session, after several movement exercises, I asked them to spend forty-five minutes exploring the meadow, woods and rock ledges. We could talk about what they saw, heard and/or touched. One of the girls, even though she lived in the area, later reported that she had seen things she had never really noticed before.

Several of the children asked almost immediately what I expected them to find. I explained that this was not a treasure hunt and that I had not put anything out there for them to discover.

On their second excursion I asked them to bring back an item which particularly interested them and could be easily brought back. They returned with various items. One girl brought a rock. I asked, "Why did you bring back this rock?"

She said, "You told us to bring something back."

I asked further, "Was this the only rock out there?"

"Oh, no! There were hundreds of rocks out there."

I pushed her further. "Why didn't you bring back one of those other rocks?"

"Well, just look at it!"

Without challenging her too strongly, I continued, "What should I find so particular about it when I look at it?"

"Don't you see the interesting rust color? And also the bumpy surface when you touch it? And don't you find the shape kinda interesting? The weight, itself, is surprising, 'cause it's so heavy for its size."

She had just discovered and shared *color, texture, shape* and even *weight* without a lecture from the teacher. In praising her discovery I asked her to expand her tactile and visual observations to the auditory potential; "You've done a wonderful job of looking and touching, but what does it sound like?"

She dropped it on the wooden floor and said, "It sounds like a thud, but I'll bet that if I knock it against another rock it'll be a different sound—more like a clang."

I could have lectured on these art principles and expected the children to remember them for a test. Instead, they were experiencing these principles for themselves.

The next time they went foraging, they were to bring back something . . . a stick, piece of bark, stone, etc. . . . to use as the raw material for an art piece.

One girl brought back an interesting brown, twisted, textured stick. She regarded it for at least an hour and reported, "I think it's fine just the way it is, so I'm not going to change it in any way, but will find something else to paint or carve."

I lauded her response.

In contrast to these classes, I attended a showing of a film documenting an arts project in Tennessee. Although all the other viewers at the Tennessee Arts Commission seemed to be impressed with the project, I asked the presenter how many artists had been involved with the project. He said, "No artists were involved."

I said, "To me that is quite obvious."

"Why?"

"I observed that you lined up the children with their fingers over their mouths. You took them to the edge of the playground where you pulled a leaf off a tree. They marched back into the classroom in a straight line, and as soon as they returned to their seats, you asked them to identify the name of the tree.

"You didn't give them a chance to explore; looking, listening and/or touching. They didn't discover. You plucked the leaf, and when you brought it back in they didn't even have the opportunity to ask if it had a name."

The kind of learning I am suggesting may take time, but it is more indelible as the cognition is existential and kinetic—not simply verbal.

One of the children in the Wisconsin summer classes, although an adult internationally-known athlete now, told me recently, "That summer was the most beneficial time of my education."

I read of an anthropologist who was studying a tribe of primitive people and was particularly interested in their pedagogy. He asked one of the leaders about their education methods, "How do you teach your children?"

"We don't teach."

"But you must teach, as your culture, your ways, are very complicated."

"We let them watch. To explain too much steals the opportunity to learn and stealing is against the law."

Frank Lloyd Wright was noted as an architectural genius, but his pedagogy was also brilliant. Even today the mantra of the Frank Lloyd Wright School of Architecture is "Learn by doing."

In my own experience, as a student in various educational venues, I should pay homage to many great teachers.

My first "home away from home" was Brevard College, a small Methodist college in the mountains of North Carolina. The professors — in particular Professor Roy in Religion, Professor Lucille Smith in English Literature, Professor Lobdell in Biology and Professor Trowbridge in German—in their pedagogical responsibilities made it possible for me to get on with my learning by *opening, inspiring* and *challenging* while providing a comforting educational atmosphere where I could take those risks.

I do not teach—I hope that I am an active participant in the learning event.

An ancient Japanese legend tells of a teacher who attempts to catch the salmon of ultimate wisdom. When he has caught it, he hands it to his student, who says, "Why are you offering the salmon to me?"

The teacher replies, "It was my responsibility to catch the salmon of ultimate wisdom, but it is not mine to eat; it is for you."

Every master teacher hopes that the student will take the musical notes captured by the teacher to compose the magnificent symphony; the vocabulary from his mentor to write the great novel; the gesture from the dance master to choreograph and dance the great Greek myths.

EXTRACURRICULAR

To limit one's teaching time and energy to the assigned schedule, is to ignore what the learning process is about. Of course, if the study is theatre, there is no way one could limit the activity to the classroom, unless you were considering only theatre history or literature.

At Union College, my first venture into college teaching, the rehearsal and performance times demanded a great deal of extracurricular commitment.

I thought the students ought to have the opportunity to see theatre at its best. So it's "Broadway here we come." The first year I made the trek to the Big Apple, I drove my '57 Dodge with four students.

I drove all night, as we couldn't afford motel rooms. When I drove into the city, I made a big mistake following a bus making a left turn. A cop blew his whistle and had me back into the intersection.

"How long have you been driving?"

"Oh, ever since I was 16."

"Don't be coy with me." He had seen the Kentucky license plate.

"You must have been driving all night. You're eyes are bloodshot."

"Yes sir." I didn't dare tell him I had just moved from the NJ/NY area only a few months earlier.

"There is a sign 'No left turn'."

"The bus was turning."

"The sign plainly says, 'Buses allowed'."

"I was right behind the bus and couldn't see the sign."

"That was because you were too close to the bus. There's a law in the city that you must drive a certain distance behind the vehicle in front of you."

Having driven in NY quite a bit, I nearly laughed at him about the distance required between cars.

I played my Kentucky hillbilly role well, so he gave me only a warning.

The purpose of the trip was to see professional theatre. That we did and had arranged to meet with Julie Harris after her performance I Am a Camera; a real thrill for all of us.

I continued that practice at Union College and subsequent teaching at Lambuth College and OSU, of taking students to see professional theatre not only in New York, but also at The Shakespeare Festival in Canada.

At Ohio State in 1984, I set up a summer session in Comedy with several invited instructors and performers. One such instructor/ performer was Stanley Allan Sherman. He received a wonderful review in *The Columbus Dispatch*. "Seriously, you must go see this clown. Parents take your kids! If you don't have any, that's no excuse . . . His show is that special."

I received a national award for innovative summer programs.

With the help of several others, I established four mythic summer workshops. My co-directors were Richard Harned (OSU Art Department) and Rick Ney (SMU and LSU). The participants were advanced students and performers.

Each year a different Greek myth would be the focus, but the participants were encouraged to explore parallel myths from other cultures

It was significant that we were able to secure fascinating natural areas for our exploration, ending each session with a public performance.

Oedipus was the focus of our first summer and was conducted at an extended SMU campus on the outskirts of Taos, NM. The following summer we studied the myth of Prometheus at Hilltop across the highway from Taliesin.

This note in the performance program gives a fair indication what all the mythic workshops were about.

> Welcome to Hilltop, a special place for creative energies and celebrations. This evening's presentation is a collaboration of Global Views and Valley Studio, which for nine years existed in the Upper Wyoming Valley.

This evening's presentation is not a finished product/production, but rather a work in progress based on the ancient Greek myth of Prometheus and similar fire bearer myths in other cultures. Our approach is eclectic, drawing upon the thought of various artists from percussionists and glass artists to dancers, actors and story-tellers.

Our work with Greek mythology is motivated by our concern with our culture's neglect of our mythic heritage. It is almost impossible to find a college student who can recite one nursery rhyme. We are bombarded constantly with TV and film without acknowledging that the roots of those dramas are rooted in the myths. The undercurrents of art are nourished and informed by Greek and other mythologies.

We ask you this evening to celebrate the gift of fire, ponder the misappropriation of that gift and retain the potential of that creative gift of enlightenment within our own lives.

In considering the myth of Prometheus the fire-bearer, we understood that this also meant fire-power. The last image of the performance was a stealth bomber with a twenty-four foot wingspan.

The plane was made of black plastic stretched over a frame of bamboo, quite manageable by two runners. They started behind the seated audience and holding the contraption just over their heads. We added another touch of verisimilitude by Richard Harned running at the tail end with a noisome gas fire apparatus.

Several people from the Frank Lloyd Wright School of Architecture attended the performance.

The celebration ended with a Promethean ball.

The final two workshops were held on Gladwin Island, a small island at the confluence of the Glady and Dry Fork rivers in West Virginia.

Those myths were Pandora and Persephone. Some of the participants were children.

In the presentation of Pandora, a beautiful Japanese dance was performed across the Glady. When the actor in full Japanese costume slowly crossed the Glady in a shallow area, floating candles were released, floating around and under the kimona and down toward the Dry Fork.

In the final performance of Persephone, one of the participants had shaved his head and covered himself with white clown make-up. He then put on a three-piece suit. A dog observing the performance started barking wildly when the actor put on the suit, even though the pooch was quite docile with earlier loud noises and weird dancing.

Before stepping into the river the actor put on a fedora and holding a briefcase, began wading Across the Dry Fork and up the Glady River in water about thigh deep.

Two unanticipated participants were a couple of fly fishermen, fishing down the Glady. They quickly reversed course and headed back up river.

Each of these events was documented with photos and film, but I no longer have access to the documentation. The significance of these explorations was the experience, itself.

Even though theatre is a natural for exploring beyond the classroom, it is hoped that other disciplines will exit the classroom.

TRANSCENDING TECHNIQUE
go beyond/move above

Having earlier exposed my predilection for the Socratic Method in education, it behooves me to account for the necessity of basic techniques or training. It must be admitted that underpinnings/basics are necessary to pursue any field of study or endeavor.

In military training, the recruit is expected to learn discipline, ranging from bed making and uniform upkeep to arms training and cooperative behavior. As rigorous as this discipline may be, it is not an end in itself. It is not combat, for which it is intended to support. One might imagine the shambles of military combat if there were no discipline of training prior to any confrontation with the opponent.

I find it interesting that *discipline* and *disciple* are derived from the same root word, *discipulus* (learner, follower). It seems appropriate to think of the discipline of training to be a follower of a program of technique. A disciple of a master is a committed follower.

Fred Buerki, a stagecraft professor of mine at the University of Wisconsin, once complained to me of his disgust with young artists, who painted only abstracts. I said, "Fred, at least they're being creative," also reminding him that the verb *created* is the first verb in the Judeo-Christian scriptures. Being an old curmudgeon of an agnostic, he didn't like to be preached to.

He countered with, "I don't care what they paint or what style of art, if they can demonstrate that they can draw the human form." If they can master the discipline, they can then pursue whatever direction they choose.

I call this transcending the technique, but there must first be a technique to transcend.

As related in an earlier story of my performing with Sadayo Kita, I was shocked when he dropped his fan before exiting, as he was performing Hagaroma, a heavenly princess.

In order to appreciate this moment one needs to understand that each Noh drama has had the same blocking for centuries and Hagaromo is not choreographed to drop her fan. In the discussion afterward I asked, "Kita-san, why did you drop the fan?"

His response: "Because I felt like it."

Kita was a master of this art form and its technique. He not only had the right to go beyond the expected movement but had a responsibility to do so, if the integrity of his performance at that moment called for it. If as a neophyte, I had done the same thing, it would have been a terrible mistake, because I had not yet mastered the technique. He, as a master of the technique was able to transcend it.

I urge my students to transcend the technique of their art form, but there must be a technique to transcend, otherwise the acting art descends into the slobber-mouth, blue jean faux-Stanislavski style. I also suggest to them that there are times when I feel I could be a fantastic orchestra conductor; the only problem is that I don't know music. I have no technique to transcend with brilliance or even with mediocrity.

There is always the danger when mastering a technique to stay at the level of the mere form of the technique. In acting we sometimes call it, "phoning it in." When technique becomes the endgame the endeavor becomes an orthodoxy which is a virus leading to lifeless paralysis.

In my research in theatre training in India, I often heard traditionalists claim that no new approaches for theatre training were needed, as everything was outlined beautifully in the Natyasastra. It is true that this ancient treatise, older than The Poetics details the requirements for acting. It would be wonderful if an Indian theatre were to establish these techniques again, but they would then need to be transcended, as India is now a modern nation no longer confined to the rule of rajahs.

As wonderful as the traditional theatre forms of Japan (the Noh, the Kabuki and the Bunraku) are, they must also continue to change, allowing transcending beyond the technique.

In the learning/teaching event, attitude of the instructor is more important than we sometimes acknowledge. In fact it is a major factor in the learning process. Both the student and the teacher must be open to the endeavor and to the moment as partners in the enterprise.

In the theatre both the director and the actor are partners in the resulting performance, as the coach and player collaborate in the final score on the playing field. This also implies that they are open to each other.

As the discipline/technique is pursued by the master/apprentice, teacher/student, director/actor, coach/player, little, if anything, is accomplished without mutual respect. It doesn't mean that the partners must love each other, but it does mean that the discipline falls apart without each participant's respect for the other.

An example of the absence of respect between actor and director took place when, a few years ago, I directed Moliere's *A School for Husbands*. One of the actors had exhibited throughout the whole summer season his lack of respect for me as the director. I had attempted to convince him to shorten his pause just before his last line in the play. After the opening night performance, I again said, "Marty, that pause is much too long."

His response was, "Well, dude, whatever works."

"That's the point, Marty. It's not working."

"It's not as though I'd forgotten my line."

"Marty, that's just it. The audience thinks you've forgotten your line, and they're feeling sorry for you, the actor, and have lost interest in the character you're portraying." Only then did the actor accept my direction. If it had been working his way, I would gladly have accepted it.

When the child is permitted and encouraged to ask a question, it may behoove the teacher or parent to say, "Let's (let *us*) search for the answer."

This brings us full-circle back to the Socratic Method in which Socrates respects the ability of the boy to answer intelligently the probing questions. The boy respects Socrates enough to accept the challenge of answering the questions.

Even when Kita-san is sharing the detailed technique of the Japanese Noh with beginning students, a major factor in the disciplined process is the substantial presence of mutual respect.

SIGNPOSTS ALONG THE WAY
Children's Lessons for Adults

As Aesop had morals with his fables, I felt that each of these foibles of children would also have a moral.

Everyday humorous or touching events are useful when attempting to make a point or persuade an audience to some kind of action or thought.

Even Jesus, when confronted by his disciples for the explanation of a knotty theological issue, told a story, which we know as parables. It is rather amusing that most of my parables are given to me by children.

When my wife, Luan, and I and four-month-old daughter, Tari, had moved to Barbourville, KY in 1959, we lived next door to a two-year-old neighbor, Danny, who loved to visit. He came so often that I had to latch the back screen door to prevent him from coming in and disturbing Tari when she would be asleep. One evening, while we were having dinner, Danny came to the back door and tried to open it. He always talked in baby gibberish and after several strong tugs on the door, he again used several completely unintelligible words.

I didn't want to be completely rude to the tot, so I said, "All right, Danny."

Then he, in perfectly good intelligible, articulate English said, "Well, open the door then."

Moral: Be sure you understand the question, before you venture an incriminating answer.

When Tari was five I was pastor of Grace Methodist Church in Belleville, Wisconsin.

One Sunday after the morning church service, she asked me a rather serious question. I don't recall the question, but I did feel that it was a little too academic for a five-year-old. But I told myself, *After all, she is my first-born.* So I gave her a quite lengthy answer. She listened carefully,

then said, "Now Daddy, are you telling the truth or are you preaching now?" Ministers always wince when I share this story.
Moral: There is sometimes a disconnect between the truth and an oration (even a religious one).

When I was in seminary in Texas, I spent the weekends with a young minister and his family in Lancaster. His five-year-old son, Paul, and I became rather good friends. One day I commented to his mother, Sarah, how different the food (Tex-Mex?) was from what I was used to in the hills of North Carolina.

Paul looked up at me and said, "Reid, you've sure learned a lot since you've been down here in America, haven't you?"

My response: "Paul, spoken like a true Texan!"
Moral: We learn early to buy into the local jingoistic propaganda.

Paul had a little friend, Polly Filgo, in his Sunday-school class. One day after church she went promptly to her room, even before Sunday dinner. Shortly, her mother heard a crash and went running to Polly's room and saw her picking herself up off the floor.

"Polly, what in the world happened?"

"I fell."

"What were you doing?"

"I was closing the window blinds."

"Why were you doing that?"

"I get tired of Jesus and Santa Claus watching me all the time."
Moral: Who watches the watchers—God and the North Pole elves?

A Union College student of mine, Hap Cawood, was from Harlan, Kentucky, where many mine strikes and wars occurred. His father was a mining engineer. His mother was from Mississippi and related an experience she had had with Hap when he was eight.

It seems that Hap would invite the striking miners, who were from up the hollows or "the Lord knows where all", to have lunch with the Cawood family. If it was late evening, he would invite them to come in for the night and sleep on the living room floor.

His mamma said, "Hap, honey, you can't do that."

Hap said, "Why not, Mamma? That's what you said in Sunday school we should do—share our portion with the poor and outcasts."

"Yes, but Hap, honey, you just don't understand."

Moral: It's often difficult adjusting our actions to our (PPP) pronounced principled priorities.

When I was in India in 1962, one evening I went to the theatre in a new, only partially developed, part of New Delhi. After the theatre, I was rushing to the taxi stand two blocks away. There were no street lights between the theatre and the taxi stand, so I was hustling to get there. After all, I was in a foreign country, the mysteries of which evoked a certain amount of anxiety, particularly *under the cloak of darkness.*

Suddenly I heard beautiful flute music. I stopped—straining my eyes to see the source of these wonderful sounds in the moonless night. Gradually I became able to see a small boy sitting on a mound of new construction dirt, playing a traditional Indian flute. I listened to the impromptu concert for about five minutes—my anxiety having completely vanished.

I'm sure the small musician was unaware of his audience of one.

Moral: We're not always aware of what guests there may be or who's listening to the music.

In January 1972 I finished my PhD studies at the University of Wisconsin. It was in the middle of the school year, and my daughters shared with their schoolmates the good news of the completion of my doctorate. However, when their friends expressed amazement at this accomplishment of their father becoming a doctor, one of my daughters—or all of them—said, "Oh, he's the kind of doctor that doesn't do you any good."

Moral: Children are assigned to us to keep our feet on the ground even when our heads are in the clouds and we're soaring with winds of praise beneath our wings.

When my younger sister, Evelyn, was seven years old, she went into business of making and selling potholders from an endless supply of loopers (discarded nylon circles from the tops of nylon hosiery from Hanes Hosiery Mill). Daddy made her a little four-sided, eight-inch square wooden frame with ten nails on each side. Evelyn would stretch the multicolored nylon rings from one side to the other then weave from the other two sides ten loopers through the first ones.

She was dedicated to this project, weaving more than two dozen of the brightly colored pot holders of various designs. I don't believe that she sought anyone else's assistance or advice.

Early one morning—it was summertime—she took her merchandise out to the front yard under a small tree, which provided a little bit of shade. Next she hung her craft items, like colorful Christmas tree ornaments, from the branches of the young maple sapling, I had transplanted there a few years earlier. She had already made penciled signs on tablet paper, which she also hung on the tree facing the road. The signs announced "Potholders For Sale: 25 cents"

The road was a dirty, dusty, bumpy rural road with only a few cars traveling it each day. She sat there patiently all morning, came in for lunch, but hurried back out to her business.

The only car I remember coming by in the afternoon was Paul Starbuck in his old Mercury, going to work on the second shift at R. J. Reynolds Tobacco Company. She waved at Paul and he returned the greeting. He was already blowing his horn before he came into sight. This was his usual ritual—whether it was his friendliness or his pride in his car or his job, we never knew. Of course, he couldn't read her signs, nor could anyone else driving up the road.

At about five o'clock Evelyn dismantled the store, putting away her goods in a cardboard box and took down the signs.

She came in to supper but, without telling anyone what her plans were, she decided to close down the business and share the potholders as Christmas gifts.

Moral: How many adults can make such a commitment with unblemished hope and then have the courage, with only a small tear, to "know when to hold 'em and know when to fold 'em?"

That was the same summer I woke up in the middle of the night when I heard Evelyn open my bedroom door. I could observe that she was sleepwalking. She stood there, quietly at first, then said, "I'm here. I don't know why I'm here. I'm just here." I picked her up and put her back into her bed. Her only recollection of the event was what I told her the next morning.

Moral: Would that adults, fully awake, could candidly admit, "I'm here. I don't know why I'm here. I'm just here."

When I was studying in New York in 1958 I often rode the subway, which was a kind of education in itself. You wouldn't dare to make eye contact with anyone. Surface walking was impersonal enough, but everyone seemed to transform into zombies when they descended the steps into the filthy, smelly, earsplitting din of the underground transportation tunnels.

One day when I took the subway to Brooklyn I noticed a small black boy across the train, sitting with his grandmother and another woman. He had on brand-new polished shoes, a suit, white shirt and tie. He was excited and very much alive. As he kept up a perpetual monologue, his grandmother's face beamed in appropriately familial adulation.

When the train emerged from the underground onto the bridge to Brooklyn, the little fellow looked up at the sunlight and fairly shouted, "Wow! See Grandma what I told ya?"

Even though he had experienced it before, it was still a Wow for

him. The adults were looking at their watches and calculating how many minutes before their stop.
Moral: Follow the child to celebrate the WOW again.

When I was in college I often attended the churches with my father in the southern mountains of Virginia. One cold Sunday morning when I was seated on the second bench from the front—they weren't fancy enough to call them pews—I was sitting, shivering with a pair of fur-lined gloves, Grover Goins, a ten-year-old mountain boy sat down next to me. Grover was poorly dressed for winter—without gloves—but looked wonderingly at my gloves. I asked him if he would like to try them on. He nodded yes that he would. They were much too big for him, but he wore them for the rest of the morning. I often wonder what may have happened to Grover in the ensuing years.
Moral: And who will clothe the children?

In the same neighborhood, I was dating a beautiful girl, Alpha, who had a younger brother, Charlie, about four. One evening when I drove into their driveway to pick up Alpha to go to the movies, Charlie greeted me first with a question: "Weed, do you dot a dime?"

I said, "Charlie, I'm not sure I have a dime."

"Well, if you ain't dot a dime a twarter will do."

Many years later when I asked of the welfare of Charlie, I was informed that he was dead - murdered. Something to do with drugs!
Moral: Where is the innocence of the child who was?

When Clayton, my oldest grandson, was fourteen, he and I exchanged love poems. I read one of my poems about the love I still had for my former wife.

He asked, "Paw-Paw, do you still love Robin?"

"Yes, Clayton, unfortunately I do."

His quick response was, "Paw-Paw, it's not unfortunate to love. It's unfortunate not to have it returned."

Moral: Lessons are provided by the children. . . even the grandchildren.

One day when he was five, my youngest grandson, Theo, and I walked to a nearby park.

While we were chatting, we both noticed that someone had removed some swings from a metal trestle. He said, "Paw Paw, why did someone take the swings away?"

My honest answer was, "Theo, I don't know."

He looked at me quizzically. "Mommy said you were smart."

Moral: Be careful of the advance publicity.

When Theo's older sister, Alexis, was four, she attended a Fourth if July celebration with me and her parents. I became a little concerned when she recoiled so strongly at each fireworks blast.

When she noticed my concern, she said, "It' all right Paw Paw, Alexis likes being scared.

Moral: One can enjoy a little shot of adrenalin.

August 1996

My daughter, Adrienne, moved with her husband, Jesse, and the boys, Clayton and Sammy, to a new house in 1996. Sammy (age 4) was trying to memorize their new address, 333 South Street, DeForest. He would then be able to tell the police where to take him, if her were lost. After repeating the address several times, his mom asked him, "Where are we going to live?" His anser was, "DeCountry." He said, "DeCountry".

Moral: Well, isn't DeForest in DeCountry?

October 1996

Clayton (age 8) tells the people looking at the house across the street that he really likes his new school because they 'challenge' him and he likes that.
Moral: A little bit of challenge can be efficacious.

April 1997

I called Clayton a 'young man'. He corrected me, and said that the way he had been behaving, and not doing his schoolwork well, that he did not deserve to be called a young man. I should instead call him a young boy.
Moral: The right terminology for the appropriate time.

Sammy said. "I am a sensitive guy and I will always be a sensitive guy."
Moral: It's good to know how "to call 'em".

Sammy said, "It just doesn't feel right in my brain that kids get left home alone without a Mom or a Dad."
Moral: This old world could use some heartfelt empathy.

Clayton said, "Words can hurt. You can write a word on a board and hit someone with it."
Moral: The old adage "Sticks and stones may break my bones, but words will never harm me." Is only half- true. Words may not break bones, but may more disastrously break someone's heart or spirit.

Clayton, (age 7) said, "I'm stronger than Superman." When asked to prove that, he said, "All I have to do is turn off the TV, and he goes away."
Moral: An Important Announdement: To be repeated on every TV Channel every hour.

July 1997

I had to take Sammy to Urgent Care. We thought he had a broken bone in his foot. The nurse asked me if he was allergic to any drugs. Sammy said, quite indignantly, "I don't do drugs! I would be dead by now if I did!" Later, when the Dr. said it was not a break, Sammy insisted on seeing the 'pictures of his bones'. He examined them for a while then said, "Wow, you don't see that every day do ya." The Dr. chuckled.
Moral: One must relish the rare internal view.

August 1997

While driving through the mountains of West Virginia, Clayton announces from the back of the Van to his aunt Karen. "Karen, I think the objective is to go slowly."
Moral: One mustn't rush these things.

Sammy told Aunt Tari last night that he does not want her to get married. Because if she does, she will have kids and she won't play with him anymore. Tari said, "Well Karen has Alexis", and Sammy said, "See what I mean."
Moral: We must consider similar circumstances.

September 1997

I started complaining because the leaves were already falling from the Maple tree in the front yard. Sammy said, "But Mom if you look closely at the leaves they are very beautiful."
Moral: We always have a choice: Drugery or Beauty.

Sammy asked Clayton what to do when a kid is picking on you on the playground. Clay had been lying in bed. He got up and said, I need to get my examples. He hauled out a big T-Rex and two guys. He proceeded to explain, with demonstrations, how one guy might pick on the other guy. But, the T-Rex, hovering overhead, was a guardian angel. This angel makes sure that the guy who does something mean will have something mean done to him by somebody else. (What comes around goes around theory or karma.)
Moral: Be sure to locate your T-Rex.

October 1997

While I was folding clothes one day Sammy looked at me and said, "Mom you are my hero." I asked what prompted that. He said, "It's because you're the best Mom in the World to me."
Moral: We have to look at the world from our own POV.

Sammy still comes to our bed occasionally. After one rather restless night, I mentioned to him that he kicked me in the head twice during the early morning hours. He responded "Mom, you know I am very active when I sleep."
Moral: To be forewarned . . .

November 1997

Clayton and Sammy are having a discussion in the back of the van as I'm doing errands. Clayton is talking about when he gets married and has children. All of a sudden Sammy says, 'But what about me Clayton!?!' Clayton reassured him, "You can live on the first floor level of my house. That way we would see each other every day, and maybe you could watch my children at times."

"Okay I'll watch your kids two times, and then I'm going to be out on dates."

Moral: "A little bit of sugar MUST go a long way."

December 1997

I had to take Sammy to see Dr. McCabe regarding all of his nosebleeds. The Dr. suggested going to an ENT Doctor. "You need to see Dr. So&So because he is good with kids."

Sammy says, "How do you know he's good with kids? You're not a kid."

Dr. McCabe says, in kind of a sheepish voice, "Well, he is a friend of mine."

Moral: Friendship doesn't top one's life position.

January 1998

In 1998, Sammy (then age 5) was watching a movie with his mom. A woman in the movie asked a man for something. He kept saying, "No", until she said, "I love you." Sammy saind, "It's those three words that always gets us guys.

Moral: Our vulnerability is exposed.

The boys are on their way to the Dr. for allergy testing. The discussion is around how much the test may hurt. Clayton said, "Last week when I got my filling, when it started to hurt I just squeezed my 'cookies' really hard so I didn't concentrate too much on the tooth. So if the allergy tests hurt, just grab your cookies and squeeze!"

Moral: A bit of distraction may at times be in order.

February 1998

I baby-sat my co-worker, Luanne's 2 month old. When she was dropping him off she warned me that he had gas on the way over to

our house. Clayton said, "That's okay, my Mom is used to guys with gas." Sammy wanted to hold the baby and see how much he weighed. He proclaimed, "He's 2 pounds and a feather."
Moral: Let's be precise here.

I took the boys in to get their haircut. Sammy was very pleased with his decision. The following day I had the boys get ready to go out. Sammy came downstairs with his hair wet and combed nicely into place. I told him, "You did a great job on your hair.
He touched his hair and said "I've never had hair this beautiful."
Moral: We should acknowledge beauty wherever we find it.

While watching a movie, a guy was tied to a pole awaiting execution (Pocahontas Disney movie) Sammy said, "His butt cheeks must be tight, when you're really scared your butt cheeks get really tight."
Moral: The point is not to get too scared or your butt cheeks will get overworked.

October 1998

We found out that Grandpa has terminal bladder cancer.
Clayton said, "I want Grandpa to go for more walks in the woods with me, but I know Grandpa is suffering. It wouldn't be fair for me to want Grandpa to live longer just for me because it would make him suffer more."
Moral: Grandpa's pain takes precedence over my hoped-for joy.

Clayton said that he feels sorry for his cousins. "I know how final death is since Grandma Lu died, but my cousins don't know how final it really is yet."

Moral: If we could only prepare others for the finality of the life of a loved one!

December 1998

We got a new puppy. While Sammy and Clay were playing with him, the dog, Willie, started humping Sammy's leg. Sammy said, "Does that mean we are married?"
Moral: But no one's made any promises yet.

The boys went to get haircuts. Two of Sammy's favorite foods are chili and baloney sandwiches. He asked for a chili bowl cut, rather than a bowl cut. Being very pleased with his hair cut, he asked me to comb his hair. I didn't comb it quite the way he liked and he looked in the mirror and said, "This doesn't look like a baloney sandwich."
Moral: It would be nice to get somewhere close to the mark.

February 1999

I'm talking with Jess on the phone and call him Babes. After I hang up Sammy says, "You shouldn't call Dad 'Babes' any more. It sounds too sexual." Mike is here and says "I like to call Amelia 'Babes' ". Sammy says, "That's okay, because Meli is not my Mom."
Moral: One's mom must be more circumspect than some else's mom.

March 1999

Sammy wants to know how come Daddy gets to cuddle with Mom every night and he doesn't—"It is just not fair."
Moral: Aren't kids as important as grown-ups?

August 1999

Sammy said, "My teacher is on the edge of the paper of being nice."
Moral: It's nice to know that she's almost there.

September 1999

During the summer I bought the boys journals. At dinner recently I asked the guys, How about your journals? I've noticed that you haven't written in them in a long time. Clayton has said he needed his to write down his feeling. "Sammy what did you originally intend for your journal?"
"So I could write down about my food."
Moral: It's important to keep one's priorities straight.

November 1999

Clayton passed a burning candle, then went back and took a long whiff and said, "That smells like Molly's hair." So Sammy came over to smell the candle then proclaimed, "I'll bet she's pretty, like a horse."
Moral: Beauty is in the eye of the beholder.

Clayton had a 3-D cell science project due. I suggested that in homework club he start working on a model as a kind of prototype, so that once I got the necessary materials, we could just quickly put it together. As we were sitting at the table assembling the cell, Clayton asked, "How did I end up with you and Dad as parents?" I thought he was joking and told him he just ended up with the short straw. Again, he said, "But how did I end up with you two as my parents?"
I wasn't sure where he was going with this. "That was just the way things happened."
Then he surprised me and said, "I would never have thought by

myself to put together a blue print before working on the cell, and it made it much easier. I think a lot of my friends could use parents like you."
Moral: Sometimes we just luck out.

January, 2000

Some kid was giving Clayton a hard time about being Mexican. Clayton's response to him was, "well, at least I have a future."
Moral: An insult can be answered with a bit of candor.

Sammy was not too happy with me for missing one of his soccer games, then he found out I was about to start ballet classes one night a week. He said, "Mom, you're breaking up the family."
Moral: Broken families are so sad.

Jess was telling the boys about his high school gym teacher who was well built with great muscle definition. Sammy said," Yeah, but I bet he picked his nose."
Moral: Nobody's perfect.

March 2000

Sammy heard that he was going to Hunter's house after school. He put his arm around Hunter's neck and said, "Cool, I get to spend some quality time with my Bud."
Moral: Quality time must be claimed.

July 2000

Sammy was climbing in a tree at Grandma's. I had to help Jesse find something around the opposite side of the barn. I told Sammy where

I would be just in case there was a problem. He said "Fine, if I have a problem you know where I'll be, under the tree."
Moral: Just to be forewarned.

August 2000

Sammy didn't want to go grocery shopping with me. I said, "You'll love Woodman's since it is full of food." He said, "If it's full of baked beans and chips, it would be paradise."
Moral: Everything in its place.

May 2001

Sammy said, "Moms are delicate and strong and Dads are just strong." I asked him where he got that from and he said he had just been thinking about it.
Moral: *Vive la difference!*

October 2001

The boys have physicals scheduled for late afternoon. I am just about to leave my office when I get a call from Clayton. He asks, "Is the Dr. going to touch my balls? I don't want her touching my balls." I told him he should call his Dad to find out. Later on at the Dr.'s office he said, "You don't need to my touch balls, because I touched them last night, and they were FINE."
Moral: Self-assessment is good.

At the doctor's office, Clayton was asked by the nurse after taking his height and weight, "is there anything else, we should go over?" Clayton answered, "My brother spaces out a lot."
Moral: It's good to know these things in advance.

Sam and I are sitting in the waiting room at the Dr. office. Out comes a couple from a 1-week infant check. They look tired; nothing is tucked in, no make-up, etc. They probably were just happy they made it in. Sammy looks at me and says, "They aren't the best looking couple are they?"
Moral: That experience will come much later.

December 2001

Sam says, "Watch how I can make my butt look like a brain." He pulls his pants down and squeezes his buns together, and indeed it looks like a brain. He shows us and his Aunt Tari with great pride.
Moral: One must be allowed to show one's assets.

February 2002

Clayton keeps asking for another snake. I tell him, "I'm looking for you to mature a little more before I can agree to that."

He says, "Mom I did some shoveling without being asked and I let you and Sam go to the Mall without me when I was feeling sick one day. I don't know how much more mature I can be."
Moral: Maturity is to be claimed and acknowledged.

Sammy said "Mom I love you so much, I love Dad so much, and I love Clayton so much. I love you more than I love my vocabulary."
Moral: It's nice to know where one stands in the order of things

PART V
THE CHURCH

My life in the church has been influenced by the community where I lived as well as from the beliefs of my grandfather, Elder Noel B. Gilbert. I must admit that my religious beliefs have also been influenced by my graduate studies in Asian Theatre. Although I have received a master's degree in religious Drama from Union Seminary, my understanding of Religious Drama comes from Asia.

There are three audiences in Asian Theatre; the audience in the seated area of the theatre and the audience shared on stage. However the most important audience is the ancestors and the gods. When people ask me why I left the ministry, my answer is, "I didn't . . . I simply expanded it."

MY METHODIST ROOTS AND MY METHODIST DISCONNECT

Some of the happiest, as well as serious, moments in my childhood and teenage years, were in the Methodist church. Even though we moved often until I was nine, my family and I always seemed to connect with a Methodist Church; in Sunday school, summer revivals, Boy Scouts, choir practice, Wednesday night prayer meetings, Vacation Bible School. Each of these activities gave me my early exposure to educational inquiry, public speaking, music, leadership, collaborative work, spiritual training and even dramatic experience in the annual Christmas plays.

It was natural then for me to choose Methodist colleges: Brevard Jr. College for an AA in English (1951), Duke University for a BA in Sociology (1953) and Southern Methodist University Perkins School of Theology (1956) for a ThM. My STM in Religious Drama was earned at Union Seminary and later a PhD in Asian Theatre at the University of Wisconsin.

As I was finishing my study at Perkins, I was told by a classmate, Jack Hampton, of an opportunity at the First Methodist Church in South Bend, Indiana. Jack had already arranged for an interview for himself as Minister of Education and suggested that I apply for the position of Associate Minister. Having chosen not to return to North Carolina to take a traditional pastorate, I was hoping to return to graduate school in a few years.

After arranging for an interview, I packed my things and drove with Jack to South Bend in June of 1956.

We were both accepted for the respective positions.

In October I traded in my little black '54 Ford for a brand new Dodge Coronet hardtop, which I assured myself would be paid for by the time I would be ready for more graduate study in four years.

I was told by a church member that the car was too fancy for a minister. I knew not to get a red car, because that would be inappropriate in a funeral cortege.

It was a new experience for me to work in a large city church, as my earlier church experiences had been in smaller rural churches, but everything seemed to go well . . . in my spiritual, professional and social life. I thoroughly enjoyed my experience there working with various groups within the church, even serving as First Methodist's representative on the St. Joseph County Council of Churches. I occasionally preached as well as conducted wedding and funeral services, until . . . In May 1957 the South Bend Methodist District Superintendent, Dr. Coble, called, requesting that I come by for a visit. I readily agreed, as there was nothing unusual to have occasional meetings with the district superintendent, who represented the bishop in appointing pastors to specific churches and who also served as the local pastor's pastor.

At the meeting, Dr. Coble cut right to the chase by telling me that he would be moving me to another church in Indiana. I was shocked at such an *ex cathedra* decision in the Methodist hierarchy without any discussion with me except the abrupt announcement, itself, and after less than nine months.

I, of course, immediately asked what was the rationale for his decision, as I was enjoying the work and the people at First Methodist. I inquired if there had been any complaints from any of the parishioners or the pastor or the Council of Churches on which I served. He assured me that my work was exemplary with accolades from all concerned.

It was then he hit me with the brickbat of his rationale. "We're having to move you because of Jack's problem."

"What do you mean by Jack's problem?"

"You may not be aware that Jack is homosexual, but he is seeing a psychiatrist regularly."

"I had no idea Jack had a problem, but what does this have to do with me?"

"As you and Jack are both unmarried, Rev. Hemphill, Bishop

Raines, Mr. Mossberg (chairman of the pastoral relations committee) and I feel it would be best for both you and Jack, that you not both be appointed to the same church, and as Jack is making progress with his healing, it seemed best to move you to another parish."

"You mean to tell me that all of you knew about this situation when I was appointed at First Methodist, but no one had the decency, let alone Christian values, to inform me of this situation until now . . . when all of you in your spiritual wisdom have decided what to do with me and my life? If I were given the opportunity to choose to serve on the same ministerial staff with Jack, I would no doubt have opted for that, but you have put me in an extremely compromising situation. Do you realize that, as there was no parsonage for either of us, Andy arranged for each of us to have a housing allowance, urging us to rent a house together, which we did?"

"I'm sorry, but I didn't know about that."

"I'm sorry, but I will not accept another appointment in this manner. I will take this opportunity to attempt to return to graduate school even though I have a heavy debt with the car I bought recently."

"Please don't say anything to Jack about the circumstances in which you're leaving, as we want to assist him in his further progress. I'm sure he'd be very upset to know that you would be leaving because of him."

"I'm not leaving because of him. I'm leaving because some pontifical church fathers have decided the course of my life for me and apparently for Jack."

I immediately left Rev. Coble's office and tracked down the Rev. Andy Hemphill at the hospital where he was visiting a church member. Andy assured me that all this was being done for Jack's benefit and that he knew I'd do well in whatever position I would be placed. He, being an amateur psychologist, opined, "I had felt that you would provide a male balance to Jack's problem."

I then recalled, but not mentioning it to him, that when we had gone on a trip together to *bond* in our working relationship, Andy wanted to save money and rented single rooms with two double beds. As he was rather large, he suggested that Jack and I share a bed. *What the devil was in his mind when he urged that?* Fortunately nothing untoward happened in our shared bed, except sleep.

Before leaving South Bend I was able to contact Union Seminary in New York, obtaining both admittance and scholarship for their religious drama master's program.

I had three weeks before leaving and only told Jack I was lucky to get into this new program at Union Seminary. In the meantime, I had wondered why Jack's degree from SMU had not been conferred, and he had kept telling me that he had an incomplete which he had not finished. It then occurred to me that Perkins Seminary knew of Jack's *problem* and couldn't afford to confer a Bachelor of Divinity degree on a homosexual.

On my way out of South Bend I stopped in Indianapolis to talk with Bishop Richard Raines, who had been aware of this situation the whole time and had delayed my application into full membership in the Indiana Conference without ever telling me why there had been a delay. His response to me was the same as the other Methodist authorities. They all wished me well and prayed that I'd have no lingering grudges against the situation and their impact on my life's calling in the ministry of the church.

A month after I left South Bend, Jack was given his walking papers and was told that I left because of *his problem*. When he contacted me, he asked why I had not told him of the real reason I was leaving. My response was that I was told by the DS it would interfere with Jack's progress if I discussed it with him. He was devastated to hear this.

We corresponded a couple of times after that, and the last I heard from him he was selling Fuller Brushes in San Francisco. How tragically—and even spiritually ironic— that San Francisco welcomed Jack, even though the Methodist Church and Perkins School of Theology had rejected him.

I still wonder how Christian church authorities can make such exclusive judgment calls in the name of the One who said, "Come unto me all ye that labor and are heavy laden . . . "

As school wasn't starting in NY until September I drove back to Dallas and worked as a life guard in a day camp. That whole summer remains a void in my memory bank, as I was so traumatized by being unexpectedly trapped in this bizarre ecclesiastical vise by officials of the Methodist Church, which I had loved so well.

I did return to First Methodist the next December and married Luan Miller, who was on the staff of the South Bend YWCA.

I went on to serve small Methodist churches while in graduate schools and taught for six years in Methodist colleges.

To add insult to injury, when I applied for pension benefits from the Methodist Church, I was told that although I had seventeen years of Methodist service. I was credited with only nine years and ten years was necessary to be vested for a pension in the Memphis Conference which was the last conference in which I had served, while teaching at Lambuth College in Tennessee.

In order to reconcile the difference between the 17 years of service and 9 years of investiture, I checked on the record. I discovered that the treasurer of Union College had contributed to only one year, instead of the three, toward my pension credit.

It was then too late for the church to reconcile with me, as they informed me, "We don't review any pension issues prior to 1982." I wonder what they do with other superannuated octogenarians.

It would be decent if they could locate Jack, if he is still living, and apologize to him and insist that Southern Methodist University confer his theology degree.

This bureaucratic entitlement was not as egregious as that of the Roman Church, but the autocratic action has impacted Jack for life.

I daresay that my path was drastically altered, as I sought other (non-Methodist) avenues for spiritual sustenance and creative involvement.

* * *

P.S. After I shared this with my oldest daughter in San Diego, she was interested in locating Jack Hampton, but the only Jack Hampton she was able to locate in Texas was, ironically, a judge who had pronounced that "Homosexuals are in the same category as prostitutes."

MY BLACK HEART
Or
GROWING UP WHITE

"Mamma, why are there two school buses?"
"One's for the colored children, and one for the white children."
"Yes, I know that, but why?"

"Mamma, when Aunt Effie comes to help when you're sick, why don't we eat together?"
"Aunt Effie is colored."
"Yes, I know that, but why?"

"Mamma, why do we have to call Mrs. Gray, Lucy, when she's older than you are?
"Honey, Lucy is colored."
"Yes, I know that, but why?'

Harry Golden was the publisher and editor of *The Carolina Israelite* and wrote often of the strange phenomenon of segregation. He editorialized that one of the problems was the act of sitting down. Blacks could be served in restaurants as long as they didn't sit down. He thought that the patrons of the eating establishments wouldn't have to be segregated if everyone simply stood to eat. He called it the "vertical plan".

Another problem was the segregated public facilities, such as water fountains. He suggested that in the hot summer dog days someone should put an out-of-order sign on the "white only" public drinking fountain in the courthouse. It wouldn't be long until the white citizens would be drinking from the "colored only" drinking fountain and finding that the water was just about the same.

One reporter wrote, "If Harry Golden isn't careful, he'll laugh segregation right out of existence."

My parents attempted to fit in with the accepted racial-social mores of the southern state where we lived. However Daddy would have punished us kids more severely for mistreating the neighbor black children than the whites, because he said, "They are already down-trodden enough without us making life any harder."

Grandma Gilbert lived in town and always hired a large black woman to help in the kitchen of her boarding house. When I was about four, we were having breakfast at Grandma's, and her new cook, Black Nancy, asked me, "Little white boy, what does you want to drink for breakfuss?"

No one had ever asked me what I wanted to eat or to drink, so I figured I had reached my majority, so I should have what other adults have. "I'll have coffee."

Black Nancy looked at me and said, "Little white boy, if you drinks that black stuff, you'll get as black as I is."

There was a lot of black there. "I'll have milk."

Both blacks and whites contributed to the racial stereotype, even though the balance was terribly uneven and uneasy.

Dick Gregory observed that "In the South they don't care how close we get, just don't get too big, and in the North they don't care how big we get, just don't get too close."

The South substantiated this observation by carefully monitoring the body language, particularly that of black men who learned how to lower their head and shuffle backwards to show their humble demeanor, as they mumbled, "Yassuh!" or "Yassum!" In the North, neighborhoods, rooming houses and hotels maintained strict regulations to prevent Blacks from getting too close. Of course, not all encounters were contentious. My brother had a black co-worker who told him, "Art if you wuz black one Saturday night, you never would wanta be white again."

As a teenager, I would raise questions about these strange arrangements, I was told, "They're just fine as long as they stay in their place."

My obvious question—with never an adequate answer—was, "What is their place? And what is my place?"

When I attended Duke University I saw that there were plenty of blacks, but they were only maids and janitors . . . not even basketball players.

Continuing my questions, I enrolled in a Sociology of the South class. In some of my research there were numerous horror stories. A really bizarre one was of a North Carolina politician. Whenever he would visit his home town, he would always go visit the old black woman who had been his wet nurse. But he clung to his segregational demagoguery even while attempting to honor his black mammy.

Durham was the capital of black capitalism in America with three large corporations, started by an ex-slave, Mr. C. C. Spaulding. After my sociology class visited the Spaulding Bank, run primarily by blacks, we returned to our seminar room. One of the girls from Georgia was so impressed with the apparent efficiency of the tellers that she exclaimed, "Why, they were running all those typewriter and calculators just like . . . just like . . . well, like people."

As the focus of a final term paper, I chose to research the legal case of black children against the Durham County Board of Education, which occurred two years before the *Brown vs. Topeka Board of Education* litigation. The attorney for the children was John Wheeler who was also the vice-president of the black-operated bank.

Mr. Wheeler met with me twice, discussing at length his tactics in winning the case. I recall that his definition of leadership was simply, "Be in front of the people where they can see and hear you, but not so far in front that they can't see and hear you."

He even let me borrow the only copy he had of his brief, which outlined and detailed the discrepancies between the white and black students in the school district. He had accounted for the number of students per drinking fountain and the number of gymnasium square feet per student. Even as a non-law student, I knew it would have been foolhardy to try to outmaneuver this documentation.

In order to have some balance in my term paper I thought I ought to interview the principal defendant, Dr. Stacy Weaver, the Superintendent of the Durham County Public Schools. After successfully scheduling a meeting, I arrived early at Dr. Weaver's office, only to be kept cooling my heels for more than an hour.

After I shared with him the focus of my visit, he wasted no time in informing me, "You schoolboys think you can solve these complicated education issues by writing papers."

I explained, "I hadn't thought I would be solving any problems. I'm just writing a term paper on an issue which I thought was important." I felt like crawling out of his office.

Several years later when I was looking for employment on a small liberal arts college faculty, I received a letter from the President of North Carolina Methodist College inviting me for an interview. It was signed, Dr. Stacy Weaver.

I had the poetic pleasure of rejecting the interview by reviewing our earlier encounter years earlier and stating, "I would not be comfortable serving on a faculty under the administration of a president who has such disdain for basic scholarly research even if a sensitive racial issue."

In the summer of 1952 while attending Duke, I worked at RJ Reynolds Tobacco Company, inspecting cigarettes and taking 1300 of them off a conveyor belt every minute. I observed to the foreman, "The only Negroes working here are janitors. Why aren't there any inspecting cigarettes?"

He said, "You know, they're not very bright. They wouldn't be able to do this work."

"Why, this is the most mindless job in the world. Handing green tobacco leaves at the tobacco barn, takes a higher IQ than this."

"Well, I'll be honest with you. If you let those black SOBs start getting these jobs you white boys would be outta work, 'cause they'd work a whole lot cheaper than you boys."

I didn't argue with him, knowing him to be right.

After graduating from Duke in 1953 I attended Perkins Seminary at SMU, which had just started integrating the student body. Of course, they started the process in the seminary because we religious types would be more tolerant and accepting.

One of my friends there was a large black student, Jim Hawkins. One day, he and I were heading to downtown Dallas. We chatted while waiting for the city bus. However, when we boarded the bus, we couldn't continue our conversation; he went to the back of the bus, while I sat at the front. I lacked the courage of a Rosa Parks.

During seminary on weekends I served as youth minister in the First Methodist Church of Lancaster, Texas. During those years, attention was given to the racial situation in the churches once a year and called Race Relations Sunday, as close to Lincoln's birthday as possible.

In February 1954 I was asked by the nearby African Methodist Episcopal Church to deliver the sermon for them on Race Relations Sunday. That was a normal thing to do . . . exchange pulpits on that special Sunday. I happily accepted, though with fear and trembling, because I was so new to conducting worship services and had never attended a service in a black church.

The service began calmly with the regular minister leading the singing, taking up offerings (three, in fact), leading the prayers of supplication and sharing the concerns of the community of the faithful. I was intrigued with the energy and sense of celebration, as I sat on the pulpit rostrum.

It was nearly noon by time for me to read the scripture and expound upon it. I had selected a passage from Exodus, because I knew many Negro spirituals were often about leaving Egypt and traveling toward the Promised Land. I read Chapter 14, with particular focus on the 12th verse, which recorded the Israelites' complaints to Moses, "Let us alone that we may serve the Egyptians. For it had been better for us to serve the Egyptians, than that we should die in the wilderness."

By the time I started reading the biblical passage, the pastor had started tapping his foot on the dais behind me and softly murmuring, "Yeah, Amen!" This unnerved me at first, until people in the congregation started doing the same thing. I took a deep breath, attempting to get on the same wavelength as the other brothers and sisters.

My remarks started by reminding everyone, "Now we all know about those Egyptian slave masters and what terrible things they had done to the Hebrew children, so I'm not gonna talk about them. The Lord will take care of them in His own way . . . in His own time. No, we gonna talk about those Israelites who were scared . . . and complaining . . . and wanting to turn back . . . and didn't want to listen to Moses or his brother Aaron, emissaries of the Lord God, himself. They wanted to stay in the comfort of slavery, and brothers and sisters, I'm afraid even today too often . . . too many of us want to stay in the comfort of slavery and forget about the comforting arms of freedom."

By the time I had become comfortable with the audible feedback to my reading and speaking, I was able to utilize the energy coming my way from the congregation. The responses never died out. *Amen . . . You tell 'em brotha . . . Dat's de way it is.* But when a point was weak or not completely understood, the volume would amp down, so I knew to back up and reiterate that proposition from another direction.

The service lasted until 2 o'clock, still in time for fried chicken, biscuits and gravy. The whole experience was as though I had been uplifted on the wings of a band of black angels.

This was only three months before the Supreme Court would be handing down the verdict of *Brown vs. Topeka Board of Education*. In the same month of my experience in the AME Church, I reminded my white congregation in a Sunday evening worship service that the Supreme Court decision on school segregation would soon be made, and that there was no option but to integrate the nation's schools. Several of my white congregants were unhappy with my political prognostication.

After SMU I took a position as associate pastor of the First

Methodist Church in South Bend, Indiana. The senior pastor, Andy Hemphill, was originally from McAllen, Texas. The year before I arrived in South Bend, Andy had welcomed into the church a black woman and her teenage daughter. He was nearly fired by the church for doing such an audacious thing, and the political intentions of the woman and her daughter were under serious suspicion. The matter had calmed down by the time I had arrived there in 1956.

Andy assigned me to represent the church on the St. Joseph County Council of Churches. One of the projects for the Council was to plan the program for the annual Brotherhood Week, which had come to replace Race Relations Sunday. At the meeting when the outline for the Brotherhood Week was reported, I discovered that plans were afoot to have a speaker come from Americus, Georgia, to report on the vandalism there at the racially integrated farm operated by the Fellowship of Reconciliation. There would be a large meeting of people from all churches, both black and white, to convene at the Central High School Auditorium, which was the only indoor space in South Bend large enough to hold the anticipated crowd.

After hearing the details of the plan, I asked "Is that it?"

The chairman replied, "What do you mean?"

"Are you simply going to have a speaker come here to tell us of the awful conditions in Georgia and take up an offering for the Fellowship of Reconciliation? The race relations are terrible there, and we should be aware of that, but Americus, Georgia is a thousand miles away. You all know very well that the main hotel in town does not allow black patrons, and the same is true for most of the restaurants. Even the churches represented here are still segregated."

The chairman asked, "What would you have us do?"

My answer: "I'm new here and I certainly can't tell you what to do, but I would urge you at least to face the fact that there is a serious disharmony in race relations here."

With the approval of the rest of the Council representatives the chairman named an ad hoc committee, appointing me as chairman of it. To the committee he then appointed Dan Fowler, the white minister of the First Presbyterian Church, and Eurilla Wills, a black social worker from the YWCA.

However, we met and began the proceedings in a rather friendly fashion. Soon one of us suggested that we examine the official race relations statements made by each of the denominations on the Council. We tweaked that a bit to recommend that:

> *Any church in good standing with the St. Joseph County Council of Churches must demonstrate that an educational program for all ages be established to acquaint their church members of the statement their own church denomination has made on the subject of race relations and the brotherhood of all believers.*

This resolution was adopted at the next Council meeting. I left shortly after that to enroll at Union Seminary in New York, but that summer I returned to South Bend and visited Eurilla. I asked her how the Council had implemented our resolution.

She said, "They didn't."

"But they passed it at the May meeting."

"Yes, but you left town . . . You weren't here to push."

Several years later I was teaching at Lambuth College in Jackson, Tennessee, just 80 miles east of Memphis, when Martin Luther King, JR. was assassinated. My wife and I joined the racially mixed march of grief.

It was also in Jackson where I met Sister Willie Mae Tyger, a black woman who had organized the Fite's Bottom Improvement Association to address the issues of that black neighborhood of dilapidated, substandard houses inhabited by blacks and owned by white landlords who couldn't fix them up because of a city ordinance which allowed the houses to be rented but not repaired or even painted.

Sister Willie Mae, not only the founder of the Association, but also the protectress of her neighbors, would march onto City Hall and confront whatever official she could find, whether mayor or chief of police, to deliver her grievance. A marvelous human being with compassion for the whole town!

Moving ahead several more years, I was in Wisconsin and participating in the summer programs of the Uplands Arts Council. Martha Smith, a tall redhead from Texas, had arranged for Fannie Lou Hamer to come and speak in Madison. She also brought her out to speak to a group of us in a hayfield next to the Uplands Art Gallery Barn.

I had never before met this stalwart of the civil rights movement, but was captivated by her stories of the injustices done to her family —even the killing of the family's mule when she was a little girl. Such a dastardly act was tantamount to starving a poor black family. As she recounted her stories, there was no sense of self-pity or hatred in her demeanor. When she started leading us in singing "We Shall Overcome," I was literally overcome and had to escape to the other side of the barn where no one could see my white tears for my black sister. I wasn't about to quote any scripture to her.

Fannie Lou Hamer had organized civil rights events, including voter registration, in Sunflower County, Mississippi, where many marches were held. At the rally for Fannie Lou I met a minister who had been on the marches and had returned to Wisconsin with several stories for sermon material. He prided himself on being "Wanted in Sunflower County."

I told him, "I would think one would want to go where one was really wanted."

He didn't see the value of my comment; after all he had a lot of sermon illustrations from his experiences there, but he didn't have to remain and work at improving the situation.

It was in the same decade—the sixties—when James Farmer, a black Mississippian enrolled in Ole Miss, thereby testing the civil rights waters. Activist students at the University of Wisconsin wanted to encourage him in his brave venture, so they set up a table in the Memorial Union with various materials about Farmer and the civil rights movement.

Seeing a stack of postcards on the table, I asked what their purpose was. I was told, "They're to send a message of support for James Farmer in his effort to integrate the University of Mississippi."

I said, "That's a wonderful idea, as he is the only one who could have done it. No white or black outside the state could have done it. I'll certainly send him a postcard, supporting his stand . . . "But what's the purpose of the offering plate?"

"That's to raise money to send Freedom Fighters to Mississippi."

"What're they going to do down there?"

"They're going to march and demonstrate against the injustices."

"Have you seen the new documentary film, exposing the landlords of student housing here in Madison and the techniques they have been using to prevent Jews and Negroes from renting from them?"

"Oh, yes!"

"What is your group doing about it?"

"Well, we feel that we can accomplish a whole lot more by being diplomatic and dealing with the problem quietly and patiently."

Pounding on the table, causing the stack of postcards to tumble over, I said, "That's the same damn thing the folks in Mississippi are saying. Now if you can go down there and demonstrate you can park your asses on State Street and march from Bascom Hill to the capitol, demanding redress to this injustice to Jewish and black students here in Madison in the enlightened state of Wisconsin."

By this time, a crowd had gathered around to listen to this street preacher (*moi*), so I thought I'd give them their money's worth . . . even though I hadn't yet taken up a freewill offering. I thought it was time for a bit of scripture: "And Jesus said, *Why beholdest thou the mote in thy brother's eye, but perceivest not the beam in thine own eye?*"

No one started "amening" or "hallelujahing," so the congregation started leaving even without a benediction.

When I would discuss these things with my friends and kin in the South, they would simply say, "Oh well, they're just all hypocrites up North."

"They may be hypocrites up there, but where are you in your response to Jesus' admonition to *"set at liberty them that are bruised?"*

Tip O'Neill once observed, "All politics is local," and we have often heard, "Charity begins at home." It is also true that we must act responsibly in race relations, both in action and attitude, where we live, even while apprising ourselves of the progress or lack, thereof, in other parts of the globe.

It is always easier to see someone else's burden which they carry on their back than to see our burdens carried on our own backs; even if we're bent over with the weight.

In response to them all, I offer a couple of couplets:

> *Oh, what hypocrites we mortals be*
> *When what's for me is not for thee*
> *And when there's need we both see*
> *It's for thee and for me.*

I neglected to mention that after my Race Relations service in February 1954, the black pastor told my colleague at the white church, "He may have a white skin, but his heart is just as black as mine."

Now, in retrospect, I must admit my fear at the time of Black Nancy's warning about the coffee turning my skin black, but I hope I value my black brother's estimation that my *heart is just as black* as his.

RIBSIDE OF THE RELIGIOUS LIFE

Never let it be said that ecclesiastical life is only spiritual and without humor, and at times downright irreverent.

When I was five years old. Mr. Styers would walk with me and my sister, Della Sue to Sunday school at Marvin Chapel Methodist Church.

One Sunday we stayed for the regular worship service:

AMEN

Eyes closed
Head tilted forward
Feet dangling off the floor
Rump squirming ever so slightly on the hard oak pew

Ears listening
Five-tear old brain waiting
Waiting for the reverend voice to end
To end the prayer, that called on the Dear Lord above
To forgive, to bless, to sanctify, to heal, to comfort the pew sitters

The end is always Amen
But he hasn't amened his end
Others have amened again and again
Ol' Man Styers yelled his amens over and over

The preacher of the morning didn't heed
Amen suggestions to end the longwinded prayer
Until a squeaky voice clamored a loud AMEN aloud

As silence hovered over the Sunday congregants

> Closed eyes opened
> Bowed heads turned toward me
> I looked up
> That cry for relief
> Didn't come from me

Did it?

    The Methodist churches in Texas, at that time, provided and furnished the parsonage for their pastor. The women's society at Lancaster Methodist purchased a new mattress for the master bedroom. Surely they were adequately thanked, but in a small gathering of the Board of Trustees, Sarah, the minister's wife, mentioned the new bed equipment. "We really do appreciate the new mattress. (Speaking directly to her husband) Have you noticed, Neyland that the bed doesn't squeak anymore?"

    Immediate titters could scarcely be hidden.

    Being aware of the implications of her statement, she tried quickly to put her statement in a proper context. "I mean when I sit on the edge of the bed to put on my shoes, there is no squeaking."

    She had tried, but to no avail. The damage had been done to the propriety of the meeting that evening.

    After seminary, I served for one year as Associate Minister of the First Methodist Church in South Bend, IN. My leaving, after only one year, wasn't fully explained to the congregation, who had difficulty wishing me on my way to return to graduate school at Union Seminary in NYC. One small boy at the farewell reception knew exactly what to say. He and I had been successful in capturing a bat which had been terrorizing the ladies in the Ladies Aid Society meeting in the Fellowship Hall. (That church had a lot of bats in the belfry.) I heard my young friend say to his mother as they stood in line to wish me Godspeed, "You know Mom, I think he's the best bat-catching preacher

I've ever met." That was one of my memorable ministerial accolades.

When I was serving that church I bought a brand new car, hoping to have it completely paid for by time I left for graduate school. It was a black and turquoise 1957 Dodge hardtop with those newly acquired fins. One of the young church ladies stunned me by seriously saying, "I don't think it's really appropriate for a Methodist minister to have a car like that." I knew the unwritten rule that forbade ministers from having red cars, because it would be unseemly leading a funeral cortege to the cemetery. I suppose those fins, though black, were also too flashy for ministerial demeanor pursuing pastoral duties.

It sometimes takes a while to decode the unwritten rules, like making sure the terribly uncomfortable donated chair to the parsonage must always remain in its assigned place in the northeast corner of the parsonage living room. A self-appointed member, usually the granddaughter of the deceased member who donated the chair, will check on its position every time a committee meeting is held there.

While at Union Seminary in NYC, I served Eastside Terrace Methodist Church, a small church in Paterson, NJ. It was the first home for my bride, Luan, and me. One Sunday after the church service had ended, Hector Young commented to me, "It looked as though Luan was wearing a maternity dress this morning."

I assured him that he was indeed correct and that we were "expecting" and noted that his young wife was also wearing "expectant" clothing.

His response was, "Yeah, but I didn't think that kind of thing happened in the Methodist parsonage."

Everyone understands that for Catholics the virgin birth, nearly 2000 years ago, was a really big deal—a once-ever miracle. Methodists continue to expect more virgin births in the Methodist parsonages.

Eastside Terrace had ninety-nine members and every time that I thought we would find the hundredth sheep with a newly enrolled member, an older member would have just previously unceremoniously passed away.

The church was an old frame building with twelve rickety front steps leading from the Vreeland Avenue sidewalk up to the vestibule. Some Methodist ministers, who are excellent at raising funds for new magnificent buildings, are said to have an "edifice complex." It was evident that no such pastor had ever served this congregation.

The Board of Trustees discussed the need for new front stairs, at least for safety reasons. One of the members even fantasized about something more attractive than wooden stairs . . . brick perhaps. We decided to ask Bill Touw, one of the church members who was a professional mason, if he could lay brick steps for the front of the church. He said that he'd be happy to do so and would donate his labor, but under one condition. He said, "As we're heading into the heat of the summer it would be a good time to add the steps, but the only way I can work in such humidity is to imbibe in a few beers during the heat of the day."

The Board agreed on Bill's caveat, even though the Methodists at that time were proud of their pledge of total abstinence. They seemed to understand that even faith-based communities must at times make some compromises with the world to accomplish needed tasks.

One of the church members was a beautiful 24-year-old blonde who attended almost every Sunday with her parents Tom and Mary Brown. Jennifer's lovely blonde tresses were accompanied with the blonde stereotype of ditziness.

One Sunday, as she and her parents were about to descend Bill Touw's new brick steps, she shook my hand and looking deeply into my eyes, she asked quite innocently but suggestively, "Reverend Gilbert, would you marry me?"

Looking into her eyes, I facetiously suggested, "Well I'll have to ask my first wife first, but I'm sure she'll agree."

Without catching the joke but with innocent approbation, she answered, "Well, all right then. I'll give you a call this week."

I officiated at the lovely wedding, and she appropriately married someone other than myself.

Due to praises from their parishioners for their priestly responsibilities and patronizing compassion, ministers can easily slip into or transport themselves onto the narcissistic dais of divinity, which we often call the "God complex". However the Good Lord, in order to avoid such competition and to prevent this apostasy, intended for His emissaries to bear fruit in the form of children. This seems necessary to keep the preachers' feet on the ground and out of the clouds . . . until it was time.

Although I was on the faculty of Union College, I was appointed there as a ministerial appointment; it being a Methodist Institution.

Several of the students served small Methodist churches in the mountains close by, as they intended eventually to enter the ministry. One such student, William Fergus, came to me with a problem. "Professor Gilbert, we had a revival at our church and a young girl came to the altar and wants to be baptized and join the church. I wonder if you would be willing to officiate at the baptism. I'm not ordained yet."

"Of course, William, I'd be honored to perform that duty."

"But she wants to be baptized the old-fashioned way."

That became an unanticipated situation, as I had never conducted such a service. It seems that her choice for the ritual would be a pond in a cow pasture on her grandfather's farm.

So William and I went to the designated place at the agreed upon time in his car. We both had dry clothes in the car, as we knew we would both be too wet to drive back to the campus.

Unfortunately it was pouring rain. We sat in the car, while the girl and her family and friends sat in two cars close by.

Finally, I said, "William, it looks as though the rain is not gonna let up. We're gonna get wet any ways, so let's do it."

When we got out of the car, the people in the other cars also got out. We all walked down the muddy red bank to the edge of the murky pond. William and the girl and I waded into the water until we were about waist deep. We quickly did the appropriate baptism, but even more quickly emerged from the water.

William and I rushed to his car, as the girl and her family went to their cars and left.

While I was in the back seat and William was in the front set changing into dry clothes, I said, "William, if a state patrolman were to stop by and ask what we're doing, we'd have a hard time convincing him that we are out here for a baptism."

Poor boy. I'm not sure he ever made it into seminary and an actual pastorate.

Several years later I served as Associate Pastor of the First Unitarian Society in Madison, WI. It was a popular venue for weddings. One reason was that it was a major architectural design of Frank Lloyd Wright's. In addition to that, many of the young couples planning weddings didn't want a church setting, but their parents did. The Unitarian Church seemed to be a valid compromise between a church and a non-church.

One Sunday after the morning service I was talking with a young church member and said something about the communion. He said, "Reid, Unitarians don't have communion."

I said, "Of course we do. The coffee hour here is more meaningful to Unitarians than the Lord's Supper is to some Methodists."

He chuckled and agreed.

On another occasion an elderly church member, after some discussion with me said, "But Reverend Gilbert, you must admit that you're not Unitarian.

"Mrs. Foster, of course I am. Just look at the plaque on the wall that states the Unitarian mission. 'All those who believe in the precepts of Jesus of Nazareth, etc.' . . . "

"Yes, but you didn't read between the lines."

It seems that even Unitarians can read between the lines.

On a Saturday afternoon wedding in early June 1971, I officiated at the wedding of a psychiatrist and his receptionist That, itself, was probably another story.

In the midst of the ceremony, with the whole wedding party assembled, I said to the bridegroom, "Please repeat after me: 'I promise under God'." His quick response was, "Oh, I wouldn't go that far." "Well they're really your vows, not mine." One young couple asked me quite anxiously, while planning the wedding, "What do you have to say?" "I don't have to say anything. I just have to sign the legal papers. If you'd like I can do it in mime." That usually inspired the couple to go the traditional route.

On a later occasion, I was conducting the wedding for my grand-nephew, Wesley

Stoltz, and his intended on a beach in Maryland. Just before pronouncing them, "husband and wife", I said, "Now that I have taken the time and traveled the miles to get here, I have earned the right to tell a story." I could see poor Wesley almost wither and probably thinking, Oh, no. Uncle Reid is going to tell one of his old boring stories. I'm sorry we asked him to perform the wedding. How will I ever be able to apologize to my Jody?

With no outward objection from anyone, I said, "In seminary I had a wonderful professor who was asked one day in a small seminar, a contentious question. It was obvious that the student wasn't looking for an answer. He just wanted to confront the professor. With a sympathetic look to the student, Professor Gealy said, 'To be perfectly honest, we don't know what we're talking about. But the point is we have to keep talking.'

"Now my advice to you is that there will be times when you will not know what you're talking about, but remember Dr. Gealy's statement, 'The point is you must keep talking.'"

I must admit that it was good advice for newlyweds, and now a few years and a couple of children later, it's apparent that Wesley and Jody are still talking.

It seems that the more hallowed the occasion or sanctified the setting, any aberration from the norm, becomes comic.

ROAD TO SALVATION

In 1956 shortly after graduating from seminary at SMU in Dallas, I interviewed for the position of Associate Minister at the First Methodist Church in South Bend, Indiana. The interview went well, and I was offered the position. Soon thereafter I visited my folks in North Carolina. When I returned to South Bend, the senior minister, The Rev. Andrew Hemphill, asked, "Reid, if one of the church members, or a non-church member, were to ask you the way to salvation, what would be your answer?"

My answer was simply a question to him, "What do you mean?"

"It's a straightforward question." (Which it was.)

Although I was already on the job, I supposed he was interested in how orthodox my theology might be.

I answered, "Well, I'd transpose the question to a more commonplace question like, 'How do I get to Chicago?', which I'd answer by saying, 'You get out on Highway 30 and head west through Hammond and Gary and on through South Chicago, and there you'd be.'"

He wasn't exactly pleased with that answer so he asked further, "But what if they say that they'd heard that there were other ways to Chicago?"

"My answer to that would be, 'I've heard that too, but Highway 30 is the only route I've taken, and to say that there'd be another way would be speculation on my part. To say that there is not another way would be arrogant.'"

I hadn't re-transposed the metaphor back to explain what the Methodist theological position to salvation might be. He probably wanted a more orthodox answer about conversion and baptism, so I dug out of my seminary training an answer given by Professor Ed Hobbs, my New Testament Professor. He explained to us young theologs, "The gospel message is to love God and do as you please."

I'm not sure this pleased Rev. Hemphill, but he asked no further questions at that time.

Many years later in 1994, I was on the theatre faculty of Ohio State University and had bought a house close to the OSU campus. One balmy spring afternoon, I answered the doorbell and encountered a couple of graduate students taking a spiritual survey. Since my South Bend days, I had not taken a spiritual survey, so I suggested to the young man and woman that we sit on the front porch swing and parapet.

After being seated—the young man on the porch railing and the young woman and I on the swing—he asked, "Do you believe that Jesus was the Son of God?"

I answered, "Yes!" While he was checking the appropriate block for my answer on his clipboard, I added quickly, "And so am I."

His surprised response was, "Huh?"

"I do believe that Jesus was the son of God and so am I—a stunned silence from both the surveyors—and so are you." Turning toward the young lady, I said, "And you're a daughter of God."

Neither of them was pleased with my answer, so the young man pushed further into his survey questions. "Do you read the Bible?"

"Yes."

"What part?"

"All parts."

"But what part do you prefer?"

"I'm not sure that I prefer one part over another."

He continued to pursue the matter. "But surely you understand that certain parts are more germane to today's reality and proclaim the gospel of Christ."

I answered, "I'm not exactly illiterate of the scriptures. I have a couple of seminary degrees."

He seemed intrigued with this information, but the young woman, focusing sharply on my demeanor, interpreted it as a challenge, which she was determined to address. Squinting her eyes, she asked, "Are you sure you're going to heaven?"

I answered, "I have no guarantee about that."

"Then why do you love God?"

Not really intending to change the direction of the communication, I simply asked, "Are you married?"

"No!"

I then delved further. "Do you ever hope to get married?"

Taken aback by this question, she sheepishly looked toward her surveying male partner. "Well, yes, some day." (I had already reckoned that they may have been on the cusp of a romance.)

Continuing the pursuit, I asked, "Are you looking for an old fellow with a million dollars, who'll probably die in a couple of months and leave you all his fortune?

"Why, no! That'd be conniving."

"You've just suggested that I connive my love of God, so that I'd receive a reward. Don't you feel that love is a reward in itself and doesn't have to be recompensed for a price you've paid?"

As the young fellow was writing some notes on his clipboard, the girl jumped up off the swing and said, "Maybe we'd better go on next door to continue our survey."

Obviously, I haven't fared well on spiritual surveys, so I'll just revert to Professor Hobbs's admonition and "Love God as well as I can, but then do as I please."

I still don't know why you must have a reward for loving. Isn't love a reward in itself?

Orthodoxy doesn't suit me very well.

PART VI
THE THEATRE

Theatre seems to have permeated much of my life whether it was in education, the church or personal enjoyment.

MY LIFE OF MIME

In 1957 I attended a mime performance at the New York City Center. Little did I realize that this casual act of responding to the enticement of a poster would lead eventually to a life of mime.

The poster was simple enough, with only a few graphic lines depicting the eyes and mouth of Marcel Marceau, whom I had previously seen in a film clip. The alluring poster and earlier fascination of the film-clip paring away of auditory images in the film clips caused me to wonder why the diminution of stimuli was so impelling. At other times, I had marveled at puppets and the dummies of ventriloquists.

Years later, I experienced a similar response to shadow puppets, performing in my back yard in Mahasarakham, Thailand. With the shadow puppets, one didn't even see the actual puppet—only the shadow cast by a single light behind the performers. And, of course, the puppets were merely silhouettes.

It occurred to me that my interest was piqued in each of these instances by the lack of stimuli by increasing my awareness of the stimulus which was provided. The poster drew me in because it didn't tell the whole story, and the performance—of necessity—caused me to focus intensely on every nuance of movement, as there was no auditory stimulus. Even with the dummies and shadow puppets, the audience was required to focus on the diminished stimuli in order to understand the story.

This selectivity of the details of reality entices the audience to become an active participant in the development of the message, by providing his/her imagination—not his/her cleverness of playing a guessing game like charades—but by accepting the given image and bringing to it one's own personal history and emotions.

As a case in point, when Marceau, in the *Ages of Man*, drops his right hand limply over his left wrist, we sense the end of life, encapsulated in that one small movement.

It was only in retrospect that I began to understand how I was so seduced by this art form.

In August 1959, my wife, Luan and new daughter, Tari, and I moved to Barbourville, KY, where I had obtained a theatre faculty position at Union College.

As this was my first college teaching job, in which I had to teach everything from stagecraft and dramatic literature to acting, public speaking and oral interpretation of literature, I had little time to think about the art—either teaching or performing—of mime.

However, it soon became clear to me that my acting students were in dire need of movement instruction to be included in their actor training. Most theatre programs at that time understood the need for vocal training and some technique of role interpretation, but the actors were generally limited to move in their respective character roles with their own normal physical attributes and tics. Thus I began to include movement in their studies, based on the movement principles of Decroux.

After three years in Kentucky I enrolled in the PhD Program at the University of Wisconsin, where again I found my mime training to be helpful in my teaching as well as my performing. Jacques Burdick, who had also studied mime with Marceau, directed me in two productions (a "A Servant of Two Masters," a *commedia del arte* play and "Streets of Paris," a mime performance). Of course, in both instances my mime background proved useful.

When in 1964 I studied and performed Noh Theatre with Sidayo Kita, my Mime background came in handy again.

In the movement classes, I was able to use the specific techniques I had learned with Decroux, including posture, physical isolations, pacing and balance. My utilization of the mime techniques became obvious when Kita-san started assigning performance roles for the public performances of *Ikkaku Sennin*.

He asked me to take the lead role. I demurred, as my assignment with the project was as the American assistant director, precluding (in my estimation) my taking a position from another actor. I then asked Kita-san why he would like for me to perform that role, as there were other actors and dancers with more professional experience than mine.

He said that the others, who had had dance training, had such definite forms of their dance, such as ballet or flamenco that he would have to deconstruct their movement style and then construct the specific principles of the Noh. And the actors without dance training had no discipline of movement at all. He then said that although he didn't know what my movement training had been, I had a kinetic understanding of movement which he could use as the base for the Noh movement requirements.

I did take the role of the Koken and had to sit silently on my heels for long periods of time. That was a wonderful experience of utilizing my mime training in the oldest extant form of theatre in the world today. Professor Robert Seaver, who had insisted several years earlier that I obtain movement training said, "Well, I still don't know how well you can move, but I certainly was impressed how you could remain immobile."

As soon as I returned to Wisconsin, my family and I started preparation for my Fulbright assignment to India. My official focus there was to research acting and dance training of India as the basis for my doctoral dissertation, based primarily with E. Alkazi at the National School of Drama in New Delhi. Alkazi, aware of my mime training, asked me to conduct a mime class, which I happily agreed to do. One of my students was Om Shivpuri, who, years later, played Nehru in the film, *Gandhi*.

Of course, I saw wonderful mimetic elements in the Manipuri dance of Manipur, the Kathak dance of North India, the Bharatanatyam dance of Madras and the Kathakali of Kerala.

I even had the chance to perform with another mime, Irshad Panjatan. The highlight of our performance was a duet we called "Tashkent," which was the recent locale of the signing of a peace treaty between India and Pakistan after their 1966 war. The piece depicted a tug of war, quite often used by two mimes. However, when Irshad and I kept pulling the imaginary rope back and forth, we stopped momentarily and Irshad took out an invisible pair of scissors from the pocket of his costume, at which time he handed it to me and I cut the rope. Both of us exited in opposite directions holding up the frayed ends of our illusionary rope like bouquets of celebration.

To be true to Decroux's principles of mime, I must admit that the performances of both Marceau and myself was pantomime, rather than mime. That was an example of how pantomime, though often comic, can also be utilized in a political statement.

Sometime later, Paul Curtis had organized the international Mimes and Pantomimists (IMP). In 1973 he asked me to lead the organization, which I did for five years. In that capacity I assumed the responsibility to confront the Spanish government for imprisoning Els Joglars, a mime troupe who had satirized a Spanish general.

After that, the US State Department held up the visas of the Afghan Exile Theatre because their mime had challenged the politics of Afghanistan. Mime was even useful for political purposes.

The most exhilarating experience I had had of Mime in India was at an all-India theatre conference. There would be one-act plays in the fourteen major languages performed by theatre groups from various parts of India. Kamaladevi Chattapadayah, the convener of the conference, invited me to perform, and I readily accepted. She said, "I'll place you at the end of the conference."

I said, "That will be fine."

Then she corrected herself by saying, "No, it won't be possible for you to perform at the conclusion of all the performances."

I was intrigued with her change of mind and asked, "Why isn't it possible for me to perform last?"

She said, "Because you're so good that no one will remember anything about any of the other performances."

I was shocked at that answer and replied, "Why do you say that? I don't believe you've ever seen me perform."

"No," she said, "but you're an American, and I feel that whenever an American decides to do something he'll do it extremely well. So I'm sure you'll be marvelous."

Muttering to myself, I thought, How can I live up to a billing like that?

At the conference all the languages and dialects of India were used. Of course, not everyone could understand Telugu or Urdu or Bengali or Marathi, etc., but each language had its own cheering audience.

Although I did perform, I don't recall whether I was last or not, but I was the only foreigner on the agenda at the conference that week.

As I was utilizing the international language of mime, I was the only performer whom everyone in the audience could understand.

Returning to the US in 1966, I again served as the Director of Theatre at Lambuth College in Jackson TN. I spent my summers teaching in the Uplands Arts program in Iowa County, WI,

Again I used the Mime principles of Decroux to teach young people in the Spring Green area.

Those summers led to the establishing of the Valley Studio with the Wisconsin Mime Theatre and School. That is well documented in the book, *Valley Studio: More Than a Place.*

Aside from offering Mime classes and performances, we also offered classes in Kathak Indian Dance, Zen Mime, Ballet, Renaissance Dance, Stage Combat, Experimental Theatre, Commedia dell'arte, Mask, Circus Technique, Corporeal Mime.

In addition to full-time students, we occasionally offered weekend workshops, particularly for high school students. On one occasion we hosted a weekend workshop for students from Cedarburg, WI. I was always fascinated by the enthusiasm and energy of the high schoolers. That weekend there was an especially excited girl. During a partner exercise , she continued to comment,"Oh I like this." "Isn't this fun?"

Being as non-judgmental as possible, I said, "It would be more beneficial to us if we did this without talking. That way we would be sharing silence."

She became admirably calmer after that until we had a sit down discussion session. Someone asked me a question, and I answered it briefly. For about ten seconds no one was saying anything, until she piped up, "Are we sharing silence now?"

"Well, we were, weren't we?"

The weekend visitors helped us to revive our own initial interest in this art form.

I was also able, within the purview of the school, to pursue my interest of folklore; music, storytelling and the craft of making play-pretties (folk toys) In fact, David Crosby and I developed a show which we called Appalachia and Other Folk. PBS filmed a half hour segment of the performance on the lawn of Valley Studio.

There were folks who thought it odd that I was dedicating so much of my life to this art of clowning. When Dad showed a magazine picture of me putting on white face makeup, a fellow said, "Pete, is this the boy you sent off to college to be a preacher?"

"Yes, and I do one of his acts, called 'Chewing gum' that I like to do for senior centers." Many folks would be surprised how many professional mimes have studied theology.

Mime was an integral part of Clown. Mime, Puppet, Dance Ministry Workshops which were held for five summers at different universities. It was the most ecumenical gathering anyone could imagine. Church doctrine wasn't broached. We were there to celebrate, and celebrate we did, even culminating the workshop with a parade in whatever town was close by. There were Catholics, Methodists, Southern Baptists, Jews and even Muslim participants. At the workshop at Oberlin University some of us men discovered a nearby lake, and four of us went skinny-dipping a Methodist minister, a Catholic seminarian, a Jewish clown and a Muslim percussionist, a virtual act of physical/spiritual ecumenicity in *holy water*.

Even after I officially left my "Life of Mime", it continued to inform me as I taught Movement for Actors for thirteen years at OSU and conducted many life enrichment classes The Self-Mask. Mime principles were utilized in all similar activities, even with a workshop for playwrights in the use of gestural notations in their scripts.

NATIONAL MIME WEEK

In 1979 Martin Kaplan set up the recognition of Mime in the theatre world, by lining up public officials as well as a parade down Pennsylvania Avenue in Washington, D.C. It would also be a special moment in my fantasy life.

It's not often that a boy meets his childhood sweetheart for the first time when they both (he and she) are in their late fifties. I was a year older than she, so the age relationship would be appropriate.

I was not quite 14 when I saw her for the first time onscreen in *National Velvet*. It was love at first sight. Unfortunately that wasn't a first sight she had of me or history might have been different. At the time I wasn't aware that it would take 35 years for my first (and only) kiss from Elizabeth Taylor.

She, of course, distinguished herself in many ways besides her beauty and violet eyes. Theatre critics have honored her theatrical accomplishments (four Oscar nominations and recipient of two). Gossip columnists have gloried in her frequent marriages (eight, including twice with Richard Burton). Film producers have profited mightily from her beauty and talents. Even comedians have gathered scads of comic material from her life and peccadilloes. The world has benefited by her efforts against HIV/AIDS. The British government, years ago, recognized her accomplishments with the honorific title of Dame; she was born in England in 1932.

But ultimately it was her fans who hoisted her onto the pinnacle of her own fame and abilities.

In 1979 while Liz was married to Senator John Warner and living in Washington, she accepted the role of Honorary Chair of National Mime Week which the International Mimes and Pantomimists were celebrating in the nation's capital. As the Administrator of IMP I was the Executive Director of the festival.

Our first public event was a parade down Pennsylvania Avenue with

Red Skelton. It was such a strange occurrence as no one knew a parade had been planned, and only a small number of mimes, jugglers and clowns were in the parade—no marching bands, elephants or parade floats. Red Skelton and Senator Inouye were riding in the back seat of a convertible. Mike Kaplan, a mime, was walking on the right side of the convertible alongside the senator. I was on the left side next to the entertainer of the hour. Whenever Red Skelton was detected in the procession, people along the way would wave and yell. One man called out to him, saying, "Thanks, Red, for bringing so much joy into our lives."

He turned to me and said in his little-child voice. "Isn't that nice!"

After the parade our rag-tag celebrants were greeted at the Corcoran Art Gallery by Mrs. Joan Mondale, who, during the Carter Administration held the arts portfolio for the White House.

The highlight of the festival was a cocktail party at the Georgetown home of Senator and Mrs. John Warner (Liz Taylor). She had been interviewed earlier in the week for a news release announcing the Mime Week. The reporter asked her, "Miss Taylor, why are you sponsoring this Mime Week and lending your prestige to such a fringe event?"

She said, "If we artists don't support each other, who is going to, and don't you suppose that we are all, in one way or another, on some kind of fringe?"

That elicited no response from the reporter.

The cocktail party was a howling success even in the parlance of the silent mimes. Everyone, who was anybody, was there. How could anyone imagine someone being invited to a Liz Taylor party and having the fortitude to avoid attending?

At the beginning of the festivities, she told me that she had engaged the services of a photographer to take various and sundry pictures during the evening. She solicited my assistance in setting up a particular photo-op.

She had invited both the Chinese Ambassador and the Taiwan Consul. Ordinarily those two political representatives would not attend the same social function, but after all, this was a Liz Taylor soiree.

What she was hoping to do was to be shaking the hand of the ambassador with one hand and then take the hand of the consul with the other. At that moment the photographer was to take a picture to be seen "around the world." Liz Taylor would have brought these two antagonistic political entities together.

She realized the power—even political power—in the glamour and art of an accomplished celebrated actress.

Unfortunately, it didn't happen, but what a fantastic idea! Perhaps I failed in my mission.

It was a wonderful evening, and yes, Liz had had a little too much Southern Comfort. However she received and shared a bit more southern comfort when she gave me a little kiss, as I was leaving.

Having been smitten so many years earlier by Elizabeth Taylor, while viewing *National Velvet*, I had no idea I would ever be so close to those velvet eyes—not to mention the thrill of those sensual lips

Shortly after that, when I was visiting my dad in North Carolina, I told him of my project with Elizabeth Taylor, and told him, "She even kissed me."

Ruminating, I suppose, over her many marriages—only six at that time—he asked, "What's so special about that?"

Of course he wouldn't understand, but it was the crowning moment of my long—but one time— (face to face or cheek to lip) relationship with Miss Taylor.

I'm reminded of John Greenleaf Whittier's poetic lines in his poem to Maud Muller:

> "Of all sad words of tongue or pen,
> The saddest are these, 'It might have been.'"

May Dame Liz, at last, rest in peace!

PERFORMING FOR BENEFITS
OR
BENEFITS FOR WHOM

Community organizations and fundraising administrators are constantly requesting performers to donate performances for various causes . . . usually worthwhile community service causes. The rationale for making these requests, I suppose, is that the performers aren't really spending any of their money; they would only be utilizing a little of their time and talent. *After all, performers love to perform, don't they?*

When I was Director of the Wisconsin Mime Theatre (1970-1979) I was consistently getting requests to perform *pro bono* for various occasions. One rather aggressive woman, organizing a benefit in Milwaukee, asked me to bring my whole theatre group to perform. She said, "Of course, as this is a benefit we won't be able to pay you and your company, but we will give you a lot of exposure."

Her use of the word "exposure" was a perfect segue for an appropriate response: "Lady, if I were exposed any more, I'd be arrested."

Another festival organizer called from Illinois, asking us to come to a special benefit performance for hospital patients. I listened carefully, as I was interested. After all, this was the kind if thing which we were committed to doing.

When I asked about the budget, she replied, "Of course, this is a benefit, and we have no funds for the performers."

"Are you donating your time and services?"

"No! I'm a professional fundraiser."

My reply was, "We're professional performers, but we will be happy to come . . . budgeting our travel, preparation and performance time . . . and contribute our performance skills whenever you and the doctors contribute your professional time and skills for the day." Reciprocity wasn't offered.

I discovered that whenever a person or organization has to pay nothing for an object or service, the recipient will regard it as worth nothing. Even when I could have accepted students into my school on full scholarships . . . they weren't requiring any more of my time or facilities. I always insisted that they contribute something for this benefit I was providing for them.

In 2016, I was asked to give a reading of my books at a senior living community in Tucson. The host told me that I could not sell any of my books, but I could pass out bookmarks to the audience. I did get a free Reuben sandwich for lunch.

At lunch I idly asked my host what was her career.

"Oh, I'm a psychiatrist."

Not completely facetious, I said, "I could probably use your services."

"Well, I'm rather expensive."

"How much should I expect to pay?"

"Two hundred dollars an hour."

"They don't pay us authors that well."

"Well, that's because I'm better educated than you."

"Oh really? Would you like to compare your education to my five college and university degrees and my two Fulbright awards?"

When I told my daughter this little story, she said, "Dad, did she apologize then?

"No, she's French."

There had been earlier times when I did perform for benefits . . . benefits for myself and my school. I performed gratis at Vice-President Mondale's Washington home as well as at a congressional wives' luncheon at Wolftrap National Performing Arts Park, where I first met Liz (Elizabeth Taylor).

During that same period of time I was in Washington fairly often, as I had a wonderful contact person there, Jere Wright, who introduced me to several movers and shakers; one being Mrs. Shouse the founder of Wolftrap. In fact, I gave Mrs. Shouse one of my hand-whittled canes.

She also introduced me to Carolyn Long, Mrs. Russell Long. Senator Long, the son of the legendary and infamous Huey Long, was the chairman of the Senate Finance Committee.

Mrs. Long and I discovered that we were from the same "neck of the woods" in North Carolina. Away from home all Tar Heels are considered actual kin-folk. She continued to insist on calling me, "Doctah Gilbert" in her slow southern drawl.

She inquired of me, "Doctah Gilbert, could I prevail upon ya to perform yoah mime act for a dinnah pahty thet Senatah Long an' Ah are hostin' for the Senate Finance Committee?"

How ironic that the Senate Finance Committee, which is responsible for budgeting billions of dollars of my taxpayer money, was asking me to perform *gratis* for their annual dinner party! I did accept, as I thought this exposure might be worth the donated effort.

At the end of the silent performance—lasting about 25 minutes and my curtain call in response to the polite applause—I demonstrated that mimes can talk. I told the assembled audience, including Senators Long, Dole and Byrd, Vice-President Mondale and several Cabinet members, "Although mimes perform in silence, we *can* talk, and on behalf of all the mimes, as well as all the artists in this country, and as honorarium for my performance this evening, I urge this prestigious committee and honorable officials to increase financial support to the arts—the creative core of our culture."

This was the first time I had met any of these individuals. Senator Byrd later became my senator when I moved to West Virginia. I was aware that Senator Byrd had fiddled his way into the Congress, as a young man, by playing his "ol' timey, foot stompin'" mountain tunes.

When Mrs. Long thanked me for my performance she said, "Doctah Gilbert, if Ah had not pervided entertainment foh the evenin', Senatah Byhd would hev taken his fiddle out, an' he would hev fiddled all night."

I should have reminded Senator Byrd some years later that I had saved him from providing a benefit performance at Mrs. Russell Long's dinner party.

I don't know if the Metropolitan Opera or the Kennedy Center or any other arts organization received a financial boost from my impassioned plea to our national financial arbiters, but within a short length of time after that auspicious evening, the Valley Studio and The Wisconsin Mime Theatre had run out of funds.

In 1979 the NEA, as well as other cultural foundations, seemed to regard most of the real estate between New York and San Francisco as a cultural dust bowl.

As my apprentices, instructors, staff and actors left for various artistic venues and global destinations, I slowly folded my tent and retreated silently—as befits a mime back to the mountains of my forbears.

BLOSSOM AND BEETHOVEN

It was summertime in Wisconsin. I had brought my family and my Lambuth College students to participate in the Uplands Arts Council 1968 Summer Arts Festival.

Robert Graves, president of the Arts Council, had arranged for my students to stay in an old farmhouse next to a barn, which was renovated into a dance studio in the upstairs hay mow and a wonderful *rathskeller* in the lower level. An outdoor amphitheatre had been built just downhill from the barn.

My family and I were to stay about a mile away in a log house, which Robert called Stonedge—so named because behind the house was a barn on the precipice of a stone cliff. The uplands area is in driftless southwestern Wisconsin; here the glaciers in the ice age had separated, leaving behind impressive rock outcroppings.

An eccentric entrepreneur, Alex Jordan, had taken advantage of the fantastic rock formations and built The House on the Rock. This successful tourist attraction was built on a stone monolith across the road, Highway 23, from the Stonedge farm. Alex's farm was on the same side of the road as our summer place. Only a small valley separated the two farms. He had several large barns where he stored various curiosities to be considered for later installment in the tourist area. The world's largest carousel and an automated orchestra had already been ensconced in the House on the Rock.

Often this major tourist attraction is mistaken for a Frank Lloyd Wright design or at least a derivative of his style. The hackles will rise immediately at Taliesin, five miles away, if you even suggest such a thing. There was a mutual animosity between these two creative, egotistical giants.

One of the student actors, Ron Baker, was a wonderful performer and beautiful human being. All the teenage girls in the community fell deeply in love with him, even though it was obvious he was about to emerge from the "closet." He was an outstanding performer—not only as an actor, but also as a guitarist and a singer of the "Memphis Hollers."

Ron was interested in "getting back to the soil," where he'd never been, but of which he harbored a marvelous fantasy. We let him bunk in the chicken house between the Stonedge house and the barn. He said it was a bit smelly, but he seemed to understand that that was a part of "getting back to the soil".

Another part of this journey to early Americana would be to have a cow. After all, we were in the dairy state. Ron prevailed on me to get a cow. I discovered I could rent one for the summer from Paul Kooiman, a dairy auctioneer, who was also on the board of the Uplands Arts Council. The cow was an adorable little Jersey, named Blossom, with beautiful large brown eyes. She would have been a perfect model for Elsie the Borden Cow. She was small, as Paul explained it, because she had "left the dance early."

I told Ron that the one condition for the rent-a-cow deal, was that he would do the milking. However, teaching him to milk was one of the challenges of the summer. Because Blossom was diminutive, her milking appendages were also miniature. Ron was more than six feet tall with rather large hands. I attempted to demonstrate how the milker had to clinch one finger at a time from the top of the teat until all the digits forced the white liquid out the bottom end of the faucet. I even tried to entice Ron with the smell of the fresh milk and the sound of the liquid stream drumming on the bottom of the metal milk pail.

The greatest part of the ordeal was to convince him of the necessity of milking at the same time each morning and evening. That was particularly difficult as Ronnie lingered in the chicken house each morning, and sometimes in the evening wouldn't come home until midnight. Therefore, out of sympathy for poor Blossom, I usually did the milking—a task which I thought I had left many years earlier at Baux Mountain, NC.

Blossom, getting lonesome for some of her own kind (kine), would get loose and run up the hill to the neighbor's dairy herd. Although I substituted at times for Ron in the milking department, I insisted that he go fetch Blossom whenever she made her frequent neighborly visits. A large hayfield lay up the hill from the house, between us and the road.

On one occasion when Ron had to bring Blossom home, it was misting rain, and halfway home Blossom got loose again. As I looked up the hill I could see tiny Blossom racing across the horizon with her tail straight out behind her. Tall Ronnie was about two yards behind her; his long blond hair flowing back, his huge bare feet jogging out of the knee high alfalfa. Where is Ingmar Bergman's film crew just when you need them?

I did enjoy the fruits of the milking effort and even churned butter a couple of times. Jersey milk was so rich that we often had real whipped cream to put on our desserts. I also thought it would be good to have some fresh butter. As we always had left-over milk, I would set aside some of it to clabber. Not only would we have butter, but also buttermilk, which I liked.

On one occasion when I tried churning with an old Daisy Churn, the butter wouldn't set or gather. What that means was under the ideal circumstance, flakes of butter fat would begin to form and then to cling together in little lumps. That's when the churner would dip the hands into the liquid and pull all the lumps together, before patting them into molds.

Being a depression child, I wasn't about to waste any food. The milk had already clabbered, so I set it aside until the whey began to separate from the curds, which I wrapped in a cheesecloth and hung up for several days.

One evening my wife and I invited Charles and Patty McCallum for a spaghetti supper. Charles was the founder and managing director of the Milwaukee Repertory Theatre. The cast was performing in

Spring Green that summer at the Gard Theatre. I decided to serve some of the drying curds. Our guests were impressed with the exotic cheese and asked where I had bought it. I had to confess it was a product of our "getting back to the soil", but basically a bungling of my efforts to churn clabbered milk for butter. It was a wonderful, though surprising, contribution from Blossom.

In the midst of this bucolic life, our arts programs were not going well financially. The Uplands Arts Council had raised only one-fifth of the funds needed to fulfill all of our fiscal obligations.

As a result of insufficient publicity the ticket sales for the Gard Theatre performances were also meager. One Saturday evening the number of empty theatre seats was extremely distressing.

When I got back to Stonedge at midnight, I walked out about fifty yards behind the house to meditate on the rock ledge. It was painfully obvious that the box office was not going to meet our financial needs.

It was a lovely night with a full moon, which seemed to dart behind small, cottony cumulus clouds. The air was still, damp and cool. Suddenly I began to hear music. It seemed to come directly out of the clouds. I looked around and up and over the rock precipice, but saw nothing unusual—only the idyllic scene in which I was already immersed. The moon was bright enough to light the bucolic green valley below my perch.

A few years earlier in North Carolina I had observed with my mother a UFO, so I was prepared for unusual celestial sights and even sounds.

What I was hearing was what seemed to be a pipe organ, playing Beethoven's music. Lacking any further manifestation, I simply opened my hands, raised them aloft and, while looking into the heavens, said, "I'm ready, Lord". I had always hoped I would be taken to my heavenly reward in this manner. An inner question was, *Is there a chariot also? Will one of the angels or saints accompany me? That will be wonderful, except don't send St. Paul. I have some issues with him.*

I waited, but nothing further happened. The organ finally played the postlude, then ceased.

The next day, while inquiring of local folks if they had heard anything unusual the night before, I was told, "You know Alex Jordan has that farm right north of you."

"Well, yes, I'm aware of that."

"He puts a lot of stuff into that barn, before installing them across the road in the sprawling House on the Rock. He's put a pipe organ in the barn, and he's been known to pretend—quite often at midnight—he's the Phantom of the Opera. That happens particularly after some Saturday- night bachelor party. He's likely to play the organ with all the stops pulled out."

So much for my theatrical heavenly ascension!

Beethoven seemed to sum up my summer of fresh milk, disappointing theatre and a thwarted heavenly chariot ride.

A SACRED VALLEY

The Wisconsin River flows south until it takes a turn westward near Spring Green, Wisconsin, before it proceeds westward then onto the upper Mississippi River. About fifty miles from the confluence of the Wisconsin and Mississippi is the small, lush valley named Wyoming Valley. It is often assumed that the word "Wyoming" was the name of an American Indian nation, but it is a Delaware Indian word meaning "mountains and valleys alternating."

The name Wyoming has been used as the name of a state, a New York state county and even a Methodist Church Conference, as well as a suburb of Cincinnati. One may suppose all of these entities have "mountains and valleys alternating."

It is certainly true of Wyoming Valley in Wisconsin, as it is a glacial driftless area, which is to say that the glaciers, for some undetermined reason, had split and avoided the whole area of southwestern Wisconsin. Madison, only forty-five miles away, was first known as "Five Lakes" because of the natural lakes there.

However, southwest Wisconsin has no natural lakes but a plethora of valleys and ridges with magnificent stone outcroppings. Being from the Appalachian Mountains, I felt right at home when in 1962 I visited Wyoming Valley for the first time.

Legend has it that Native Americans sensed a spiritual presence in the valley and therefore, out of respect, stayed out of the valley even though it is lush with edible plants, such as watercress, may apples, various mushrooms and much more—as well as abundant prey for carnivores. There is also a belief that when a river turns back on itself, as the Wisconsin River, as described above, that spot holds great spiritual meaning.

In the early to mid-nineteenth century, Europeans began settling the valley, including the Lloyd-Jones family from Wales. The settlers were impressed with the potential for new homes and substantial farms.

It seemed, right from the beginning and extending into the following century, that there was indeed a powerful energy in the valley—sometimes creative and at other times destructive.

One of the stalwarts of the Lloyd-Jones family was Jenkin Lloyd-Jones, a rhetorician and Unitarian minister, who began a summer series of Chautauqua performances at Tower Hill, which, in later years, became a state park.

Although Tower Hill, on the bank of the Wisconsin River, had been the site for making cannonballs for the Union Army in the Civil War, it became a venue for the creative presentations of orators, opera singers and educators.

Another scion of the Lloyd-Jones family was Frank Lloyd Wright, born in 1867.

Even before his stellar achievements in the international architecture arena, his aunts, Aunt Nell and Aunt Jane, established the first co-educational boarding school in the country. In fact, in 1902 young Frank designed a school for them, the Hillside Home School which still today houses various activities of the Frank Lloyd Wright School Foundation and School of Architecture.

In 1911 when a young recent college graduate, Mary Chase, applied for a position in the school, Aunt Nell and Aunt Jane asked her only two questions: *Do you know the names of the wild animals and plants where you come from in Massachusetts? Do you find children fascinating?*

Mary Chase answered in the affirmative to both and years later wrote in her memoirs that "They asked the two most important questions for elementary education."

That same year Wright designed and built Taliesin—a Welsh word meaning *shining brow*, as it stood on the brow of a hill on the family farm. That structure and its subsequent reincarnations have received accolades worldwide.

Seven years after Wright's death in 1959, Robert and Derry Graves formed the Uplands Arts Council with arts instruction, performance and exhibitions in the valley and the rocky ridge at the southern end of the valley. Young students could be seen dancing in the daisies, all ages attending outdoor performances and visitors attending art exhibits hung on snow fences in a hay field.

It was during the summers of the 1960s that I became involved with the Uplands Arts Council and brought my family and college students from Tennessee to be an integral part of the creative life of the valley and uplands.

In 1970 I established Valley Studio and the Wisconsin Mime Theatre and School in a small spur of the Wyoming Valley. My architect was one of Wright's apprentices, Herbert Fritz. Herbert had a marvelous ability to take an old barn, move the farmhouse close to it and tie the two structures together with wide eaves and porch overhangs.

He also designed two small dormitories in the same elegant primitive style. We bought and moved the old Kritz School (where Edna attended elementary school) and renovated it into a dance studio.

Although we were ensconced in such a small out-of-the-way spot, we were recognized by the *New York Times* as the center of mime training in the U.S., attracting summer instructors from France, England, Italy, India and Japan, as well and from various arts centers in the US.

During all of these decades since the valley has been inhabited, the Great Spirit respected by the Native Americans must have influenced the fantastic energies, both creative and destructive. Aside from the aforementioned activities, farming and hunting have continued from the awakening of the spring, the creative growth of the summer, the harvesting and reaping in the fall and the hunting and resting during the snows.

Steven Wasson, a mime student of mine, left my school in 1976 to study in Paris with my teacher, Etienne Decroux, who was also Marcel Marceau's teacher. He and his wife, Corinne Soum, were the last assistants Decroux had before his death, and they carried on the mission of the school and moved it to London.

In 2010, after many years of being out of contact, Steven googled me and said that he felt it was about time for him to return to the Valley with his school. I told him to get in touch with Robert Graves, who with his wife, Derry, had brought me to the Valley in the mid-60s to teach and perform in the Uplands Arts Council summer programs.

Robert told them at that time that he didn't know of any available facility for a mime school. Shortly after that Wyoming Valley Methodist Church was put up for sale at which time Steven and Corinne bought it and began refurbishing it. They even installed plumbing in the Ladies Hall, as there had never been more than an outdoor toilet at the church.

Some locals expressed their feelings that "it doesn't seem appropriate for a Mime theatre to be housed in a church." I responded to them by saying, "It is not a church. When there is no congregation, the building becomes a beautiful edifice, waiting for some creative activity. We should recall that the first verb in the Bible is CREATE. *In the beginning God created the heavens and the earth.* The creative act is also a spiritual act."

A quarter of a mile south of the White Church is the Wyoming Valley School, designed by Frank Lloyd Wright (whose own Taliesin was only two miles away) was also abandoned and was donated to a non-profit organization as a cultural/educational center. Robert and Derry Graves provided leadership as well as maintenance and landscaping for the new re-newed venture.

The next summer (2011) afforded me the opportunity to hold a Sunday service at Unity Chapel, the home church of Frank Lloyd Wright's family. I had shared the Valley with Taliesin during the 70s, and this summer I was invited at formal night (special guests in formal evening wear) to perform in its Hillside Theatre after the dinner. I performed four short mime pieces and then demonstrated with kimono and mask how mime is used in the Japanese Theatre.

During all this time I saw my old friend, Robert Graves, several times, but his health seemed to be deteriorating even though he continued when able to work on landscaping at the Wyoming Valley School of which he was president of the board. Every summer Thursday evening in Spring Green the community holds what they call "Local Night" in a small park in the middle of town. Live music is performed on a small stage, and food and drinks are available. One evening two of my daughters came out from Madison for Local Night, and it was one of the few times that Robert and Derry were there. Later my daughters and Robert and Derry had said how very fortunate they had been to make that connection that evening.

On the last day I was there I went by the Graves's to leave a copy of a rough draft I had written for a grant for the Wyoming Valley School. Derry, Robert and I sat on their veranda facing the ridge across the creek. When I left, knowing that I would be leaving the next day for Arizona, Robert, while still seated, gave me his usual hug and said, "It's always difficult saying goodbye to you, Reid." I realized that there was a more consequential message than usual from him.

The next day I left the Valley for a two-day driving trek back to Arizona with Clayton, my grandson. It was a wonderful, though fast-paced trip, and we learned a lot about each other . . . learned a great deal more than we would ever have learned if we had not been confined in a metal cage, hurtling sometimes at eighty-five miles an hour across the Great Plains.

After I had settled back into the rhythms of home in Tucson, having been away for three months, Tia, one of Robert and Derry's daughters, phoned and said that her dad was fading fast, as they were told it would be only a few days until his passing. She asked me if I would be able to conduct his memorial service, which he had requested. I, of course, agreed even though it would be extremely difficult as Robert has been like a brother to me for more than half a century. She called again on Labor Day, saying that Robert had passed away that morning with his wife, son and four daughters with him.

The service was held in the same church, the Wyoming Valley Methodist Church, which my student had bought . . . the church where Robert's parents were leaders and where Robert and his siblings, as well as his children, had attended church and Sunday school, so many years earlier . . . and where I had officiated at the wedding for my daughter, Karen, in 1985. The reception after Robert's memorial service was to be just up the road at the Wyoming Valley School, where Robert and Derry had lal-labored during the summer to get it ready for classes and performances.

I include here a poem I wrote, inspired by Robert's life and to include the benediction at the end of the service:

DEATH IS MORE

Death is more than passing over.
though it is that and much more.
It is a cessation of shared work and play
as we have enjoyed so oft before.

But there will be times in days ahead
when those of us left here behind
will remember past times of joy
vividly bringing those moments to mind.

There will be occasions in the days ahead
when great wisdom will be received
by the ones on this side of the mysterious door,
as spoken directly by the one gone on before.

And as we lay to rest the mortal frame
may we be comforted by memories of his life,
and now embracing each other in his name
be comforted in our present joy or strife.

"Now cracks a noble heart. Goodnight, sweet prince, and flights of angels sing thee to thy rest."

That summer was truly a celebrational homecoming and a grief-filled parting!

WITWEN

In the summer of 1969, I brought several of my Lambuth College Theatre students from Tennessee to Wisconsin to participate in the arts activities of the Uplands Arts Council. They were involved in several theatrical productions, including *The Conversion of Buster Drumwright*, the premiere of a drama about a family's commitment to revenge.

A memorable experience of the summer was a Mime performance in the small rural community of Witwen for their Fourth of July celebration.

The local Methodist minister had been assigned the task of booking entertainment for the community Fourth of July bash. I use the term "bash" advisedly, as the term "celebration" would be much too tame. He asked if I would bring my acting students to perform. I agreed . . . for a small fee, which would contribute to the summer upkeep of the student actors.

Some of our Uplands Arts Council friends in Spring Green also went along to enjoy the day's festivities. Although they were from another community, they wanted to see the Mime performance. It became obvious rather quickly that we needed a supportive audience.

When we arrived at the township of Witwen, we saw that it was a setting of three houses, an abandoned service station, a crossroads and a Methodist church with a cemetery and picnic pavilion close by. I felt that the setting—not just the physical setting but also the human setting—was not quite conducive to the silent art of Mime. The stage area was too small for much movement. I used its physical inadequacy as a good reason to cancel the performance part of the day's celebration. I was most concerned about the huge firecrackers and general unruliness of the older children and teenagers in the crowd.

I told the pastor-impresario that, "We really won't be able to perform in this space."

"What's wrong with the space?"

"It's fine for a speaker, but the altar rail at the front of the platform would hide the feet of the performers, and it's really important to see the feet of Mime performers. You know . . . when they walk in place, and things like that."

"We'll just rip that out."

"No, no, don't do that. Anyway the wall at the back makes the performing area too small. We don't have to perform. We can just . . . "

"That can easily be moved. It's just temporary."

"Well, my performers are rather modest (They weren't modest at all, but that was a good excuse.), and there's no place for them to change into their costumes."

"I'll just have the boys move that wall back into the corner to make a kind of dressing room."

During this verbal exchange, I followed him around, as he began gathering up hammers and crowbars as well as a couple of boys to help with the architectural renovation from a picnic pavilion to a theatre. They immediately began ripping out the altar rail and prying up the wall to move it back towards the stage right corner.

There was simply no way to avoid performing, so I told the actors to put on their costumes and white-face make-up.

By the time we were ready to start, only adults and small children were sitting at the picnic tables inside the pavilion. All the older children and teenagers were outside shooting off fireworks, but peering in through the wire screen enclosing the pavilion. Even before the performance started, the outside audience of youngsters had started hooting, booing and yelling obscenities.

When one of the mimes was miming a shower bath, one of the kids started yelling, "Don't laugh at him. He's just got a hernia." Of course he got a laugh from *his* audience.

When two performers, a boy and a girl, were miming a love scene, there were various catcalls, "Kiss her. Go ahead . . . kiss her. Smack one on her. Go ahead," . . .

There was no effort made by the adults to rein in the misbehaving youngsters. In fact, the parents seemed to appreciate the cuteness of their offspring. What angered me so much about this situation was that I knew these Wisconsin farmers were extremely critical of the students protesting the Vietnam War over in Madison, only 45 miles away. Yet they made no effort to control the misbehavior of their own children at home.

We left immediately after the performance . . . without even changing costumes or removing the make-up.

I met the pastor later the next week for our monetary reward for performing in such a hostile environment. I had decided to say nothing about our dismay with the behavior of the audience, but the pastor asked, "What did you think of our audience? They were really something, weren't they?"

After a moment's hesitation, I replied, "They *were* really something, but something I have never experienced before. I have performed in various places and venues, even in Asia, but I have never experienced such a rude, boorish, hostile audience as we found in Witwen."

"I'm surprised that you'd say that. I was very pleased with them, as it was the best and most attentive they've ever been."

I wondered what the previous years' celebrations must have been like.

If that community had been named in a Renaissance play it would be called "Witwould" (would that they had some wit). Years later, one of the young girls (not one of the actors) accompanying us that day said, "That was the most frightening day of my teenage years."

When I talked with my actors about their horrible experience at Witwen, they expressed their sense of devastation with the audience response they had received.

I told them, "Every performer has to experience a Witwen at least once in his/her performance life. You have now experienced yours."

USA MOON LANDING ON THE GARD THEATRE STAGE

On June 20, 1969, the world was anticipating an incredible event to transpire on the moon . . . a heavenly ball revered for millennia by earth inhabitants. TV channels were excited to be able to share the occasion ("A small step for man. One giant leap for mankind.") with their avid viewers.

That summer, I had brought to Spring Green, WI several Lambuth College theatre students with me for the summer arts program of the Uplands Arts Council. In addition to establishing the summer art fair at the Uplands barn and several arts classes, Robert and Derry Graves had secured the use of the Gard Theatre, which at that time had not yet been given that name.

Many local people had spent hours refurbishing the old movie house. Rudy Kraemer and Bud Keland had helped finance the purchase of the theatre. David Kraemer and several Spring Green young people had helped clean and paint it. Robert Graves painted the gold medallions on the ceiling. We accused him of pretending to be Michelangelo.

Several plays were staged that summer including the premiere of THE CONVERSION OF BUSTER DRUMWRIGHT, written by Jesse Hill Ford, a novelist and film writer from Tennessee.

However the most memorable production must have been LITTLE MARY SUNSHINE as it coincided with the Apollo Moon Landing. The script was written by Rick Besoyan, and our production was directed by Stanley Godfrey, who had performed on Broadway with Yul Brynner in THE KING AND I.

The play was a spoof on the old time operettas, like those in which Jeanette McDonald and Rudy Valle had performed. In our rendition of the musical, Monona Rossol played Little Mary Sunshine, proprietress of the Colorado Inn, and John Juhl played Big Jim Warington of the Forest Rangers.

Lynn West, our tech director and a Lambuth College student, played the cameo role of Fleetfoot, a name which stuck with him both on and off the stage.

There were many musical numbers, highlighting the theme of sweet romance, including ONCE IN A BLUE MOON. As it was also the evening when everyone anticipated the first human beings landing on the moon, the actors, when not on stage, would slip out and into the corner bar to watch the TV to see if the moon landing was actually going to occur.

There were numerous skeptics, assured that it wasn't going to happen. "Aw, it's just gonna be staged on one of those Hollywood movie lots, tryin' again to convince us that the gov'ment is doin' somethin'."

Probably we would have had a larger audience that night, if people weren't so interested in watching the historical event on the moon.

In every performance when ONCE IN A BLUE MOON was sung, a cut-out bright yellow full moon, rigged by the stage techies, would slowly rise behind a canvas hedge. On that particular moon landing night, as the song began, the make-believe moon started its slow rising arc over the painted Rockies. However, this time when the BLUE MOON came into full view, it was sporting a waving American flag, celebrating John Glenn and his crew, represented by Lynn West and his cohort, David Pyron.

The audience laughed and cheered wildly.

On July 20, 1969 while the whole world witnessed that spectacular interstellar event, the Spring Green audience applauded its own unique moon landing on the stage of the Gard Theatre.

INSUFICIENT EVIDENCE

In the winter of 1981-82 my nineteen-year-old daughter, Karen, and I moved from Wisconsin to West Virginia where I had already bought a large apartment building, *the flats*, down the street from an old theatre, the Cottrill's Opera House, which I had hoped to restore to its former glamour. The flats had five storefronts and twelve apartments inhabited by various tenants, mostly elderly.

That winter, along with several other actors and directors, I had a favorable contract with a local ski resort to produce five theatre productions to be performed every weekend over a period of ten weeks. The productions were *The Fantastiks, Glass Menagerie, an Evening of Mime, Stand-up Comedy* and *Improv Theatre*.

Even though the size of the audiences was small, the response to the performances was wonderful.

The small troupe of actors consisted of four women and five men. One of the young men, Fred Alley, some years later became a playwright, writing a marvelous musical, *Guys on Ice*, about two fisherman spending a day ice fishing on a frozen lake in northern Wisconsin. Later, he won the Richard Rodgers $100,000 award for the outstanding musical of 2001, *Spitfire Grill*. One of the actors thought he, himself, was a clone of John Travolta. Another was probably the only black person in the whole county. One of the actresses kept "hitting up" on the ingénue. We all shared two large apartments.

At the end of the ten-week run I thought we ought to have a little party celebrating our questionable success in enduring the theatre—as well as the winter—season without any bloodshed from either the weapons or each other.

One of the apartments had a commodious living room, adequate for a gathering of about twenty actors and guests. After the last Saturday night's performance, we changed clothes, struck the set and props and headed ten miles into town for a quiet little party in Apartment 11. It was late, so I explained to the actors that it was an old creaky building and as we were on the fourth floor, we ought to take off our shoes and boots and keep the music amped down low.

Shortly after everyone had arrived and we'd brought out some snacks and had opened a few beers, I got a phone call. It was from a tenant in Apartment 6 directly under our party space. It was Charles Woods, who obviously had been drinking—but then, at any point of time, that would have been the reality.

He yelled into the phone, "Reid Gilbert, I want to know what in the hell is goin' on up there?"

As an aside, hopefully without too much of a digression from the story, I should explain that Mr. Woods, whom everyone called "Woody," was a kind of building superintendent when I bought the building, and he and I had tacitly kept that arrangement after I moved in. He paid only $38 a month for his seven-room apartment.

I replied to Woody. "We're just havin' a little party after the close of the theatre season."

"Well, why in the hell didn't you tell me somethin' about it?" He generally felt that he should be informed of anything that happened in the building, even from the landlord, himself.

"Woody, there was no need to tell you that I was havin' a party. After all, I do own the building, and I can have a party whenever I wish. If we're disturbin' you, I'm sorry. I've had everyone take their shoes off and we've kept the music low."

"Well, if you don't shut the hell up, I'm callin' the cops."

"That's fine, Woody."

About fifteen minutes later, the phone rang again. I knew who it was at the first ring. "Dammit, Reid Gilbert, I swore I'd call the cops if you didn't cut out that damn racket up there."

"You do that, Woody."

"I swear if I hear anything else up there I'm not callin' next time. I'm bringin' my rifle up to take care of matters . . . I got a gun, an' I know how to use it. You know what I'm asayin'?"

"I do know what you're sayin', but you'd better get back to bed and sleep it off."

In a few minutes there was a knock at the door of the steps to the two fourth floor apartments.

Standing at the door was a state patrolman, whom I knew just by his last name, Bonner, usually pronounced, "Bonnard."

"Mr. Reid, I've had a complaint from one of your tenants, Mr. Woods, about the noise your party is making."

"Well, come on up and meet my guests."

After he came up and looked around and howdy'd everyone, he said, "After I received the complaint, I sat in the patrol car out on the street and listened for any noise, but I didn't hear anything. If I had, I'd have to give you a ticket for disturbing the peace."

"I appreciate your keeping the peace. It must be a quiet night, so why don't you just stay for the rest of the party?"

"No, I'd better get back to my duties."

The next morning, I went downstairs and knocked on the door of Apartment 6. When Woody came to the door, I said, "Woody, you're movin' out."

"Whadda ya mean, I'm movin' out? You can't just move me out."

"Woody, I own this building, and we (you and I) have no lease, and I'll not have you threatenin' me or any of my guests. I'll give you ample time to move, but I'm evictin' you."

It took Woody and his family several months to find another place, but in the meantime I was served a subpoena to appear before the local justice of the peace to answer to a complaint of "disturbing the peace," of course having been brought by Woody.

At the appointed hour, Karen and I walked down the back alley to the small city hall. When I looked in the front door to the conference room, I saw that there was no one there yet, except the janitor. At least, I figured it was the janitor, as he was elderly, unshaven and wearing a tattered coat. He was also sweeping around the conference table which would be used by the justice of the peace. I told Karen that since we were early, we should simply walk around the block and not disturb the janitor's duties.

It took only a few minutes to walk around the block, but when we returned, several people were in the room, including the janitor who was sitting behind the table where the justice of the peace was supposed to sit. It turned out that the janitor was A. J. Carr who was the justice of the peace and the mayor and whom I had not met before. Karen and I took seats immediately.

Mr. Carr opened the proceedings. "Well, hit looks like we may all be here." He turned toward Bonnard, the investigating officer and said, "Bonehead, what're we doin' here?" As it was apparent A. J. was nearly stone-deaf, Bonnard had to lean over to him and yell into his ear.

"We're here to hear a complaint of disturbing the peace which Charles Woods has brought against Mr. Gilbert."

Looking straight at me, the justice of the peace said, "Is Mr. Gilbert thet feller in the brown coat, what come in late?"

"Yeah, that's Mr. Gilbert."

I was sure my goose was sure enough cooked, even without an oven.

Mayor A. J. continued the proceedings with swearing in Woody and asking him to explain his complaint. "Well, thar was this terrible racket from a party Mr. Gilbert was throwin' in the apartment right above my apartment. Hit woke up my mother-in-law . . . "

"I thought she was deef."

"Well, yeah she is , but thet's what I'm atellin' you about. Hit woke up my daughter an' her boyfriend. I mean they wuz settin' on the couch an' hit disturbed them somethin' terrible awful."

Officer Bonner next had a chance to explain that when he investigated he'd heard no noise from out on the street. "I sat in the patrol car for 'bout twenty minutes, then went to Mr. Gilbert's apartment."

"Did he cause you any trouble?

"No he was real nice, and as a matter of fact he invited me to stay for the rest of the party."

"Did you do thet?"

"No I went back to the car to continue my nightly duty."

"I'm certainly glad to hear thet. A conscientious public servant."

Moving his sights to me, the Honorable Justice of the Peace, said., "Mr. Gilbert, you're directed at this time by this court to take the stand."

It wasn't much of a stand—just a chair at the end of Mr. Carr's conference table. I slid out of my chair and sat in the stand, while leaning in as closely as possible to the hard-of-hearing justice of the peace-judge-mayor. Then of course the usual swearing in.

"How do you plead . . . guilty or not guilty?"

"Not guilty, your honor."

"Would you please give the court your account of the evening?"

"Yes, your honor. If it please the court this is my account of the evening. I was especially careful to keep the noise down and explained to my guests that they should take off their shoes and boots, as it was such an old building and the noise carried a long ways. I also explained to them that I didn't want to disturb any of my tenants at that late hour of the night. I'm sure Mr. Woods' complaint was that I hadn't checked my schedule with him."

Dave Hart, was called forth as my witness. He was usually called Pearl because of his taste for Pearl Beer, which he featured in his bar No Le Hace. As some diversion from his business he had been the tech guy for our theatre season.

Justice of the Peace: "Were you at Mr. Gilbert's *late night* party?"

"Yes, your honor, I attended the party,"

"Well, now tell me what it wuz like."

"There wasn't a great deal goin' on. In fact, it was undoubtedly the most boring party I'd ever been to."

I don't know if any other host may have liked to hear that their party was a boring success, but I was delighted with Pearl's testimony.

At the conclusion of the hearing, the justice of the peace said to me, "Young man, can you come down to city hall next Monday mornin' at nine o'clock?'

"Yes your honor I will surely be there."

"Well when you come by on Monday mornin', I'll render my jedgement."

The next Monday morning I was there—on time this time.

Justice of the Peace Carr said, "Well, I'm gonna hafta throw the case out of court fer insoofficient evydence."

"Mr. Carr, I'm glad to hear that and greatly appreciate it."

"Well thet's jest the way I see hit—Insoofficient evydence," as he wrote his conclusion in his official ledger book, which was kept open on the city hall lobby table so that everyone could read it. It was Tucker County's policy of Open Government.

Shortly after that incident, I joined the theatre faculty at Ohio State University, but on one of my frequent trips back to Thomas to check on my apartment building, I was told about Woody's activities and recent demise.

Walt Ranalli, the fellow looking after my building and my antique store, had been a student of mine at Davis and Elkins College. He had also run for mayor and was elected—the youngest mayor in the state of West Virginia. It seems that Woody had pursued his earlier foray into the political scene and neighborly complaints, so had run for city council and was elected by a few votes—of course, there were only a few votes in the whole election.

After a short time in office, Woody up and died, and Walt, being the mayor, was obliged to attend the funeral on a raw, rainy day. After the brief funeral proceedings were over, everyone left immediately, because of the weather.

In his official capacity as mayor, Walt felt he was obliged to wait until they lowered the casket.

As they lowered the casket, the rain continued even more determinedly. Walt turned to leave but slipped on the mud banked up at the edge of the grave and slid into the grave right on top of Woody's casket.

When he related this event to me, knowing of my earlier conflict with my former tenant, Walt said, "Well, I guess Ol' Woody had the last word after all."

THE OLD TIMER

In 1990, I established Valley Ridge Theatre in the backyard of an apartment building I owned in Thomas, West Virginia. It was primarily a summer variety show with scenes from Shakespeare, an original *commedia del arte* romp, local kids' instrumental and vocal music, some mime sketches, monologues and solos by visiting established actors.

A homespun character I developed for these revues, the Old Timer, would interrupt (prearranged of course) a particular performer at the end of his or her set. The Old Timer wore an old fedora hat, clean but unpressed bib overalls, a flannel shirt and brogans (work shoes).

There was some precedence for this character. When I was in high school we didn't get an auditorium until our senior year. The first play our teachers produced and directed had a hillbilly character, which was assigned to me. At the auditions for the next production I was away on a school trip. When I returned I was told that I got the part of Uncle Alex, another hillbilly character.

I recreated that character at the Valley Ridge Theatre, where I would enter with a battered suitcase, behind the performer on stage, but facing the audience, and would ask in my best Appalachian dialect in a very loud voice, "Is this the Greyhound bus station? I'm gonna ketch the Greyhound bus to Roanoke to visit Mamma."

The performer, as solicitously as possible, would say, "No, the Greyhound bus station is down the street. This is a theatre and we're expecting a storyteller to come and perform, but he hasn't shown up yet."

"A storyteller? Why, I got lotsa stories" as I settled myself into the only seat on stage. I set my suitcase down beside me and declared, "An' I got lotsa play-pretties here in my travelin' case."

With that intro I'd begin my Appalachian tales and a few mountain songs while demonstrating some of the handmade toys, such as the pop gun and limberjack.

On one occasion, when the performances took place in an open air space behind the apartment building, I wandered up the walking alley between two buildings, and it was rather believable that I might be someone who had walked to town from one of the secluded hollows from across the river. As I had taken out my dentures, I couldn't speak in any dialect except the Appalachian twang. It took the audience a while to realize that I was simply a plant and not a lost hillbilly.

On another occasion, we were performing in the theatre space inside the building. My wife, Robin, was just finishing a dance on the stage when I wandered into the back of the small audience space with my suitcase. She was finishing her bows, when I started a loud whisper to those on the edge of the aisle: "Is this the Greyhound bus station."

The quiet answer was, "No, this is a theatre, and we're watching a performance."

"Oh, good, I'll set down right chere in front uv you, if you don' min'."

So I set myself on the aisle right in front of my new friend. I looked at the performer, my wife, in an elegant Asian costume, then leaned back and said, "Ain't she purty!"

The woman sitting right next to me turned to her husband on the other side of her. "Bill, get that hobo outta here. He's ruinin' Robin's performance." Although she was a neighbor, she hadn't recognized me.

I even got the Old Timer involved with politics. Senator John Blair Hunter and I had become good friends, and when he ran for reelection to the state senate, I served on his committee and offered my theatre space as a good place for a political rally for him. The committee liked the idea and thought it would be great fun, and not so boring, if I were to bring the Old Timer to have a dialog with the candidate.

After I discussed the plan with John, I noticed he was a little reticent, but he said, "Well, if that's what the committee wants, it should work out okay."

"Just think, John; I'll ask you some questions pertaining to your platform to give you a chance to explain your plans without having to lecture about what your hopes may be."

"Yeah . . . I guess that'll work."

At the rally, John and I and the rest of the committee greeted folks as they came in. While refreshments were being served in the art gallery lobby of the theatre, I slipped quietly away to get into costume. This time, instead of using an old suitcase as a prop, the Old Timer decided to bring along an old broken lantern.

Shortly after John, standing in front of the stage, greeted the audience, I meandered in through a side entrance only a few feet from John. He truly acted surprised, but instead of displaying his acting abilities it may have been genuine fear of pulling off this little prank with the crowd.

He looked at me and said, "Could I help you?"

I said, "I been lookin' fer a honest politician jest like thet Greek feller did a long time ago. An' look (as I held up the old lantern) my fahr has gone out an' the globe is busted."

John hesitantly answered, "Well, I'm running for the West Virginia Senate."

"So you're a politician?"

"Yes, I guess so." (Almost as though he didn't want to own up to it.)

"Well now, could I ast you some questions?"

"I think that would be fine."

"Do you mind if I set hyar in this hyar cheer righchere on the platform?"

"I'm sure that will be okay."

"I'm shore I'm much obliged," as I sat on the chair forcing John to turn toward me and away from the audience. I felt badly that I was upstaging him even though unintentionally.

"Now I onderstan' thet you're innerested in Little Orphan Annie roads."

"Well, I am concerned about so many folks living a long distance from state-paved roads even when there are several families living in that area. I do call them "orphan roads" and plan to introduce legislation that will require the state to maintain a road into any neighborhood with at least three inhabited houses."

This dialog continued for about forty-five minutes until the crowd was dismissed to do some more political hobnobbing.

I pulled John aside to apologize for upstaging him and explained to him that that meant the person downstage (closest to the audience) would have to turn away from the audience to carry on a conversation with the person upstage (me). This, of course, would put the downstage actor at a great disadvantage. That's why you've seen cartoons of ham actors all standing right next to the upstage scenery.

John listened carefully to my explanation and graciously accepted my apology, and said, "I have never been so frightened in my whole life."

There are few rewards in this life, but when you have been able to frighten the B.S. out of a politician, you could chalk up a significant accomplishment.

TUCKER TALES

Chuck Nichols and I were writing and rehearsing a performance for part of the 1999 summer season of the Valley Ridge Theatre in Thomas, West Virginia. We had performed together a few times before; once when I directed Foxfire, he was in the musical group featured in the second act. Our new production was to be called Tucker Tales, featuring songs and tales of Tucker County from the past 150 years.

We both knew Cleta Long, a local poet, who had received a great deal of attention because of her reading her poetry on NPR (National Public Radio), and we thought it would be great to have her read her poetry in our performances.

Her poems were truly down-home writing, providing heartwarming accounts of the natural and human wonders of Tucker County. She had told me that after she had read one of her poems on NPR she received a phone call from a woman, saying she had heard Cleta reading her poem of the '85 flood and that she had to stop her car as tears had clouded her vision. The caller said she could even smell that old wet hound dog, described in the poem about spending the night in a fodder shock (dried cornstalks stacked together in the cornfield, looking like Indian tepees).

Raised in a poor Appalachian family, who lived in various places along the Dry Fork River in Tucker County, Cleta started writing at an early age. The home where she began her writing was an old schoolhouse with an attic, but no stairs. There was a ladder, which she found that gave her access to her private place in the large upstairs. There she wrote daily in her diary, as well as letters to God and President Truman.

She readily accepted my invitation to our performance ensemble. After our first gig of my tales, Chuck's music and Cleta's poems, Chuck and I realized that he and I were simply a warm-up act for Cleta.

While still a teenager, Cleta married Norman Long after his return from the battles of Vietnam. When she was only a child, Norman, who was ten years older, told her mother that when Cleta grew up he was going to marry her, and if he didn't marry her, he'd marry no one.

Her mother warned her not to marry one of those Longs, "Why, Honey, they're such mountain people that if you was to marry Norman, he'd take you a way off in the hills yander, an' we'd never see you no more."

Theirs was such a beautiful love story that even two years after Cleta's death, when I visited Norman, he was still grieving over the "most prettiest girl I'd ever seen. I was shore the good Lord would've took me long afore he'd taken my Cleta."

Many years after their wedding vows Cleta wrote of Norman and their marriage:

About Norman
Deep set eyes under bushy brows
have a knowledge not taught in school.
The long square set of the lower jaw
won't allow for bending the rules.

See, he won't settle for bakery bread
or frozen potatoes or beans
everything has to start from scratch
or else he gets cranky and mean.
But, we've put up with each other
for thirty-seven years
and the reason is truly plain
no one else would have either of us
and so, it was God ordained.

Norman would always bring her, whenever Cleta would perform with us, as she could no longer drive, due to her MS. Most often he would simply sit in the car until the show or celebration would be over; sometimes for several hours. When he would come in for the performance, Cleta would ordinarily read something about him and say, "My husband, Norman, is sittin' in the audience, way towards the back." When people would turn around to look, he'd stoically turn around and look toward the back to avoid being identified as the center of curiosity.

Cleta once told me of an incident Norman experienced where he worked as a day laborer for the US Forest Service at the Nursery Bottom near Parsons, WV. One of the concerns at the forestry experimental facility, in addition to planting trees, was to determine the most efficient way to harvest trees with the least damage to the fragile ecosystem of younger trees and the forest floor, itself.

So the professional foresters developed a contraption they called the "chew-ball." When Cleta got this far with her story, I accused her of readying this tale for the annual West Virginia Liars Contest. She said, "Nauw, Reid, now this is the sure 'nuff truth."

The chew-ball was a huge steel sphere, weighing several tons, and manufactured in two halves which would be assembled on the work site. They would put the assembled chew ball at the top of a ridge, chain it to a felled log, then roll it down the hill towing the fresh timber to the top of the ridge. For some reason the researchers had not anticipated the damage this behemoth would incur on its downhill flight. Occasionally it even broke apart and diverged in two directions, crushing all kinds of spindly saplings and other desirable undergrowth.

One morning Norman came to work early, as was his wont, long before the professionals with their nine-to-five mentality. He noticed lots of little dead woodland critters. Because the small gnawing animals were prone to gnaw through the gas, vacuum and electric lines of the power equipment, the researchers put out poison to prevent them from disabling the machinery. As a spur-of-the-moment idea, Norman picked up the small carcasses, placing them in a perfect circle around the chew-ball.

When the foresters, biologists and other researchers arrived on the scene, they were flabbergasted at the perfect circle of corpses around the chew-ball. They discussed all kinds of theories about what might have happened. They expected the chipmunks, field mice, et al to be killed, but they were puzzled about how and why they had arranged themselves in this pattern while in their death throes. They argued all sorts of theories about such an unusual occurrence.

The engineer: "Do you suppose the electromagnetic field of the chew-ball had anything to do with it."

The biologist: "It's a well-known fact that when the fauna anticipates an imminent death, they seek a sheltered place. Perhaps they sensed that the chew-ball provided a kind . . . "

The mechanic: "Now, that don't make much sense. Why would they circle themselves so perfect like . . . "

The foreman: "Norman, do you know what happened here?"

Norman was sitting on a tree stump a short distance away. He took his time in answering his boss.

"Well, Norman, do you know . . . ?"

"Yeah!" he drawled.

A fellow ought to know better than to ask a mountain man a question that can be answered in one word, when you're wanting a more definitive response. Norman would have left his cryptic answer at that, if they had not pursued the matter further.

"Well, what in the hell happened? Why are all the dead vermin in a perfect circle around the 'chew-ball?"

"The little critters kilt theirselves tryin' to bury the damn thing."

I told Cleta that, in addition to her poems, she had to tell that story to our audiences, which she gleefully did.

The last time Cleta performed with Chuck and me, she was in a wheelchair and wearing a wig, due to the chemotherapy she was bravely enduring. She remained determined to share her stories and poems as long as she could.

One of the poems she loved to read was a Deep South poem–not hers at all, about a young girl who wanted to get married, so she talked with her father about her plans. The poem was a little racy, and I was at times afraid the audience might be offended, but I would never try to curtail any of Cleta's enthusiasm. As the poem goes, it seems the girl's father cautioned her about marrying a certain boy, because "He's yore brother, but jest don't tell yore mother."

After a few tears and a few weeks, the girl talks with her father again about another boyfriend, but was again advised, "You can't marry him nuther, 'cause he's also yore brother." She was so crestfallen that she confided in her mother who assured her, "Honey, you marry any boy you want; you ain't no kin to Pap."

Cleta would always laugh right along with the rest of us.

After her death, I wrote a play about a brother and sister at the beginning of the Twentieth Century based on stories, events and writings in Tucker County. At the end of the script, "Coming of Age," I had the brother and his son poring over the papers of his departed sister, who had lost her fiancé in World War I. As they started reading her last poem, her spirit appeared in a blue light and sang the poem to a tune which I had composed.

Norman gave me permission to use Cleta's last published poem as the epilogue to my script:

>	The book is finished, the work is done,
>	And life like the river continues to run
>	Through seasons of calm or wild with elation
>	Toward its ultimate destination,
>
>	Its cardinal path is already set,
>	Its course according to plan,
>	Though sometimes altered by circumstance,
>	Just like the journey of man.

A time to be born a time to die,
A time to laugh and a time to cry,
A time of darkness and a time of light
With the rhythm of rivers these rhymes I write.

With the rhythm of rivers these rhymes I write.

Goodnight, Cleta!

VALLEY RIDGE THEATRE

In 1980, I bought THE FLATS, a dilapidated apartment house with 12 apartments and four storefronts; the largest building on Front Street in Thomas, WV. In earlier years when the coal-mining center had 30,000 people, the building was known as The Mansion. Each apartment had a balcony overlooking the main thoroughfare, which bustled with throngs of people. As the town was largely Italian, the street was often the route of extensive, colorful and raucous parades. The balconies provided the tenants perfect seats. The Fourth of July fireworks were right across the street, the railroad and the North Fork of the Blackwater River.

By the time I had bought the building, the coal industry had dwindled, the population had decreased to 3,000 and the rails were being taken up by the railroad.

A few doors down the street from The Flats was the Cottrill's Opera House, which itself was in serious deterioration. I had bought the Flats because of the opera house, and I felt it was my mission to assist in restoring the opera house and begin the rejuvenation of the town, itself. It's doubtful that operas were ever performed there, but in those days the word, "theatre" was not very respectable, but "opera" was not only an acceptable term but even elevated, particularly with the Italian citizens.

Apparently some local folks also had hoped that I might be able to contribute some activity in the town. Down the street was the Colobrese Hardware Store. It was owned by two bachelor Colobrese brothers who lived down at Coketon with their spinster sister. They were wonderful people, and every time I went into their store one of them would say, "Mr. Gilbert, you're gonna help this town. God bless you! God bless you!"

Another old Italian in town would often visit with me at the coffee shop down the street. One morning, as I was about to sit down with him he said, "And how is Mr . . . " He stopped abruptly. I knew what he was about to do. He then said, "No! How is Doctor Gilbert today?"

"Mr. Sagace, don't do that."

"Yes, you earned that and everyone should call you Dr. Gilbert."

"Mr. Sagace, were you in the military?"

"Oh yes!"

"What was your rank?"

"I was sergeant."

"Now if you're going to address me as Dr. Gilbert, I'll call you Sergeant Sagace. After all you earned that title."

He hesitated for a moment, apparently surprised by my remark. He then said, "Okay! Let's do that."

The opera house was built in 1902, by Hiram Cottrill and was the center of social activity in the whole county. Its design was rather fascinating as the stage and seating were on the second floor. On the street level was the bar. That was quite convenient for stopping by for a drink after the film or stage show upstairs.

With the opera house down the street from my digs, it served as an inspiration for my wife, Robin Pyle, and myself. We established the Valley Ridge Theatre in the Flats by converting a store front into a small theatre. It was 1995 right after my retirement from Ohio State University when I could devote my attention and energy, as such a venture required.

It was a communal experience for the actors and crew. There was enough space in the apartments upstairs, just above our small theatre to house everyone. We scheduled the rehearsals and openings, so that everyone's energy could be accommodated.

During the ten years of the run we produced plays from Shakespeare and Greek dramas to Asian theatre and modern comedy.

In 2000 we produced The Mystery of Irma Vepp, which was a great hoot, played by only two actors, Jay Painter and Allen Talbott, talented actors from Elkins (almost local). They played all the roles, so there were many quick backstage costume changes, switching ages and genders.

That summer we also produced Tennessee Williams's A Streetcar Named Desire. Before opening, someone asked who was going to play Marlon Brando. I explained that no one was playing Brando, but Allen Talbott was playing Stanley Kowalski. He was wonderful, and the actress playing Blanche was as good as I had ever seen.

Opening night went so well that after the curtain call, the actors trekked down to the Sportsman's Club, the local bar three doors down the street. They overindulged and Marlon, pardon me, Allan, came back to the flats and decided to climb the stone wall behind the building. Unfortunately when he got to the top of the 12-foot wall, he slipped, sliding down the wall. When he hit the bottom, he broke his right leg. Stanley Kowalski for the rest of the run, wore a full leg cast. The audience seemed to accept the possibility that the character of Kowalski could have broken his leg in some foolish escapade.

At the end of the play Blanche must be sent off to a mental health facility. I didn't go to the expense of hiring an actor for the summer for just the role of the counselor, so I played the part myself. When Blanche, Robin my wife, looked into my eyes and said, "I've always depended on the kindness of strangers", our neighbors tittered a little. Unfortunately sometime after that we did become strangers.

We even produced a script, which I had written, Coming of Age. I focused on the oral history of Tucker County from the beginning to the middle of the twentieth century. As people from thirty-two nationalities were naturalized in the county, there was plenty of material for holding an audience.

An interesting facet of the history was the existence of the Black Hand, which was a kind of mafia organization that attempted to keep everyone in line, which was quite often a regretful line. As there was always plenty of coal dust, there was no problem in getting enough to daub one's hand for leaving a black imprint of a hand on the door of some hapless individual. Such a person was well advised to leave town as soon as possible.

At the bottom end of the mountain county were two communities across the Dry Fork River from each other. On one side was Hendrix, a working family community. Across a foot bridge was Brooklyn Heights, notorious for sins of the flesh and general carousing.

It was said that on Monday mornings the children in Hendrix would run to the bridge to see how many bodies had been deposited in the Green Hole just under the bridge during the past weekend. As the corpses had on heavy work shoes, the feet stuck to the bottom of the river, but the body would be erect and moving back and forth with the flow of the river . . . an eerie sight, indeed, for the ghostly beings swaying back and forth at the bottom of the Green Hole.

In the 2002 season we decided to celebrate the founding of the opera house. We discovered that the first production in the new theatre was *Ten Nights in a Barroom*. Wouldn't it be wonderful to be able to produce that script again, but where would we be able to find that antiquated script? I belonged to the National Theatre Conference, and a fellow member ran a bookstore in New York, featuring old theatre scripts. Voila!

A script . . . so we were in business. We were even able to find a photo of the original production and used it for our brochure that summer.

The production went quite well, but I'm not sure that the temperance message was ever heeded. It still amazes me that a production of a temperance play could be successfully produced in the theatre space above, but the theatre goers could drop in to the saloon downstairs and toast the actors and the success of the performance upstairs . . . even if the message wasn't honored.

WHY THE GATHERING?

One might understandably ask, "Why should I pay fifty dollars or even five dollars to attend a professional performance of Shakespeare's *King Lear*?" We already know the story; of the conflict as well as the resolution. If we were from the Appalachian Mountains we may even have heard our grandfather tell the tale, as it was an English folk tale before Shakespeare used it to write his classic.

Obviously we wouldn't go to the theatre just to learn the story. Perhaps we would like to enjoy the poetic words. But we could read the words, as there are available publications of the poem of *King Lear*.

It would be fascinating, wouldn't it, to hear the words and rhythms orally recited? So perhaps we could purchase or borrow a CD for a rousing vocal rendering of the poetry.

As intense as such an intonation might be, it would not reach the apex of the presentation of Shakespeare's script.

Wouldn't it be wonderful to see actors embodying the words and physically portraying the actions of the story? I could always get a DVD and watch wonderful actors with agile movement and mellifluous voices retell this ancient tale, while honoring the visuals of an English heath, accompanied by the audio track of roaring winds and blasting rains. We could watch it repeatedly in the comfort of our own home and marvel at the words of the poet and the ability of the actors.

We could attend a film presentation of the drama more cheaply than a live performance would cost, and it would certainly provide a certain aesthetic satisfaction, as we would be sharing the event with a number of other appreciative, breathing audience members. We do understand that the mutual experience with other audience members has great benefit, when we are enveloped in the darkened cinematic atmosphere, focused on the larger-than-life drama.

So, we're still going to take the theatre trip, with its various costs, to see the expensive live production of *King Lear*, the crowning expression and unfolding of the story, even if the current actor is less than a stellar performer. *But why?*

It's more than an interesting story, poetically written, rhythmically intoned, energetically acted while filmed in theatrical, yet realistic, settings.

When the live interactive actors parading, jostling, orating before the live individuals in the gathered audience, they breathe together in the all-too-human story of ingratitude, whereby the ultimate drama of the tragedy is attained.

The truth of the alchemy (of words, action, breath) is borne out by another Shakespearean character, Hamlet, " . . . the play's the thing wherein I'll catch the conscience of the king," when both the king and actors, as well as the gathered audience, are present, breathing the same air.

Well Hamlet knew, and here reminds us, that it is the actual performance with live actors before a collective audience that the ramifications of the telling of the tale would be definitively achieved, breathing together the same air.

We are gathered here to breathe together the communal breath of life, hoping that something extraordinaire will happen.

fini

graduation cap used by permission: https://www.123rf.com/profile_pixelrobot

CHRONOLOGY
After *The Twelve Houses*

1949-51	Brevard College (English)	AA 1951
51-53	Duke University (Sociology)	BA 1953
53-56	SMU (Theology)	THM 1956
56-57	First UMC Church, South Bend, IN	
57	Married Luan Miller	
57-59	Union Seminary NYC (Religious Drama)	STM 1961
59	Tari Born	
58-59	Studied with Charles Weidman (Modern Dance)	
59	Studied with Etienne Decroux (Mime)	
59-62	Union College (teaching)	
60	Adrienne born	
62-65	Grace Methodist Church	
62	Karen born	
64	Studied with Sidayo Kita (Japanese Noh)	
65-66	Fulbright in India	
65-66	National School of Drama (teaching)	
66-69	Lambuth College (teaching)	
67-70	Summers at Uplands Arts Council (teaching)	
67	Founder & first President Jackson TN Arts Council	
69-71	University of Wisconsin (Asian Theatre)	PhD 1971
71-78	Founded and directed Valley Studio	
70-79	Wisconsin Mime Theatre and School	
74-79	Administrator, International Mimes and Pantomimists IMP	
76	Married Julia Sutter	
79-82	West Virginia	
81-82	Founded and directed Mountain Players	
82-95	Ohio State University (teaching)	
89	Married Robin Pyle	
95-2005	Founded and directed Valley Ridge Theatre in WV	
90-95	Founder & Executive Director Thomas Education Center	
97-98	Fulbright to Thailand	
2005-Present	Tucson (Writing seven books)	

KIN - Part I

Stella Mae Brinkley Gilbert

Peter Reid Gilbert

Clarissa Jane Brinkley

Robert Brinkley

Elder Noel Byron Gilbert

L to R: Samuel Green Gilbert, Nell Gilbert, Mattie Fain Gilbert

L to R: Tari, Adrienne, Karen and Reid in back (then)

L to R: Karen, Adrienne, Tari and Reid (now)

L to R: Reid, Luan, Tari, Adrienne, Karen

Smokey

Primitive Baptists Preachers, 1911, Green Hill Church Association, Including Grandpa Noel Gilbert, Uncle Lemly Gilbert and Cousin Lorenzo Dow Gilbert

MY MENTORS - Part II

Weidman Dancing God of the Mountain

Shilo Methodist Church

Collection of Richard Chase's Stories

First Row left to right: Ted Bowman, Gene Gray James, Gene Bowman, Arthur Gilbert, Kenneth Holt, Carlton Tesh, Gene Winebarger, unknown, Tom Tesh. Second Row: Cleve Smith, Reid Gilbert, Carl Marshall, unknown rep from the Old Hickory Boy Scout Council, Carlos Marshall, Jesse Wilkins, Rev. Ralph Reed

OTHER FOLKS ALONG THE WAY - Part III

Stoneledge

Stoneledge Entrance

Stoneledge White Oak Inlay in Entrance

Roy Mallow, Master Builder

Stoneledge Black Walnut Wall

Verna Mae Slone

Edna Meudt

Edna Meudt reading her poetry to some of the summer students at Valley Studio

The Old Hendrix Swinging Bridge

Cleta Long

EDUCATION - Part IV

Gina Lalli, instructor of Kathak Dance

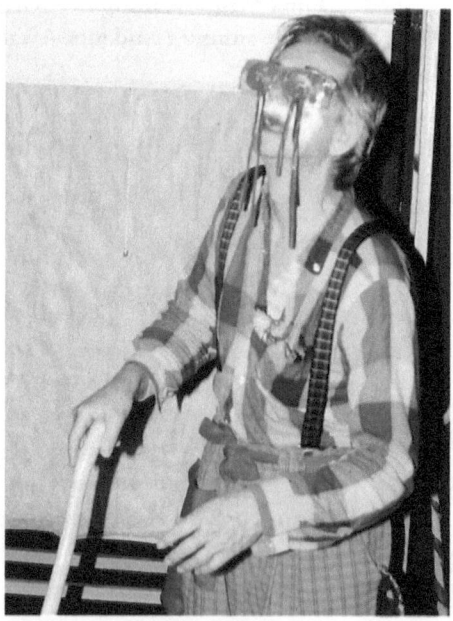

Oedipus after blinding

Mythic Workshop, Demeter at Gladwin Island

Exploring with Self Mask at Gladwin Island

Setting the Stage for Prometheus Mythic Workshop, Hilltop, Spring Green WI

E. Reid Gilbert performing Oedipus at a Mythic Workshop

Robin Pyle Dancing the Fire Goddess at the Hilltop, Spring Green WI

Shinko Kagaya dancing the Japanese Water Sprite at the Pandora Mythic Workshop on the Glady Fork River in Tucker County, West Virginia

THE THEATRE - Part VI

The Production of Ten Nights in a Barroom at the Cottrill's Opera House in Thomas, WV

William Burdick Teaching a class in Period Dance at Valley Studio in Spring Green, WI

Robin Pyle dancing the role of Madea

The Bus—Lee Dreyfus Candidate for Governor

Renaissance Dance Performance at Valley Studio

Reid Gilbert   Donn Reeder juggling at Valley Studio

Valley Studio Period Dancers

Publicity beyond the Classroom

Our involvement with other mimes

Reid Gilbert and Ben Rogner in Early Valley Studio Performance

Senator Russell Long, Mime Reid Gilbert and Vice-President Walter Mondale

www.ingramcontent.com/pod-product-compliance
Lightning Source LLC
Chambersburg PA
CBHW021352290426
44108CB00010B/207